The
Harcourt
Brace

S T U D E N T
THESAURUS

The Harcourt Brace

STUDENT
THESAURUS

Harcourt Brace & Company

San Diego   New York   London

Credits and Acknowledgments

Editor: Christopher Morris

Project Editor: Elinor Williams

Senior Editor: Daniel Hammer

Staff Editors: Gail Rice, Amy Rosen, Charles Allen

Cover Design: Michael Farmer

Illustrations: See page 312 for illustration credits.

First printing this edition 1994
Copyright © 1991 by Harcourt Brace & Company

Library of Congress Cataloging-in-Publication Data
The Harcourt Brace student thesaurus/[editor, Christopher Morris].
p. cm.
Updated ed. of: The HBJ student thesaurus.
Includes index.
ISBN 0-15-200186-7
1. English language—Synonyms and antonyms—Juvenile literature.
[1. English language—Synonyms and antonyms.] I. Morris, Christopher.
II. Harcourt Brace & Company.   III. HBJ student thesaurus.
PE1591.H39   1994
423.1—dc20   94-15603

Printed in the United States of America

G F E D C

Introduction

The Harcourt Brace Student Thesaurus has been created to help young people use the English language more effectively. It will serve as an aid in writing, a guide to correct usage, and a source for vocabulary building. Used along with its companion volume, *The Harcourt Brace Student Dictionary,* this book will provide students with a lifelong foundation for language use.

For adults, the dictionary and the thesaurus have long been regarded as companions, to be placed next to each other on the shelf and consulted at the same time. Among students, however, the use of a thesaurus is not as well established. Certain elements of the traditional adult thesaurus have made it difficult for students to use such a book. In *The Harcourt Brace Student Thesaurus,* we have set out to offer the wide range of information found in a traditional thesaurus but to present it in a format that is easy for students to use and understand.

Single A-Z List: *The Harcourt Brace Student Thesaurus* places all its main entries in a single alphabetical list. This means that the reader needs to look in only one place to find a given entry. The A-Z list is supplemented by an index of synonyms, which is an alphabetical listing of all the different synonyms that appear in the book. For example, the word *location* is not a main entry itself, but it is listed in the index on page 192, where it will be found as a synonym for *place.*

Useful Synonyms: For students, it is not useful to place an entry under *obtain* or *acquire* and offer the more basic term *get* as a synonym. The students' need is for word choices that are more exact, more emphatic, or more sophisticated than the familiar words they already have at hand. In *The Harcourt Brace Student Thesaurus,* each entry appears under the most common term within a group, because that is the word most likely to be looked up for a synonym. The synonyms for this entry word are then listed in order, according to how closely they relate to the word.

Example Sentences: Knowing that a given word is an appropriate synonym is only the first step. There are virtually no words in English that are completely synonymous with each other in every context. The student therefore has to know not only that a certain word could be used as a synonym but when and how it should be used. *The Harcourt Brace Student Thesaurus* therefore does not simply list synonyms; it provides one or more example sentences for every synonym in the book.

Appropriate Context: The context of each example sentence shows how the word is properly used. For an informal word used in conversation, the example will be someone's casual remark to a friend. For a formal word used in serious writing, the example will be taken from history, science, politics, business, or the like. For example, in the entry for *miss,* the informal synonym *skip* describes a busy shopper skipping lunch, while the more formal word *abstain* deals with a vote in the U.S. Senate.

Functional Illustrations: *The Harcourt Brace Student Thesaurus* uses artwork not to decorate the page but to give information about words. Each of the illustrations in the book has been created with two contrasting elements, one element depicting the entry word and the other depicting a synonym. For example, *hide/camouflage* shows on the left the general word with a young boy behind a rock and on the right the specific synonym with a rabbit blending into its surroundings.

THE EDITORS

Sample Page

Entry Word

Synonyms

Part of Speech

Definition

Examples
with key word
in italics.

Usage Note

coast shore beach bank

NOUN: the edge of land touching a body of water.

coast Acapulco is a popular resort city on the Pacific *coast* of Mexico. People who lived along the *coast* were warned that a hurricane was on the way.
shore They pulled the canoe up on the *shore* so that it wouldn't float away.
beach Their home is right on the *beach,* and they can walk out their back door down to the ocean.
bank The city of St. Louis grew up along the *banks* of the Mississippi River.
▶ Any body of water can have a *shore* or a *beach.* But only a body of salt water—a sea or an ocean—can have a *coast.* And only a river or stream can have a *bank.*

Illustrations
contrast two
related words.

Captions
with key word
in bold.

Gail was feeling **cold,** so she
put on her heavy sweater.

Chuck was **freezing** outside as
he brushed the snow off the car.

Entry appears
under most
common term.

Synonyms
progress
in difficulty.

Examples
show correct use
of key word.

Antonyms
follow entry.

cold freezing chilly icy frigid

ADJECTIVE: having a low temperature; not warm.

cold As soon as the fire died down, the room grew *cold.* The state of Minnesota is known for its long, *cold* winters.
freezing The sky was clear, but a bitter, *freezing* wind kept most people indoors for the day.
chilly Fall is now here, and we are starting to have some *chilly* nights.
icy He left the front door wide open when he came in, and an *icy* blast of air swept into the room.
frigid Over the years the Eskimo people developed effective methods of dealing with the *frigid* weather conditions of their homeland.
Antonym: **hot.**

47

How to Use Your Thesaurus

Entry Word: The words in this book are called ENTRY WORDS. They are printed in heavy black type to make them easy to see, and they are listed in alphabetical order to make them easy to find. An entry word, and all the information that is given about the word, make up what is called an ENTRY. The sample page here has the entries **coast** and **cold**.

Guide Word: At the top of each page, above the long line, is a single word in black type. It is a GUIDE WORD that will help you find entry words more easily. On a left-hand (even-numbered) page, the guide word is the first entry on the page. On a right-hand (odd-numbered) page, it is the last entry. This sample is page 47, a right-hand page, so the guide word is **cold,** the last entry on the page.

Synonyms: The entry word is followed by a list of synonyms for this word. A SYNONYM is a word that has the same, or nearly the same, meaning as another word. Synonyms are printed in black type, but are not as heavy and dark as the entry word. In the sample, the entry word **cold** has four synonyms: **freezing, icy, chilly,** and **frigid.**

Part of Speech: Below the synonyms, there is a word in capital letters. If you look at **coast** in the sample, you will see this: NOUN. This is the PART OF SPEECH for this entry. It tells how the word is used in a sentence. A noun such as **coast** is the subject of a sentence.

Definition: After the part of speech, there is a DEFINITION of the synonyms. This is a short statement telling what these words mean. **Coast** and its three synonyms all mean "the edge of land touching a body of water."

Examples: Below the definition, the synonyms are all listed again in heavy black type. They appear in the same order as on the first line above. Each synonym is then followed by one or more examples. The EXAMPLE is a sentence that shows how this word is best used, or most often used. In the example, the synonym is printed in *italics* to make it stand out. In this sample, the synonym **chilly** has the example, "Fall is now here, and we are starting to have some *chilly* nights."

Usage Notes: At the end of some entries, there are short articles telling you about the proper use of one or more of the words in the entry. These articles are called USAGE NOTES. In the sample, there is a usage note for **coast** and its synonyms. Watch for this special black triangle: ▶ It tells you that a usage note will follow.

Antonyms: This Thesaurus gives words that have the same meaning as the entry word, but it also lists words that have the opposite meaning. These "opposite" words are ANTONYMS. They appear at the very end of the entry. The sample has the antonym **hot** for the entry **cold**.

Illustration: Every pair of facing pages in the Thesaurus has an ILLUSTRATION. This is a color picture that shows the entry word and one of its synonyms. The picture shows the difference between the two words. The sample shows an illustration for the entry word **cold** and its synonym **freezing.**

Caption: Below each illustration, there is a CAPTION to explain what is shown in the picture. The words in darker type are the ones featured in the picture.

able   capable qualified competent willing

ADJECTIVE: having the power or the skill to do something.

able When babies are very young, they are not *able* to walk. My sister is 18 this year, so she will be *able* to vote in the election for President.

capable Mary is a very *capable* babysitter, and people feel safe leaving their children with her.

qualified Because he is very new to politics, many people think he is not really *qualified* for the office of senator.

competent Though she isn't a great soccer coach, she is *competent,* and her team should do fairly well.

willing I'm sure that Dan knows how to fix the lawn mower, but I don't know if he'd be *willing* to do it unless we pay him.

Antonyms: **unable, incapable.**

about   concerning relating referring regarding

PREPOSITION: having to do with; on the subject of.

about Megan decided to write her science report *about* black holes in space. The two brothers sometimes argued *about* which television show to watch.

concerning A policeman arrived to question the students *concerning* the accident that had just taken place in front of the school.

relating The newspaper has been getting a lot of letters to the editor *relating* to next week's election for mayor.

referring There was a note at the bottom of the page *referring* to an article in another part of the magazine.

regarding The principal is going to meet with the parents *regarding* the plans for the new school.

above over overhead aloft

ADVERB: in a higher place; higher than or on top of.

above On a traffic signal the red light is *above* the green light. I live on the third floor of the building, and my friend Maria lives two floors *above* us.

over There is a big fan *over* the stove to draw smoke out of the kitchen.

overhead To show that a touchdown has been scored, the referee holds both his hands straight *overhead.*

aloft The balloon stays *aloft* because it is filled with a gas that is lighter than air.

<u>Antonyms:</u> **below, under, beneath.**

accident chance coincidence mishap

NOUN: something that happens suddenly, without being planned or expected.

accident There was an *accident* on Main Street when a truck skidded on the ice and bumped into a parked car. Hitting that home run was a lucky *accident*—I just closed my eyes and took a swing.

chance Just by *chance,* the first name that the teacher picked from the grab bag happened to be mine.

coincidence It's a *coincidence* that Larry has the same birthday as his older sister.

mishap When Andrew and his friends eat together, there is always some *mishap* such as someone spilling the milk or dropping his plate on the floor.

By **accident,** she bumped into someone while she was going into the store.

It was a **coincidence** that she met an old college friend in the store.

across   over opposite beyond

ADVERB: from one side to the other; on or to the other side.

across Our house is right *across* the street from the school. It took her about an hour to swim *across* the lake.

over The George Washington Bridge goes *over* the Hudson River to connect New York to New Jersey.

opposite In football, the two teams line up *opposite* each other before the play starts.

beyond The tree hasn't been trimmed in years, and the branches have grown *beyond* the back fence into the neighbor's yard.

act   behave work operate function

VERB: to do something in a certain way.

act Stephanie was afraid her little brother would *act* silly and embarrass her in front of her friends. Firefighters must learn to *act* quickly in an emergency.

behave My father insists that we *behave* properly when we eat dinner out in a restaurant.

work Our refrigerator isn't *working* right—the container of orange juice I put in this morning still isn't cold.

operate Barbara's grandmother showed her how to *operate* the foot pedal on her old sewing machine.

function The movie theater had such a low budget that the owner of the theater also *functioned* as the ticket seller and ran the movie projector.

add   include join attach increase

VERB: to put something more with a thing; put something with another thing.

add The house is too small for their family now, so they want to *add* another bedroom. The recipe for cookies said to *add* the nuts to the cookie dough right at the end.

include When you count how many girls there are on your team, be sure to *include* yourself in the total.

join Neil likes to play the drums and wants to *join* the marching band at his school.

attach On modern passenger trains the engine is often *attached* at the rear of the train instead of at the front.

increase If he orders the new car with air conditioning and a radio, that will *increase* the price of the car by about $1,000.

Antonyms: **subtract, remove.**

admit   confess acknowledge concede disclose

VERB: to say against one's will that something is true.

admit Mom checked the facts in the encyclopedia and *admitted* that she was wrong and I was right. I hate the way he shows off on the field, but I have to *admit* he's a good player.

confess When the police questioned him about the bank robbery, the man *confessed* that he'd been the one who did it.

acknowledge After the Bay of Pigs invasion of Cuba failed, the United States government *acknowledged* that it had trained and supported the rebel forces.

concede As the last voting results came in, the candidate finally had to *concede* that he had lost the election.

disclose The value of the company's stock dropped sharply after the company *disclosed* that it had lost millions of dollars in the past three months.

Antonym: **deny.**

advantage   benefit asset edge

NOUN: something that is helpful or useful.

advantage Being tall is an *advantage* in the game of basketball. One *advantage* of this house is that it has three bedrooms while our old house only had two.

benefit Cutting down the amount of salt you eat can be a *benefit* to your health.

asset Richard Burton's greatest *asset* as an actor was his beautiful speaking voice.

edge The fact that Diane has played the role of Lady Macbeth once before gives her an *edge* over the other girls who are trying out for the part.

Antonyms: **disadvantage, drawback, handicap.**

advice   recommendation suggestion warning

NOUN: something said to a person about what to do.

advice Dave's eighth-grade teacher gave him some *advice* about what courses to take in high school.

recommendation The author followed the editor's *recommendations* and made several important changes in the last chapter of her book.

suggestion When I was trying to decide what to be for Halloween, Mom made the *suggestion* that I go as Dracula.

warning As the heavy snow continued, a traffic reporter on the radio gave a *warning* to motorists to drive slowly and carefully.

▶ **Advise** has the same basic meaning as **advice,** but it is used in a different way. *Advise* is a verb; *advice* is a noun. The soccer coach *advised* me to keep my head down when I kick. I took her *advice* and now I'm kicking the ball much better.

Laura was **afraid** as she watched the horror movie. Her little brother was **terrified.**

afraid   scared frightened alarmed terrified

ADJECTIVE: feeling upset and worried about what will happen; feeling fear.

afraid Some young children sleep with a light on, because they are *afraid* of the dark. My sister just learned to drive, and she is *afraid* to take the car out on the main highway.

scared Eddie says that he liked going on the roller coaster, but he looked *scared* all through the ride.

frightened She sat reading in the quiet room, when suddenly she was *frightened* by a loud noise as the door banged shut behind her.

alarmed Some passengers became *alarmed* when the pilot said the plane had to land immediately, so he explained that it was because someone on board was ill.

terrified As the ground shook violently from the earthquake, he was *terrified* that the building he was in was about to collapse around him.

<u>Antonyms:</u> **calm, unafraid.**

again   over repeatedly

ADVERB: another time; once more.

again The rain stopped and the sun came out *again.* I liked the movie so much that I stayed to see the whole thing *again.*

over He didn't play the song properly, so the piano teacher had him do it *over.*

repeatedly The bank has *repeatedly* sent him letters about the money he owes, but he still hasn't paid it back.

against opposed contrary versus

PREPOSITION: in a way that is opposite; not agreeing or on the same side.

against Riding your bike on the playground is *against* the school rules. Four members of the city council were in favor of the new law, and one was *against* it.

opposed Many local parents are *opposed* to the plan to build a large shopping mall near the junior high school.

contrary When the scientist Copernicus stated that the earth and other planets move around the sun, that idea was *contrary* to what people believed at the time.

versus For today's pro football games, Channel 2 is showing the Lions *versus* the Bears and Channel 4 has the Browns *versus* the Jets.

Antonyms: **favoring, supporting.**

The children were able to **agree** right away about which puppy they wanted.

They got their parents to **consent** to buying it.

agree consent concur conform

VERB: to have the same idea about something.

agree The boys didn't *agree* on which movie to rent, so their dad had to choose. I asked if I could do my science project on desert plants, and my teacher *agreed*.

consent For many years the government of West Germany *consented* to having United States Army troops stationed in its country.

concur The Supreme Court *concurred* that the lower court had made the correct ruling, so it let the decision stand.

conform That high school makes its students *conform* to a dress code that states what kind of clothing can be worn to school.

Antonyms: **disagree, differ.**

agreement   deal contract treaty pact

NOUN: an understanding or arrangement between people or groups to act in a certain way.

agreement The two countries made a trade *agreement* to buy certain products from each other. Everyone on the committee was in *agreement* that the nickname of the new school should be the "Wildcats."

deal The XYZ Computer Corporation has just made a *deal* to buy Explorer Software Company for 150 million dollars.

contract The Smiths have a *contract* with the company that is building their new house, stating how much it will cost and when it will be finished.

treaty Although fighting in World War I stopped in 1918, the war did not end officially until 1919, when the opposing nations signed the *Treaty* of Versailles.

pact If two countries have a "nonaggression *pact*," this means they have agreed not to attack each other.

ahead   before forward

ADVERB: in a more advanced position; in front.

ahead Annie ran well *ahead* of the others in the race and took first place. Let's get to the movie *ahead* of time, so that we won't have to wait in line to get in.

before He's not used to speaking *before* a large group, and he was very nervous. Will always seems to finish his work just as the bell rings, never *before*.

forward The captain ordered his troops to move *forward* toward the enemy. It's Daylight Saving Time now; set the clock *forward* from one o'clock to two o'clock.

Antonyms: **after, behind.**

alert   watchful wide-awake attentive vigilant

ADJECTIVE: watching very carefully; ready for something to happen.

alert She's a very *alert* baby and notices right away when something happens in the room. An *alert* motorist spotted the license number of the stolen car.

watchful The *watchful* eyes of the policeman on the corner took in everything that went on around him.

wide-awake A soldier who is on guard duty at night has to stay *wide-awake* at all times.

attentive Each of the clues needed to solve the mystery is given in the story, but only readers who are very *attentive* will be able to find them all.

vigilant Thomas Jefferson warned Americans that in order to remain free, they had to be *vigilant* at all times against threats to their freedom.

Antonym: **unaware.**

alive   live living existing vital

ADJECTIVE: having life; active.

alive Grass needs more water than almost any other kind of plant to stay *alive.* World War I ended over 70 years ago, and very few people who fought in it are still *alive.*

live Next to the supermarket fish counter there was a tank filled with *live* lobsters for sale.

living The elephant is the largest *living* land animal, although some kinds of dinosaurs were larger.

existing *The Last of the Mohicans* is a famous book about the last *existing* member of an Indian tribe.

vital Actions of the body that are necessary for life, such as breathing or blood circulation, are called the "*vital* functions."

Antonyms: **dead, lifeless.**

all   each every any

PRONOUN: everyone or everything; the entire group.

all It was Sunday night and *all* the stores in the mall were closed. By law, *all* new cars sold in the United States must have seat belts.

each The teacher said that *each* child would get one guess as to how many pieces of candy there were in the jar.

every The soccer league has a rule saying that *every* player who is on the team must play at least half the game.

any That book is number one on the best-seller list, so you should be able to buy it in *any* bookstore around here.

Antonyms: **no, none.**

almost   nearly about approximately

ADVERB: very close to, but not actually; not exactly.

almost Andrew keeps the money he gets from recycling soda cans and has saved *almost* $50 so far. Our city is really growing quickly; it now has *almost* 100,000 people.

nearly *Nearly* all of the 50 U.S. states joined the Union before 1900; only five states came in after that date.

about The ancient Middle Eastern city of Babylon was very powerful *about* 4,000 years ago.

approximately One hundred meters is *approximately* the same distance as 100 yards—it's 109.36 yards, to be more exact.

alone   single-handedly unaccompanied unaided

ADVERB: without another or others; by oneself.

alone I offered to help Jimmy with his math homework, but he insisted on doing it *alone.* The baby isn't old enough yet to play outside *alone.*

single-handedly Sergeant York was a famous American war hero who captured 132 enemy soldiers *single-handedly.*

unaccompanied In the 1800's, women were not supposed to go into restaurants *unaccompanied* by men.

unaided His leg is now healed and he is finally able to walk *unaided* by crutches.

along   beside alongside

PREPOSITION: by or at the side of; near.

along Is there a good place to eat anywhere *along* this highway? Wildflowers were growing all *along* the fence.

beside The big oak tree *beside* the house keeps my bedroom cool in the summer.

alongside "Double parking" is when you park your car *alongside* another car that is already parked.

There is a bike path **along** the river. They stopped for a picnic **beside** the river.

a lot

▶ If you can, replace **a lot** with a more exact description. Instead of "A lot of people live in this city," make it "More than 100,000 people" (or whatever). Also, if you do use *a lot* remember that it is two separate words, not one word "alot." "Alot" is not a correct spelling.

always forever regularly consistently

ADVERB: at all times; all the time.

always Running water will *always* flow downhill, never uphill. Thanksgiving falls on different dates, but it is *always* on the fourth Thursday in November.
forever The ancient Greeks believed in a number of gods that they thought were able to live *forever*.
regularly Mr. Stevens takes a walk *regularly* at three o'clock every afternoon.
consistently It's very unusual for a weekend golfer to get a score below 75, but professional golfers *consistently* score that low.
Antonym: **never.**

and also besides plus

CONJUNCTION: in addition; along with.

and Tell me which of these books you want to read, *and* I'll let you borrow it.
also This recipe for cookies is easy to make; *also,* it's really delicious.
besides I don't feel like watching that show; *besides,* I have some work to do.
plus Our soccer team will play ten games this season, *plus* two practice games.

angry mad irate furious

ADJECTIVE: showing or feeling anger.

angry The rude way that the store clerk spoke to him made him *angry*.
mad Ellen was *mad* at herself for forgetting to bring her lunch two days in a row.
irate The newspaper got a letter to the editor from an *irate* reader that began with the words, "Dear Stupid Editor."
furious When I got home two hours late last night, my mom was really *furious*.

Mrs. Lewis was a bit **angry** when the man hit their car, but Mr. Lewis was **furious.**

animal   mammal beast creature

NOUN: any living thing that is not a plant.

animal A zoo is a place where you can go to see wild *animals.* All the different foods that people eat come from either plants or *animals.*

mammal Although whales live entirely in water as fish do, they are actually *mammals* that give birth to live young, rather than laying eggs.

beast The lion's large, impressive size and its fierce behavior have given it the name of "the king of the *beasts.*"

creature Many strange and exotic *creatures* live in the Amazon rain forests.

▶ **Mammal is** a more exact word than **animal** and is used in science. *Animal* is an older word that can include birds, reptiles, fish, and even insects as well as mammals. It goes back to an earlier time when all beings other than humans were thought of as belonging to the same group.

answer   reply respond retort

VERB: to speak or write in response to something.

answer The teacher asked if anyone knew the capital of Georgia, and Maria correctly *answered* "Atlanta." Sometimes when Alex is very busy, he doesn't *answer* his phone.

reply The judge told the witness that he had to *reply* to every one of the lawyer's questions.

respond I guess the new girl is very shy, because she didn't *respond* at all when I smiled at her.

retort When the librarian asked him to please stop talking, he *retorted* angrily, "Why should I?"

Antonyms: **ask, inquire.**

apart   separate isolated aloof

ADVERB: away from another or others; at a distance.

apart The kindergarten has its own classroom building *apart* from the rest of the school. The umpire spread his arms wide *apart* to show that the runner was safe.

separate When Cliff did the wash, he kept the white and dark socks *separate,* so that the white ones wouldn't get discolored.

isolated The zoo kept one elephant *isolated* from the others in a different pen because it was afraid he might injure them.

aloof While the others in the movie crew ate lunch together in the studio cafeteria, the star of the picture remained *aloof* in her dressing room.

Antonyms: **together, united, joined.**

appoint   name designate nominate elect

VERB: to choose a person for some office or position.

appoint The news story said that the President will *appoint* a new ambassador to Spain this week.

name The soccer coach *named* Nikki and Cathy as the captains for today's game.

designate Each U.S. state has two senators; the one who has served longer is *designated* the "senior senator" from that state.

nominate The Republican and Democratic parties each *nominate* a candidate to run for President.

elect The basis of a democracy is that leaders are *elected* by the people, rather than gaining power by force.

area   region zone belt district

NOUN: any particular extent of land that is named or set off in some way.

area It is surprising how much animal life is found in desert *areas*. New York City and the smaller towns around it form the Greater New York *area*.

region The Middle East *region* was the home of many great ancient civilizations, such as the Mesopotamians and the Egyptians.

zone The roads near a school make up a school *zone* where cars have to go slow.

belt The part of the midwestern United States where a great deal of corn is grown is sometimes called the Corn *Belt*.

district A *District* Court deals with all the cases that take place within one certain part of a city or state.

▶ Try not to overuse *area* in the sense of "I find science to be a very interesting area." Just say "I'm very interested in science." Instead of saying "She's an expert in that area," be more exact: "She's an expert on wild animals."

argue   discuss debate dispute

VERB: to give reasons for or against something; give one's point of view.

argue The children sometimes get upset and *argue* when they can't agree on which TV show to watch. The mayor *argued* that the new school should not be built on Grant Avenue, because there is already too much traffic there.

discuss When the class couldn't decide on a name for their new pet rabbit, the teacher asked them to sit down and *discuss* it among themselves.

debate On our trip to Washington, we were able to hear members of the Senate *debate* on whether there should be a new tax law.

dispute A leading magazine recently stated that Robert Peary was definitely the first man to reach the North Pole, though some experts still *dispute* that idea.

army force troops host legion

NOUN: a large group of people who act or function together.

army The ancient Roman *army* won many battles over its enemies. "Coxey's *Army*" was a band of poor people who marched to Washington in 1894 to demand government aid.

force During a recent crisis in the Persian Gulf, the United States sent a large naval *force* to the area.

troops The German "lightning war" strategy of World War II involved attacks from the air and also advances by ground *troops.*

host When the city announced Clean-up Day for the town park, a *host* of people showed up to help out.

legion That singer has *legions* of fans in England, and her concerts there are always sold out.

Grandma **arranged** the flowers she had picked.

Grandpa keeps his tools **organized** in the garage.

arrange organize sort classify

VERB: to put into some order; place in a certain way.

arrange Doctor Wade sees a lot of patients each day, and she has to *arrange* her schedule very carefully.

organize Dave always has enough time to do his homework projects, because he *organizes* his free time very well.

sort Mom *sorted* the wash so that the dark clothes were separate from the white.

classify The giant panda looks very much like a bear, but scientists actually *classify* it as a different kind of animal.

Antonyms: **disarrange, disorganize.**

ashamed   embarrassed humiliated disgraced

ADJECTIVE: feeling shame for what one has done or what has happened.

ashamed   When he saw how upset she was, he felt *ashamed* that he'd been teasing her so much. I know you missed a few questions on the test, but that's nothing to be *ashamed* of; you did your best.

embarrassed   Right in the middle of the play I forgot what my next line was supposed to be—was I *embarrassed!*

humiliated   The former chess champion felt *humiliated* after he lost a match to a young boy.

disgraced   They were *disgraced* when their son was sent to prison for robbery.

Antonym: **proud.**

ask   inquire question interrogate query

VERB: to put a question to someone; try to get information from someone.

ask   When I leave for school Dad always *asks* me, "Did you remember your lunch?" Bobby wanted to know the time, and *asked* a man standing nearby.

inquire   Mom called the airline to *inquire* about the cost of a flight to Florida.

question   The store manager thought the man was trying to steal some books, so she stopped him and *questioned* him about what was in his shopping bag.

interrogate   The police called him down to headquarters and *interrogated* him for several hours about what had happened that day.

query   The professor put a note on Helen's paper to *query* her about a statement she had written that wasn't clear to him.

Antonyms: **answer, respond, reply.**

assemble   meet gather congregate convene

VERB: to come together or collect in one place; get together.

assemble   The law of the United States allows American citizens to *assemble* in a group whenever they want, as long as they remain peaceful.

meet   All those who are going on the summer trip to Washington should *meet* at 3:00 this afternoon in the school library.

gather   It was well past ten but the store still hadn't opened, and a small crowd had begun to *gather* outside the door.

congregate   When people realized she was a famous movie star, they *congregated* around her, asking for her autograph.

convene   This year's meeting of the Reading Teachers' Association is over, but they will *convene* again next year in Chicago.

Antonyms: **disband, disperse.**

assistant   helper aide associate

NOUN: any person who gives aid or support.

assistant The store manager is not here today, and his *assistant* is in charge of the store. The high school has a principal and two *assistant* principals.

helper The man who cut down the old tree had two *helpers* who carried the wood away.

aide Teachers often have parents work as *aides* in the classroom to help children who are having trouble with their reading or math.

associate In a law firm, lawyers who have been there a long time are partners in the firm, and the younger lawyers are called *associates*.

attention   thought concentration study consideration

NOUN: the act or fact of fixing one's mind on something.

attention The movie was very exciting and my *attention* didn't wander at all. She paid close *attention* to the magician to figure out how the trick was done.

thought He had to give a lot of *thought* to the math problem to get the answer.

concentration When I play right field the ball never seems to be hit out there, and I have a hard time keeping up my *concentration*.

study People complained that the city was not clearing the streets of snow, so the mayor said that he would make a complete *study* of the problem himself.

consideration The college newspaper needs a new sports reporter, and they said that everyone who applies will be given full *consideration* for the job.

Antonym: **inattention.**

The class's **attention** was on what the teacher was saying.

Tim showed a lot of **concentration** as he worked on the math problem.

audience   spectators   observers

NOUN: a group of people who watch and are interested in something.

audience   The outdoor theaters of the ancient Greeks had rows of stone benches on which the *audience* sat.

spectators   The city has a new baseball stadium with seats for 60,000 *spectators*.

observers   The United Nations sent military *observers* to the troubled area, to make sure that the terms of the peace treaty were being carried out properly.

authority   power   control   influence   command

NOUN: the ability or right to act, command, or make decisions.

authority   The President of the U.S. does not have the *authority* to declare war on another country; only Congress does.

power   Because of its great success in business, Japan has a lot of *power* in the world today.

control   In the year 2000 the U.S. will give up *control* of the Panama Canal.

influence   The rock concert was supposed to be sold out, but my uncle used his *influence* with one of the singers in the band to get us some good seats.

command   The company of soldiers was under the *command* of a captain.

available   obtainable   accessible

ADJECTIVE: that can be had, acquired, or used.

available   Books in the school library are *available* for any student to take out. I want to buy this now; after today it's not *available* at the special low price.

obtainable   Milk comes in many different-sized containers; one gallon is the largest size *obtainable* in a regular supermarket.

accessible   The kitchen cabinets are arranged so that they are all easily *accessible* to someone who is working at the stove.

award   honor   prize   medal   trophy

NOUN: a thing that is given for doing something good or for winning something.

award   Nancy did not miss a single day of school and got an *award* for perfect attendance. The best play of the year on Broadway receives the Tony *Award*.

honor   Being named to the Hall of Fame is a great *honor* for a baseball player.

prize   The judges chose Kara's speech as the best, and she won the $50 first *prize*.

medal   The city gave Jennifer a *medal* for saving the life of a boy who was drowning.

trophy   Everyone on the team that won the soccer tournament got a big *trophy*.

It was cold and we stayed **away** from the water. We saw snow on the **distant** mountains.

away   absent distant remote

ADJECTIVE: not close at hand; not here; far off.

away I'm going to feed the Johnsons' dog while they're *away* for a week. Mom told us to play somewhere *away* from the house so we wouldn't wake the baby.

absent A student who has to stay home sick is said to be *absent* from school.

distant Sometimes at night I can hear the *distant* howling of coyotes from the woods behind our house.

remote He lives in a *remote* area and has to ride a bus 20 miles to get to school.

awful   horrible terrible dreadful

ADJECTIVE: causing fear or terror.

awful The tornado left an *awful* trail of destruction through the countryside.

horrible The idea that the United States could be involved in a nuclear war is a *horrible* thought.

terrible The lion leaped against the bars of his cage and let out a *terrible* roar.

dreadful The movie is about a *dreadful* monster who rises from the ocean to attack a city.

▶ It's also possible to use **awful** to mean simply "bad," as in "I had an *awful* day at school today" or "We've been having *awful* weather lately." This is not really wrong, but there are other good words you could use instead. *Awful* is a much stronger word if you use it in its original meaning, the one described above.

back   support sponsor endorse promote

VERB: to give aid or help to; be on the side of.

back The local newspaper has *backed* the plan to build a new city library. The labor unions are *backing* the mayor in his bid for reelection.

support Senator Jones thinks that income taxes are too high, so he *supports* a proposed new law that would lower the tax rate.

sponsor Peppy's Pizza House is going to *sponsor* our baseball team, and their name will be on our uniform shirts.

endorse TV commercials for new cars often show famous stars *endorsing* the cars and telling why people should buy them.

promote The company decided to *promote* the sale of their new electric toy by offering free batteries to go with it.

Antonym: **oppose.**

Whoever knocked over the mail box did a **bad** thing.

It was **naughty** of Kate to grab her sister's magazine.

bad   evil wicked naughty

ADJECTIVE: not following what is right to do; not good.

bad Charles has been really *bad* in school this week; twice he was sent to the principal's office for fighting with other students.

evil King Richard III was thought of as an *evil* ruler; it's believed that he had his own nephews murdered so that he could be king.

wicked Cinderella's *wicked* stepmother treated her in a very cruel way.

naughty Missy was acting *naughty* and kept making funny faces just as the photographer was about to take her picture.

Antonyms: **good, virtuous.**

bag   sack   pouch

NOUN: a soft container for carrying or holding things, usually open at the top.

bag   At the supermarket you can pick out your own vegetables and put them in a plastic *bag*. My sister has a sports *bag* to keep her soccer equipment in.

sack   Dad went to the Farmer's Market and bought a big *sack* of potatoes.

pouch   Riders on the Pony Express carried letters in a large leather *pouch*.

▶ Many people carry their lunch in a brown paper **bag.** This can also be called a paper **sack.** Which word you choose can depend on where in the U.S. you live. People in the East say *bag;* people in the South and the West usually say *sack*.

ball   circle   globe   sphere

NOUN: a round object or figure.

ball   Many popular games are played with a *ball,* such as baseball, football, tennis, and soccer. The cannons used in the Civil War fired huge metal *balls.*

circle   The full moon looked like a huge silver *circle* in the night sky.

globe   The teacher showed us where the Indian Ocean was by pointing out its location on the large *globe* on her desk.

sphere   Photographs taken from outer space show that the Earth is a *sphere.*

bare   naked   nude   stripped   undressed

ADJECTIVE: having no covering or clothing.

bare   She put on a long-sleeved shirt so that she wouldn't get sunburned on her *bare* arms.

naked   Mikey jumped out of the tub and ran *naked* down the hall to get a towel.

nude   The famous sculpture *David* by the Italian artist Michelangelo shows the *nude* figure of a young man.

stripped   It was a broiling hot day, and the men on the highway crew were *stripped* to the waist as they worked.

undressed   The patient got *undressed* so that the doctor could examine him.

<u>Antonyms:</u> **dressed, covered.**

base   camp   fort

NOUN: a place where many ships, planes, or other military forces are kept.

base   Recruits are not allowed to leave the *base* until basic training is completed. Japanese war planes bombed a U.S. naval *base* in Hawaii on December 7, 1941.

camp   The troops halted their advance and set up *camp* for the night.

fort   The U.S. Army built many *forts* in the West to defend against Indian attack.

basically   mainly   primarily   essentially   fundamentally

ADVERB: for the most part.

basically He can be rude at times, but he's *basically* a nice person. This book says that good cooking is *basically* a matter of having good, fresh food to cook.

mainly A great deal of wine is produced in the United States, *mainly* in California.

primarily Herman Melville wrote a number of books, but he is *primarily* known for his great novel *Moby-Dick.*

essentially There are still a few things to do, but the building of the house is *essentially* finished.

fundamentally Though he made a few spelling mistakes, his ideas were excellent and it was *fundamentally* a good report.

▶ Don't use **basically** just to fill out a sentence. "A desert is basically a place with no rain." "Basically, this book is a mystery story." *Basically* doesn't contribute anything to those sentences. It's only useful when there are two differing ideas: "The book has a few funny scenes, but *basically* it's a mystery story."

basis   base   root   foundation

NOUN: an important idea that supports or proves something.

basis You say that students who watch a lot of television get poor grades—what's the *basis* of that statement?

base It may sound like an interesting new plan, but at *base* it's just the same old way of doing things.

root This article says that the *root* of the city's air-pollution problem is that there are too many automobiles in too small a space.

foundation The theories of the Polish scientist Copernicus were the *foundation* of the modern field of astronomy.

beat   defeat   conquer   overcome

VERB: to get the better of in some contest or competition.

beat Green Bay *beat* Kansas City by a score of 35-10 in the first Super Bowl. "I'm going to run again," the mayor said, "and I'll *beat* anyone who runs against me."

defeat Although they were *defeated* by the South in the early battles of the war, the North went on to win the Civil War.

conquer In 1519 the Spanish explorer Cortés *conquer*ed the Aztec Indians, and Spain became the ruler of Mexico.

overcome Scott Hamilton had to *overcome* a severe physical handicap to become an Olympic figure-skating champion.

because since for due

CONJUNCTION: for the reason that.

because I ride my bike to school *because* it's too far to walk. *Because* today is a holiday, there is no mail delivery.

since They had to park across the street, *since* there were no spaces left in the parking lot.

for She stood in the doorway looking embarrassed, *for* it was obvious that no one had told them she was coming.

due The Laurel Street bridge will be closed for a month, *due* to repair work on the road surface.

Because her radio was so loud, Lin didn't hear the phone ring.

Mom thought no one was home, **since** the phone just kept ringing.

become develop turn evolve

VERB: to grow or come to be.

become That tiny bud on the bush will *become* a beautiful flower. It's almost impossible to *become* a lawyer without going to law school first.

develop This is Andrew's first year playing baseball, but it looks like he's going to *develop* into a really good player.

turn The day started out sunny, but by mid-afternoon it had *turned* cold and cloudy.

evolve Many different people work on a movie script as it *evolves* from one writer's first idea to a finished screenplay.

beginning   origin source inception onset

NOUN: the first part of something; what comes first.

beginning The *beginning* of the play was so boring that half the audience had walked out by the middle of the first act.

origin Basketball had its *origin* in a gym in Springfield, Massachusetts in 1891.

source Latin, the language of the ancient Romans, is the *source* of many words we use in English today.

inception The United Nations has been an important world body ever since its *inception*.

onset The *onset* of chicken pox is marked by itchy red bumps on the skin.

Antonyms: **end, finish, conclusion.**

behavior   conduct manner

NOUN: a certain way of acting.

behavior The teacher sent a note to Joe's parents about his bad *behavior* in class. The psychiatrist Sigmund Freud is famous for his study of human *behavior*.

conduct In the Army, a soldier who always carries out his duties in the proper way can receive a medal for good *conduct*.

manner The mayor put her visitors at ease with her warm and friendly *manner*.

behind   after

PREPOSITION: at or toward a place or position in the rear.

behind She looked *behind* her before she backed the car out of the garage. Our team is in third place so far, *behind* the Eagles and the Wildcats.

after Terry grabbed his sister's hat from her, and she chased *after* him trying to get it back.

Antonym: **ahead.**

Marty is hiding **behind** a tree. He doesn't want his dog to follow **after** him all the time.

belief   opinion view theory conviction

NOUN: an idea held in the mind and thought to be true.

belief The Muslim religion has the *belief* that Muhammad was the messenger of God. There's a popular *belief* that getting chilled will cause you to catch a cold.

opinion Some of my friends like to watch that show, but my *opinion* is that it's childish and silly.

view My mom wrote a letter to the newspaper to give her *views* on next week's election for mayor.

theory No one really knows why the dinosaurs died out—one leading *theory* is that it was because of changes in the earth's climate.

conviction The experiment did not work at first, but the scientist had the absolute *conviction* that he was right and kept on trying.

bend   curve arch bow arc

NOUN: a turn or movement away from a straight line.

bend As soon as we get around this *bend* in the river, we'll be able to see the campsite up ahead.

curve The road up the mountain had many sharp *curves*.

arch The entrance to the highway tunnel is in the shape of an *arch*.

bow Cowboys of the Old West were said to have *bow* legs, because their legs turned outward from sitting on a horse all day.

arc When the moon is new, it seems to form a narrow *arc* in the sky.

best   greatest finest supreme

ADJECTIVE: of the highest quality; most excellent.

best Wayne Gretzky is often said to be the *best* hockey player of all time. I like a lot of different flavors of ice cream, but I think chocolate chip is the *best*.

greatest Vivien Leigh was in many movies, but most people consider her role in *Gone With the Wind* to be her *greatest* performance.

finest For many years the Plaza in New York City has been rated as one of the *finest* hotels in the United States.

supreme A "Renaissance man" is someone with vast knowledge and skill in many fields; Leonardo da Vinci is the *supreme* example of this type.

▶ Do not use **best** in place of **better**, as in, "We saw two movies, *Battle of the Planets* and *The Lost Ship*. I thought *The Lost Ship* was the best." You are only comparing two things, so say "*The Lost Ship* was *better*." *Best* is for more than two things. "*The Lost Ship* is the *best* movie I've seen this year."
Antonym: **worst**.

bet   wager gamble stake risk

VERB: to try to gain money on the chance that some event will turn out in a certain way.

bet People go to horse races to *bet* on which horse will win the race. Mike *bet* 50 cents with his friend that the Giants would beat the Raiders in the Super Bowl.

wager To win at the game of roulette, you *wager* as to which number a little ball will stop on as it rolls around the roulette wheel.

gamble Many people *gamble* a few dollars each week on a state lottery, hoping to win millions.

stake The real estate agent told them the house was a great buy, and he said he'd *stake* his entire bank account that its value would go up.

risk The experts say that buying this stock is not a good investment, but she doesn't mind *risking* a few dollars on it, because the price may go up.

better   greater finer superior

ADJECTIVE: of higher quality.

better I liked the first "Ghostbusters" movie, but I thought the second one was even *better*. Dana is a *better* tennis player since she spent a week at tennis camp.

greater William Shakespeare and George Bernard Shaw both wrote famous plays about Julius Caesar, but Shakespeare's is considered the *greater* of the two.

finer Cashmere sweaters are very expensive, because the wool is of much *finer* quality than ordinary wool.

superior The honors English class is open only to those who have shown that they are *superior* students.

Antonym: **worse**.

between   among

PREPOSITION: in the same group or category as another or others.

between There was an argument at the school board meeting *between* the people who want year-round schools and those who do not.

among Heather, Laura, and Beth counted the money they collected for Girl Scouts and found they had $25 *among* them.

▶ Use **between** when you refer to two things. For more than two, **among** is a better choice. "There are four people running for class president, and it's hard to choose between them." There are four of them, so the correct word is *among:* "It's hard to choose *among* (or *from among*) so many good candidates." Notice the sentence above for *between*. Even though many people may be arguing about year-round schools, there are only two sides in the argument.

beyond past

PREPOSITION: farther on than something else in space or time.

beyond The cabin is on a narrow dirt road about five miles *beyond* where the highway ends. It was a holiday, so Matt got to stay up *beyond* his usual bedtime.

past He drove *past* her house by mistake and had to turn around and go back. Don't bother to send in an entry for the contest now; it's already two weeks *past* the deadline.

A tiger is a **big** animal.

An elephant is **enormous.**

big large huge enormous gigantic immense

ADJECTIVE: having great size, or more than the usual size for its kind.

big Your older brother is really a *big* boy—I bet he plays on the high school football team. I can't wear that jacket; it has a *big* paint spot on the back.

large The best-known feature of the Arabian camel is the *large* hump that it has on its back.

huge The Statue of Liberty is a *huge* figure of a woman that stands on an island in New York Harbor.

enormous The official home of the Queen of England is Buckingham Palace, an *enormous* building with nearly 600 rooms.

gigantic Each year for the holiday season a *gigantic* Christmas tree is placed on the lawn of the White House.

immense An *immense* desert makes up much of the continent of Australia.

Antonyms: **small, little.**

bill   measure act proposal

NOUN: an action or suggested action by a law-making body.

bill There is a *bill* before the Senate now to raise the cost of a first-class stamp.
measure The senator is concerned about health care costs and thinks the government must enact some *measure* to deal with the problem.
act Yellowstone National Park was declared a special protected area by an *act* of Congress in 1872.
proposal The mayor is preparing a *proposal* to control rent costs in the city.
▶ While an action is still being considered by Congress, it is a **bill.** Once it has been approved by Congress, it then takes effect and becomes a **law.**

bit   particle crumb chip iota

NOUN: a very small piece or amount.

bit He used the vacuum cleaner to get up some *bits* of paper from the floor.
particle She picked up the old book and sent *particles* of dust flying into the air.
crumb Everybody must have liked that cake I baked; only a few *crumbs* of it are left on the plate.
chip There were *chips* of wood scattered around after the tree was cut down.
iota The lawyer said that the state had not produced one single *iota* of evidence to prove her client was guilty.

black   African-American Afro-American Negro

ADJECTIVE: of a race of people originally living in Africa.

▶ It once was correct to call this group the *Negro* race. In the 1960's, that word became unpopular, and it was replaced by *black. Afro-American* also came into use then, especially to describe features of African culture found in the United States. Later, the term *African-American* was recommended as the most suitable name of all, on the grounds that it is similar to *Irish-American, Italian-American,* and so on. It is not now possible to tell if *African-American* will replace *black.*

block   check obstruct hinder

VERB: to stop the progress of; keep from moving or acting in the proper way.

block A stalled truck was *blocking* the entrance to the tunnel, and traffic was tied up. He put out his foot to *block* the way as I tried to walk by.
check She was about to answer, but she *checked* herself for fear of being wrong.
obstruct There is a rule in soccer that you cannot *obstruct* another player who is trying to go past you to get the ball.
hinder The deep mud *hindered* their movements as they tried to climb the path.

body   shape form figure

NOUN: the main part of something.

body Following this diet and exercise plan will give you a strong, healthy *body*. After the crash, the wings of the plane were damaged, but the *body* was intact.

shape There was a big cloud overhead that seemed to have the *shape* of a house.

form A fossil allows you to see the *form* of an animal or plant that died many thousands of years ago.

figure It was hard to tell in the darkness, but I thought I saw the *figure* of a man standing by the lake.

boring   dull monotonous tedious tiresome

ADJECTIVE: not lively or exciting; causing a person to lose interest.

boring Let's go out and do something; it's *boring* just sitting around the house all day. The movie had no action scenes, and I thought it was very *boring*.

dull It will be a *dull* paper if you only list a lot of facts; you have to give some interesting details and tell what you think.

monotonous In speech class he learned to put some life and expression in his voice, rather than always speaking in one *monotonous* tone.

tedious She finds that job to be very *tedious* because she does the same thing over and over all day long.

tiresome When they ride to school, Debbie spends the whole time talking about her boyfriend, which is very *tiresome* for the other girls.

<u>Antonyms:</u> **interesting, exciting, lively.**

We thought the speaker was **boring.** He went on and on in the same **monotonous** voice.

27

Craig was **bothering** his sister while she was studying. She was **annoyed** at him.

bother   annoy disturb irritate pester

VERB: to disturb or upset a person.

bother He's just trying to be friendly when he teases you like that—don't let it *bother* you. It *bother*s me that I can't remember her last name.

annoy It really *annoys* Dad when people talk during a movie and he can't hear what the actors are saying.

disturb Their house was very close to the airport, and the noise of the big jets *disturbed* them day and night.

irritate The passengers were very *irritated* that the train was running so late.

pester Whenever the boys hear the bell of the ice cream truck, they *pester* their mother to buy them something.

Antonyms: **please, soothe, comfort.**

box   package parcel container receptacle

NOUN: something that is used to hold other things.

box The washing machine was delivered to their house in a large cardboard *box*.

package People keep *packages* of frozen food in the freezer part of a refrigerator.

parcel Cindy got a small, brightly wrapped *parcel* in today's mail—I bet it's a birthday present.

container Dad has a metal *container* in the garage that holds gasoline for the lawn mower.

receptacle The sign said to put all papers and garbage in the trash *receptacle*.

boy   youth youngster lad

NOUN: a male child who is not yet an adult.

boy There are five children in the family, two *boys* and three girls. The great Mozart was already composing music when he was just a *boy* of five.

youth The city has started a new "Get Straight" program to try to help troubled *youths* in the community.

youngster Grandpa knows these hills really well; he says he's been camping out here ever since he was a *youngster*.

lad The old folk tale of "Dick Whittington and His Cat" tells about a bold young *lad* who becomes the Lord Mayor of London.

brag   boast gloat crow

VERB: to speak highly about yourself or something that you have done; praise yourself.

brag Jerry's baseball team is in first place in the league, and he's always *bragging* about what a good player he is. Karen never *brags* about being rich, even though her family lives in a huge mansion.

boast Professional wrestlers often go on television to *boast* about how they are going to win their next match.

gloat It was bad enough when Chip beat me at chess, but the way he *gloated* about it afterward really made me mad.

crow My dad said that the award I won in math was really something to *crow* about.

brave   courageous fearless bold valiant

ADJECTIVE: having the will to do something dangerous; showing courage.

brave The people who hid fugitives from the Nazis during World War II had to be very *brave*. The pilot Amelia Earhart disappeared during a *brave* attempt to fly a small plane around the world.

courageous Martin Luther King's *courageous* leadership inspired the members of the civil rights movement in the 1960's.

fearless Even though they knew they had no chance to survive, the *fearless* Texans at the Alamo refused to surrender.

bold No one would volunteer to cross the enemy lines, until finally one *bold* soldier said he was sure he could get through.

valiant "The Song of Roland" is the story of how a small group of French knights fought a *valiant* battle against a huge enemy force.

Antonyms: **cowardly, fearful.**

break   crack shatter snap smash

VERB: to come apart; go into pieces.

break Don't play ball so close to the house; you might *break* a window. The door was locked tight, and the firemen had to *break* it down to get into the building.

crack Before Mom buys eggs, she opens the carton to make sure that none of the shells are *cracked.*

shatter The mirror fell to the floor and *shattered* into hundreds of shiny little pieces.

snap Danny stretched the rubber band too tight, and it *snapped* in two.

smash He was so mad that his toy car wouldn't work any more that he took a hammer and *smashed* it to bits.

Stacy **broke** the stick in half.   The ice **cracked** when Greg put his foot down.

bright   brilliant glowing gleaming vivid

ADJECTIVE: giving off or showing much light.

bright As the plane came down, the *bright* lights of Los Angeles were spread out below us. Very *bright* stars can be seen from Earth without a telescope.

brilliant He had to shield his eyes as he stepped from the dark movie theater into the *brilliant* afternoon sunshine.

glowing The fire had almost gone out; nothing was left but a few *glowing* coals.

gleaming We saw the *gleaming* body of a fish as it suddenly jumped out of the water right in front of our boat.

vivid The Dutch artist Vincent van Gogh is known for his use of strong, *vivid* colors in his paintings.

Antonyms: **dark, dim, dull.**

build construct erect frame

VERB: to make something by putting parts or materials together.

build The Wilsons plan to *build* a vacation home on their property by the lake. Birds *build* nests from dried grass and twigs.

construct It is amazing to think of how precisely the ancient Egyptians were able to *construct* the Pyramids without modern equipment or measuring devices.

erect The city is planning to *erect* an overpass so that children can walk safely over the highway on their way to school.

frame Early settlers in America lived in log cabins that were *framed* by hand.

building structure edifice

NOUN: something that is built for use by people, or to store things.

building Our doctor has her office in an old brick *building* downtown. The Empire State *Building* in New York City is a very famous skyscraper.

structure Their garage is not attached to the house, but is a separate *structure*.

edifice The Parthenon in Greece is a huge, impressive *edifice* that was built in ancient times as a place to worship the Greek goddess Athena.

bump knock jolt collide

VERB: to move or hit against suddenly and heavily.

bump She didn't look where she was going and *bumped* into the door. The two outfielders *bumped* into each other when they were trying to catch a fly ball.

knock The kittens chased each other across the kitchen table and *knocked* a glass onto the floor.

jolt The passengers were *jolted* as the plane made a rough emergency landing.

collide The car did not stop for the red light and *collided* with another car.

burst explode erupt

VERB: to break open suddenly and with force.

burst Every time Jimmy blew a big soap bubble, his sister Lindsay would *burst* it with her finger.

explode The fireworks *exploded* into glorious color in the dark summer sky.

erupt People who live near Mt. St. Helens know that the volcano could *erupt* again at any time.

▶ **Bust** is sometimes used in place of **burst,** as in "He used a long pin to bust the balloon." This use is not correct in school writing. It should be "He used a pin to *burst* (or *break*) the balloon."

business sales trade industry commerce

NOUN: the buying and selling of goods, or the exchange of services for money.

business The stores at the mall do a lot of *business* during the Christmas season. He wants to leave the job he has now to go into *business* for himself.

sales *Sales* of personal computers have gone way up in the past ten years.

trade The European Common Market was set up to encourage *trade* among the countries of Europe.

industry The "Big Three" of the U.S. auto *industry* are General Motors, Ford Motor Company, and Chrysler Corporation.

commerce The Federal government regulates *commerce* between one state and another.

busy active occupied engrossed absorbed

ADJECTIVE: engaged in some activity or operation.

busy Melissa couldn't play because she was *busy* doing a book report for school. All the clerks were *busy* and there was no one to wait on us.

active Grandma still does all her own cleaning and cooking; she says she likes to stay *active* around the house.

occupied Mrs. Ellis won't be able to help with the school picnic this year; she's completely *occupied* with a big project at her office.

engrossed Peg was so *engrossed* in her book that she didn't know I was there.

absorbed The doctor told him that he is getting too *absorbed* in his work and that he should take up a relaxing hobby.

Antonyms: **idle, unoccupied.**

Mom was **busy** with the sign. Dad was **engrossed** in the TV show and didn't notice her.

but   nevertheless however yet

CONJUNCTION: on the other hand.

but I'd like to go to the movie with you, *but* I have to babysit for my little sister. People always say that it's hard to get into that restaurant, *but* we didn't have to wait at all.

nevertheless Arnold Palmer doesn't play in many golf tournaments any more; *nevertheless,* he is still one of the most famous players in the game.

however It rained most of the day; *however,* the game went on just as scheduled.

yet She works long hours in a bank, *yet* she still finds time to go for a three or four mile run every day.

▶ The words **but** and **and** are both used to join the parts of a sentence together, and sometimes it's hard to tell which one to choose. Use *but* when the second part of the sentence seems to be a surprise or contrast from the first part: "I've read four books by that author, *but* I don't think she's a very good writer." If you said you had read four different books by a certain writer, people would assume you liked that writer. *But* is used to show that a surprise is coming.

buy   purchase acquire obtain

VERB: to pay money to get something.

buy Our car has been having trouble lately, and Mom wants to *buy* a new one. Did you *buy* Elena a birthday present yet?

purchase Many foreign airlines *purchase* the American-made Boeing 747 jet for use on overseas flights.

acquire In recent years several well-known American companies have been *acquired* by Sony, the huge Japanese electronics corporation.

obtain The commercial said that this record album is only available by mail and cannot be *obtained* in any record store.

Antonym: **sell.**

by   with through

PREPOSITION: in a certain way; because of.

by The sign is attached to the wall *by* two large screws. She doesn't like to drive to the city and prefers going *by* bus.

with He got the ice off the windshield *with* a plastic scraper. Many authors now write *with* a word processor instead of a typewriter.

through Dad got us these tickets *through* a friend of his at the office. Many businesses advertise their products *through* the mail.

call   invite   summon

VERB: To request or command to come; send or ask for.

call We have to *call* a taxi to take us to the airport this afternoon. I may be *called* as a witness in court about that traffic accident I saw last month.

invite The principal will speak tonight about the plans for the new school, and all parents who are interested are *invited* to attend.

summon The President *summoned* his advisors to the White House immediately for an important meeting.

Antonym: **dismiss.**

Russell **called** his dog
to come into the house.

Mrs. Evans **summoned** Russell
to the front of the classroom.

calm   peaceful serene tranquil placid

ADJECTIVE: quiet and still; not disturbed or excited.

calm There was no wind and the sea was flat and *calm.* The pilot spoke in a *calm* voice so that the passengers would not become upset.

peaceful When the twins are playing video games in the living room, my bedroom is a *peaceful* spot away from all the noise.

serene I thought Mom would be angry about what had happened, but she kept the same *serene* expression on her face.

tranquil After a long week of work in the city, she likes to escape for a *tranquil* weekend at her cabin in the mountains.

placid The store clerk is a *placid* man who always answers "Have a nice day" even when a customer is very rude to him.

Antonyms: **excited, restless.**

campaign   drive effort push

NOUN: any series of actions to reach a certain goal.

campaign The Republican and Democratic candidates will debate each other three times in their *campaign* for President. The television networks always put on a big advertising *campaign* to introduce their new fall programs.

drive The high school is going to have a fund-raising *drive* to get money for new uniforms for the school band.

effort As soon as the hurricane had passed by, the town began to carry out its clean-up *efforts.*

push The City Theater Company is putting on a big *push* to get as many people as possible to sign up for season tickets.

can   may

VERB: to be able to or be allowed to.

▶ Ben asked, "Mom, can I read your magazine?" She said, "Of course you *can* read it." But as he reached for it she said, "Yes, you *can* read it; you know how to read. But you *may* not read it. I'm not through with it." She's trying to show him that people who want to be exactly correct use *can* and *may* in different ways. **Can** means you know how to do something, or are able to do it. **May** means that you are allowed to do it. However, this difference is only for school writing. In ordinary conversation with friends, "Can I read this magazine?" is correct.

capital/capitol

▶ Both these words have to do with the center of a government. The **capital** (spelled with an **a**) is the city where the government of a country or state is located. The *capital* of the United States is Washington, D.C. The *capital* of the state of Iowa is Des Moines. The **capitol** (spelled with an **o**) is the actual building in that city in which the lawmakers meet. The U.S. *Capitol* is a large white building with a dome.

car   automobile limousine

NOUN: a passenger vehicle with four wheels and a motor.

car Robert washes and waxes the family *car* every Saturday morning. The price of a new *car* is higher than that of a used one.

automobile No one person is given credit for inventing the *automobile,* though Karl Benz and Gottlieb Daimler both developed gas-powered vehicles in 1885.

limousine On Academy Award night many movie stars arrive at the ceremonies in long black *limousines.*

care   concern worry anxiety stress

NOUN: a feeling of being troubled about what may happen.

care Even though he has a big test this morning, he's going around the house laughing and singing, as if he doesn't have a *care* in the world.

concern We know that the house needs a lot of minor work, but our main *concern* right now is that the roof is leaking.

worry When they were first married they didn't have much money, so they had a lot of financial *worries*.

anxiety Cathy didn't know what high school would be like, and she felt a little *anxiety* about starting out as a freshman.

stress In Mrs. White's job people are always calling up to complain, which causes her quite a bit of *stress*.

carry   transport convey transmit tote lug

VERB: to move something from one place to another.

carry In some Asian countries, elephants are trained to *carry* heavy loads. The defense in football tries to tackle the player who is *carrying* the ball.

transport During World War II, famous ocean liners such as the *Queen Mary* were used to *transport* American troops to Europe.

convey The giant Alaska Pipeline *conveys* oil across the Alaskan wilderness.

transmit A fax machine is a modern device that can quickly *transmit* words and images from one location to another over phone lines.

tote Susan always *totes* her purse around with her wherever she goes.

lug Joey has a bunch of empty bottles that he wants to return, and he asked me to help him *lug* them to the store.

case   matter example instance situation

NOUN: one certain thing that can be discussed or dealt with; one of a certain type.

case You usually have to pay for your ticket ahead of time, but in this *case* it won't be necessary. The doctor told her she has a *case* of measles.

matter The reporters asked the mayor what he intended to do about the *matter* of the missing city funds.

example A number of U.S. Vice Presidents have gone on to become President; Theodore Roosevelt is one famous *example*.

instance Parents have asked the city to put a traffic light at that corner near school, because there have been several *instances* of near accidents there.

situation I think you did the right thing; it's what I would have done in the same *situation*.

casual   informal relaxed sporty

ADJECTIVE: not formal or fancy; not dressy.

casual You don't have to dress up for the party; just wear some *casual* clothes like you wear around the house on weekends.

informal It was an *informal* dinner and the guests served themselves on paper plates and sat on chairs on the patio.

relaxed That computer company has a *relaxed* atmosphere; people wear jeans and sweaters to work instead of suits or dresses.

sporty Grandpa was wearing his favorite holiday outfit, a necktie with figures of reindeer on it and a *sporty* red and green plaid vest.

<u>Antonyms:</u> **formal, dressy.**

The Smiths' party was just an **informal** get-together, so Carl wore his **casual** clothes.

catch   capture trap seize

VERB: to take hold of something that is moving.

catch The ad says that this special bait is sure to *catch* a lot of fish. In the game of tag, the person who is "it" has to chase after and *catch* the other players.

capture Stevie ran up and down the beach, trying to *capture* sand crabs in a paper cup.

trap The American Indians used hidden snares to *trap* rabbits and other small animals for food.

seize Two policemen *seized* him as he was leaving the bank with the stolen money.

<u>Antonym:</u> **miss.**

cause   affect determine influence

VERB: to make something happen.

cause The brush is so dry that even the smallest spark could *cause* a forest fire. The discovery of gold in California *caused* many people to move there.

affect The type of food that you eat is bound to *affect* your health.

determine Colleges say that a student's high school grades and test scores are the main factors that *determine* whether or not he gets into a certain college.

influence The Senator had been in favor of the bill, but a number of letters from voters who were against it *influenced* him to change his mind.

celebrate   honor observe commemorate

VERB: to observe a certain day or time with special activities.

celebrate Our family always *celebrates* Thanksgiving with a big dinner at my Aunt Marie's house. Josh went to Florida to help his great-grandfather *celebrate* his ninetieth birthday.

honor Memorial Day is set aside to *honor* Americans who died serving their country in wartime.

observe Ramadan is a special month of the year in the Muslim calendar, which Muslims *observe* by not eating any food during daylight hours.

commemorate The Fourth of July holiday *commemorates* the signing of the Declaration of Independence on July 4, 1776.

Antonyms: **ignore, neglect, dishonor.**

Mrs. Ruiz **celebrated** her 25th anniversary at the company. They **honored** her with a gift.

center   core hub focus heart

NOUN: the main area of activity or attention; the middle point or part.

center I bet Jason will be an actor when he grows up, because he always wants to be the *center* of attention wherever he goes.

core To graduate from high school, students have to take courses in the *core* subjects of English, math, science, and history.

hub In earlier times Boston was nicknamed "the *Hub*," because people who lived there thought of it as the most important American city.

focus The local basketball team has been the *focus* of everybody's conversation this week, since they are in the finals of the state tournament.

heart The company's offices are at One Wall Street, in the *heart* of the American financial community.

certain   sure positive definite inevitable

ADJECTIVE: known to be true or right.

certain *Tom Sawyer* was written by Mark Twain; I'm *certain* of that. Don't seal the envelope until you've made *certain* that all the necessary papers are inside.

sure We're allowed to have our books open for the test—are you *sure* that's what the teacher said?

positive I am *positive* that the recipe calls for lime juice, not lemon juice; check the cookbook if you don't believe me.

definite The plans for the team party are *definite*—it will be at Pizza Palace at 6:00 this Saturday evening.

inevitable Once Adolf Hitler ordered the German army to invade Poland, it was *inevitable* that Great Britain would declare war on Germany.

Antonyms: **uncertain, unsure.**

chance   opportunity occasion break

NOUN: a time when it is possible or favorable to do something.

chance The first-string quarterback is hurt, and this is Eric's big *chance* to show the coach what he can do. If you don't pass the driving test the first time, you have a *chance* to take it again.

opportunity She is excited about going to New York, because it will be the first time she has the *opportunity* to see a live Broadway play.

occasion When all the students were seated and quiet, the principal said, "Let me take this *occasion* to thank all the parents who helped us with the show."

break We found a parking space right in front of the store we were going to, which was a lucky *break*.

change alter vary modify transform convert

VERB: to become or make different.

change Bobby has really *changed* since the last time I saw him—I bet he's grown six inches. She wants to *change* her sixth-period class from cooking to typing.

alter Sometimes a different hairstyle can greatly *alter* the way a person looks.

vary Mom *varies* what she puts in our school lunches, so that we won't get tired of having the same thing.

modify The computer's keyboard has been *modified* slightly because people complained that the old one was too hard to use.

transform It was the night of the Senior Dance, and the high school gym had been *transformed* into a tropical paradise.

convert When they visited England, they had to *convert* their American money to British pounds.

character personality disposition nature temperament

NOUN: the qualities that are distinctive to a person and that distinguish him or her from other people; what a person is like.

character That judge has a strong *character* and would never do anything dishonest. The dramas of the ancient Greeks often tell how a ruler loses power because of a flaw in his *character*.

personality She finds it easy to make friends because of her lively, outgoing *personality*.

disposition Mom says that I had a good *disposition* when I was a baby; I hardly ever cried or fussed.

nature Dave isn't the kind of person who would pick on someone smaller— that's just not his *nature*.

temperament The coach is known for his even *temperament* and never gets angry or excited during a game.

charge accuse indict arraign

VERB: to blame someone for a crime in an official way.

charge The district attorney has *charged* the man with setting fire to his own store for the insurance money.

accuse The police had *accused* him of that crime after they found an empty gas can behind the store.

indict The grand jury *indicted* the man for arson when the assistant district attorney presented her evidence.

arraign The man will be *arraigned* next Monday in Superior Court.

Mr. Tate bought a **cheap** umbrella. His wife bought an **inexpensive** one.

cheap   inexpensive   low-priced   cut-rate

ADJECTIVE: not having or charging a high price.

cheap   They're selling fresh corn for just fifteen cents an ear—that's really *cheap.* I want to buy a good watch, not some *cheap* thing that will break after a week.

inexpensive   La Pietra is a good, *inexpensive* restaurant that serves simple Italian-style meals.

low-priced   That company builds the only *low-priced* homes in town, and its houses are often sold before they are even finished.

cut-rate   He runs a *cut-rate* bookstore in which all the current best-sellers are offered for 40 percent off the list price.

Antonyms: **expensive, costly.**

cheat   swindle   deceive   trick

VERB: to act in a way that is not right or fair; be dishonest.

cheat   He tried to *cheat* on the test by looking at another student's paper. The gambler was *cheating* at the card game and was hiding an ace up his sleeve.

swindle   They were *swindled* out of $1,000 by a man who sold them a "diamond" that actually turned out to be glass.

deceive   Before he escaped, the prisoner put a dummy in his bed to *deceive* the guards into thinking he was still in his cell.

trick   My friend tried to *trick* me when he called up, by pretending I had won money in a contest.

check   examine inspect test evaluate

VERB: to look carefully at something to see if it is right or as it should be.

check When the night guard goes around the building, he *checks* to see if all the doors are locked. The teacher *checked* my paper and marked the answers that I got wrong.

examine The bank clerk carefully *examined* the signatures on the two checks and saw that the handwriting matched.

inspect When the City Department of Health *inspected* the restaurant, they found that the kitchen was not being kept clean.

test This liquid is used to *test* the water in the swimming pool and make sure it has the proper chemicals in it.

evaluate The school is going to choose new reading books for next year, and the teachers are now *evaluating* three different programs.

The nurse **checked** her height and weight.   Dr. Wu **examined** the patient's ear.

chew   bite gnaw nibble

VERB: to grind or crush food or other things with the teeth.

chew At our school no one is allowed to *chew* gum during class. A little baby isn't able to *chew* things and can't eat hard food.

bite I always peel apples before I eat them, because I don't like to *bite* into the skin.

gnaw Beavers *gnaw* around the trunk of a tree to cut it down.

nibble The squirrel sat watching us and *nibbling* on a nut in its mouth.

child   kid youngster juvenile

NOUN: a young person.

child Michael is the youngest *child* on his soccer team; he's five and all the other boys and girls are six.

kid A lot more *kids* came to our house for Halloween this year than last year.

youngster Henry's grandfather patted him on the back and called him a fine-looking *youngster.*

juvenile This town has a rule stating that all *juveniles* under the age of 16 must be home by 11:00 P.M.

▶ The word **child** should be used instead of **kid** in school writing. "President Harry Truman had one *child* (not 'one kid'), a daughter named Margaret."

choose   pick select opt

VERB: to decide on one or several from a larger group.

choose In Little League baseball everyone goes to a tryout, and then the coaches all *choose* the players they want for their teams.

pick Each player *picks* a card from the deck, and the high card goes first.

select The President has *selected* Senator Jones to be the new Secretary of State.

opt Everyone else wanted to go out to a movie, but Karen *opted* for staying home.

Antonyms: **reject, refuse.**

church   chapel cathedral

NOUN: a building for the public worship of God.

church Their family goes to St. John's *Church* every Sunday morning. The town has five different *churches,* four Protestant and one Catholic.

chapel A large church often has a *chapel,* a room or separate building in which smaller services are held.

cathedral Many large and impressive *cathedrals* were built in Europe during the Middle Ages, such as Notre Dame in Paris.

circle   surround encircle ring

VERB: to draw or form a circle around.

circle *Circle* either "A" or "B" on your paper to indicate the correct answer.

surround At the Battle of Yorktown, General Washington's army *surrounded* the British troops led by General Cornwallis.

encircle The flag of Rhode Island shows an anchor *encircled* by 13 gold stars.

ring The lake is in a beautiful valley *ringed* by snow-covered mountains.

city town village metropolis community

NOUN: an area where many people live and work.

city New York has been the largest *city* in the United States since the 1700's. The *city* of Rome controlled a powerful empire in ancient times.

town In the Middle Ages, most people spent their entire lives in the *town* where they were born.

village The artist Norman Rockwell lived in a small New England *village* and often painted scenes of the people and places there.

metropolis Many Americans have moved to California in the years since World War II, and Los Angeles has become a huge, sprawling *metropolis*.

community As London, England grew over the years, it absorbed many smaller *communities* that had once been separate.

civil civic public

ADJECTIVE: having to do with a citizen or citizenship.

civil Citizens of the United States are guaranteed certain *civil* rights, such as the right to vote. People who work for a city government are called *civil* servants.

civic Mom always keeps up with city politics; she says it's a person's *civic* duty to be aware of what the government is doing.

public Anyone living in this town can take out books from the *public* library.

▶ **Civilian,** although it is close in form to **civil** and **civic,** does not share the same meaning. *Civilian* means "not military." *Civilian* matters are those things that do not have to do with the armed forces: When the sergeant retired from the Army, he felt strange at first wearing *civilian* clothes all the time instead of his uniform.

clap applaud cheer root hail

VERB: to make a loud noise of approval or encouragement.

clap After the play was over, the audience *clapped* so loudly that all the actors came out to take an extra bow.

applaud The principal asked the parents not to *applaud* until after all the students had gone up to receive their awards.

cheer The fans rose to their feet and *cheered* wildly as the winning home run sailed over the fence.

root The girls' soccer team has a big game Saturday, and the coach asked all the parents to come out and *root* for them to win.

hail When Charles Lindbergh returned to the U.S. after making the first flight across the Atlantic, he was *hailed* by a huge crowd at a parade in New York City.
Antonyms: **boo, hiss.**

clear   obvious plain apparent evident

ADJECTIVE: easy to see, hear, or understand.

clear Our teacher explains the science lessons in *clear,* simple language and no one gets confused. Let me make myself *clear*—I just don't want to buy that jacket, even if it is on sale.

obvious Mom didn't say anything, but the frown on her face made it *obvious* that she didn't agree with me.

plain "Don't even think of parking here!" was what the street sign said—that's putting it in *plain* English.

apparent The questions may seem difficult now, but if you read the chapter carefully, the answers will become *apparent.*

evident It's now *evident* that the city's plan to ease traffic tie-ups is not working.

Antonyms: **vague, obscure, hidden.**

close   shut fasten seal

VERB: to cover up a space or opening; bring together the parts of.

close She *closed* her book and put out the light for the night. The door was *closed* but not locked, and the wind blew it open.

shut Justin forgot to *shut* the gate, and the dog got out and ran into the neighbor's yard.

fasten This necklace *fastens* in the back with a metal clasp.

seal Be sure that you *seal* the envelope tight before you mail it.

Antonym: **open.**

Mr. Bogues didn't **close** the car window and he was getting wet.

When Mr. Bogues got home, he **shut** the door and locked it tight.

clothes   clothing garments garb attire apparel

NOUN: things worn to cover the body.

clothes When we go from Southern California back to the East for Christmas, we have to get out all our winter *clothes.*

clothing Brooks Brothers is a well-known old store in New York City that sells business suits and other *clothing* for men.

garments Because they lived in desert climates, the Arabs came to wear loose-fitting, flowing *garments* that would not trap hot air.

garb Teenagers in the Soviet Union are now often seen wearing Western *garb,* such as blue jeans, T-shirts, and sneakers.

attire "Beau Brummel" was an English nobleman of the early 1800's who was famous for his elegant *attire.*

apparel The train to the mountains was filled with vacationing college students in their brightly colored ski *apparel.*

clown   comedian comic joker

NOUN: anyone who tells jokes or acts in a foolish way to make others laugh.

clown Lucille Ball of "I Love Lucy" was a popular *clown* who amused audiences with her funny faces and the silly things she did.

comedian The host of the show was the *comedian* Bill Cosby, who began the program by telling jokes about his family.

comic *The Gold Rush* is a famous old movie starring the silent *comic* Charlie Chaplin.

joker Sam is a real *joker* and is always fooling around at practice when the coach is trying to explain something.

clumsy   awkward gawky ungainly

ADJECTIVE: not moving smoothly.

clumsy The badger's short legs and thick body make it look *clumsy* when it runs. Jon made a *clumsy* attempt to open the car door for Ann and ended up bumping her on the head with it.

awkward Tony had never been on ice skates before, and he moved along the edge of the ice in a slow, *awkward* way.

gawky When a horse is first born, its legs are too long for its body and it takes hesitant and *gawky* steps.

ungainly That professional wrestler is a huge, *ungainly* man who can hardly move around the ring.

Antonym: **graceful.**

coast shore beach bank

NOUN: the edge of land touching a body of water.

coast Acapulco is a popular resort city on the Pacific *coast* of Mexico. People who lived along the *coast* were warned that a hurricane was on the way.

shore They pulled the canoe up on the *shore* so that it wouldn't float away.

beach Their home is right on the *beach,* and they can walk out their back door down to the ocean.

bank The city of St. Louis grew up along the *banks* of the Mississippi River.

▶ Any body of water can have a *shore* or a *beach*. But only a body of salt water—a sea or an ocean—can have a *coast*. And only a river or stream can have a *bank*.

Gail was feeling **cold,** so she put on her heavy sweater.

Chuck was **freezing** outside as he brushed the snow off the car.

cold freezing chilly icy frigid

ADJECTIVE: having a low temperature; not warm.

cold As soon as the fire died down, the room grew *cold*. The state of Minnesota is known for its long, *cold* winters.

freezing The sky was clear, but a bitter, *freezing* wind kept most people indoors for the day.

chilly Fall is now here, and we are starting to have some *chilly* nights.

icy He left the front door wide open when he came in, and an *icy* blast of air swept into the room.

frigid Over the years the Eskimo people developed effective methods of dealing with the *frigid* weather conditions of their homeland.

Antonym: **hot.**

collect   accumulate amass gather

VERB: to bring together to form a group or unit; come together.

collect After the test, the teacher walked around the room *collecting* all the papers. Cathy likes Princess Diana and *collects* pictures of her from magazines.

accumulate They were away on vacation, and a week's worth of mail had *accumulated* in their mailbox.

amass John D. Rockefeller *amassed* a great fortune in the oil business.

gather The coach told the players to *gather* around him so he could talk to them.

My brother Andrew likes to **collect** baseball cards.

He has **accumulated** quite a few baseball souvenirs.

college   university

NOUN: a place of higher learning, for students beyond high school.

▶ A **college** offers courses to students after they finish high school. A **university** is larger, and may have several colleges within it. It also has programs for students who have graduated from college, in fields such as medicine, law, and business.

color   shade tint tone hue

NOUN: the quality of a thing that comes from the way light strikes it and then is sensed by the eyes.

color The *colors* of the American flag are red, white, and blue.

shade Adding a little bit of black to green will produce a darker *shade* of green.

tint "Baby blue" and "sky blue" are both light *tints* of blue.

tone The room was decorated with cool *tones* of the sea, such as blue and green.

hue The paint store had many different *hues* of yellow to choose from.

come   arrive appear approach near

VERB: to move toward or get to a place.

come Mom called to Billy to *come* into the house because it was time for lunch. A big package from Grandma *came* in the mail today.

arrive Our plane leaves Los Angeles at 8:00 A.M. and is expected to *arrive* in New York at about 4:30 P.M.

appear As soon as you open the refrigerator door, the dog *appears* and tries to get at the food.

approach The judge asked the two lawyers to *approach* the bench so that he could say something to them in private.

near As the runner raced around the last turn and *neared* the finish line, the fans stood up and began to cheer.

Antonyms: **go, leave, depart.**

committee   board bureau

NOUN: a group of people who work together for a common purpose.

committee The principal formed a *committee* of parents and teachers to plan the school's Halloween Carnival.

board Most large American companies have a *board* of directors who are elected to control the way the company is run.

bureau The Federal *Bureau* of Investigation is responsible for dealing with crimes in which federal laws have been broken.

common   typical ordinary everyday familiar widespread

ADJECTIVE: happening or appearing often; generally seen or met with.

common Don't be upset that you spelled *separate* as "seperate;" that's a *common* mistake. There's a big pond near our house, and wild birds are a *common* sight there.

typical Maureen was late for school again today—that's *typical* of her.

ordinary French champagne is made by a special process from selected grapes, and it is much more expensive than *ordinary* table wine.

everyday I stopped getting excited about seeing snow when I spent a winter in Buffalo, because it's such an *everyday* occurrence there.

familiar The Dodgers ran onto the field, wearing their *familiar* white and blue uniforms.

widespread Ten years ago, not many people had personal computers, but now their use has become *widespread.*

Antonyms: **uncommon, rare, exceptional.**

community neighborhood district area vicinity

NOUN: an area where people live together; a certain part of a city or town.

community North Beach is a well-known Italian-American *community* in San Francisco. The Garden Club holds its meetings at the local *Community* Center.

neighborhood When we visit New York City, my dad likes to go back to visit the old *neighborhood* where he grew up.

district Anita's grandparents live in the older part of town, near City Hall and the central business *district.*

area Randy just moved to this *area,* so he still needs help sometimes in finding his way around.

vicinity Because of the flooding, all the families in the *vicinity* had to leave their homes.

company business firm corporation

NOUN: a group of people who join together to provide goods or services.

company Most television sets sold in the U.S. are now made by *companies* from Japan. She loves the world of books and would like to get a job with a publishing *company.*

business My mom is a teacher, and she and my aunt also have a small *business* publishing newsletters on their computer.

firm When Senator Smith retires from office, he plans to become a partner in a large *firm* of Washington lawyers.

corporation Chevrolet, Oldsmobile, Pontiac, Buick, and Cadillac are famous brands of cars made by the General Motors *Corporation.*

compare contrast

VERB: to find out or show how a thing is different from something else or like something else.

compare We've had some rain this summer, but *compared* to the past few summers it's been really dry. The teacher explained the term "inflation" to us by *comparing* the price of food this year and in 1950.

contrast In her book *The Proud Tower,* Barbara Tuchman showed how the easy life of upper-class people in 19th-century England *contrasted* with the hard life of working-class people.

▶ When you **contrast** two things, you always show how they are different from each other: That book *contrasts* life on a farm with life in a big city. (It shows the differences.) When you **compare** two things, you may show either how they are the same, or how they are different: This book *compares* life on a farm today with farm life in 1940. (It may show similarities, or differences, or both.)

The other boys **complained** that Jerry would never pass the ball.

The coach **criticized** Jerry for not being a team player.

complain   criticize grumble whine nag

VERB: to say that something is wrong or unfair; be unhappy or annoyed.

complain The Martins' neighbor *complained* to them about their dogs barking all the time. My sister *complains* a lot about how much homework she has to do.

criticize The local newspaper has *criticized* the mayor for spending too much time away from the city.

grumble Chris is always *grumbling* that Mom never fixes what he wants for breakfast.

whine The little boy kept *whining* that he wanted another piece of candy.

nag I was surprised to see Darryl with a short haircut, and he told me that his parents had been *nagging* him that his hair was too long.

complete   finish conclude terminate

VERB: to bring or come to an end; bring to the final or stopping point.

complete The teacher said we will *complete* the first unit of our science book this week. The pilot *completed* his check of the plane's instruments and was ready for takeoff.

finish My older sister wants to go on to college after she *finishes* high school.

conclude The City Orchestra always *concludes* their Fourth of July concert by playing "The Stars and Stripes Forever."

terminate When Dad realized it was a salesman calling, he *terminated* the conversation with a quick "I'm not interested, thank you."

complicated   complex intricate involved

ADJECTIVE: hard to do or understand, because of its many different elements.

complicated The bicycle came in parts, with a *complicated* set of instructions, and it took several hours to put all the parts together.

complex Movie making is a *complex* business that requires bringing together the talents of many different people.

intricate He took off the back of the computer and saw that inside was a very *intricate* system of circuits and wires.

involved The book's *involved* plot made it hard to follow what was going on.

<u>Antonym:</u> **simple.**

compliment/complement

▶ **Compliment** and **complement** sound alike, but have different meanings. To *compliment* is to say something nice: When I met the author, I *complimented* her on how good her books were. To *complement* is to make a thing more complete: I bought the latest book in her series to *complement* the four books I already have.

conceited   smug arrogant egotistical

ADJECTIVE: having too high an opinion of oneself; too proud.

conceited Rich is very *conceited* and is always commenting on how smart he is, or how much money his family has.

smug Jason says that his sister is acting *smug* about being voted "Class Athlete" in the school yearbook.

arrogant Several people at the meeting had good suggestions, but the boss was so *arrogant* that he insisted on using only his own ideas.

egotistical When asked who deserved the upcoming Academy Award for Best Actress, the *egotistical* movie star replied, "I do, of course."

concern   pertain relate apply

VERB: to be about; have to do with.

concern *Sarah, Plain and Tall* is a book that *concerns* a young woman who comes from the East to live with a pioneer family.

pertain The rule about not parking near the school only *pertains* to the time when school is open.

relate The students really paid attention to her talk, because it *related* to what was going on in their own lives.

apply Everyone has to wear a seat belt; that *applies* to a baby in a car seat too.

condition   state circumstance situation

NOUN: the way something or someone is; what something is or is like.

condition The dog was chewing on my baseball mitt, and when I got it away from him it was in pretty bad *condition*. The actor said that he would agree to be in the movie, on one *condition*—his name had to appear first on the cast.

state When the climbers finally reached the top of the mountain, they fell to the ground in a *state* of complete exhaustion.

circumstance The policemen were told to guard the door and not to let anyone leave, under any *circumstance*.

situation "If you have a lemon, make lemonade" is a saying that means "Make the best of a bad *situation*."

confused   bewildered puzzled perplexed

ADJECTIVE: not understanding or thinking clearly; not sure of what is going on.

confused He had never been on the subway before, and he got *confused* as to which train he was supposed to take.

bewildered By mistake Kerry was put in the advanced French class instead of the beginning class, and she was *bewildered* by what the teacher was saying.

puzzled Matt couldn't figure out why the VCR wouldn't work, and he kept pushing the buttons with a *puzzled* expression.

perplexed Many people are so *perplexed* by the income tax form that they pay someone else to fill it out it for them.

John was a bit **confused** by the two road signs.

He was **bewildered** by the math problem.

connect   attach join link fasten

VERB: to bring together or unite two things, or a series of things.

connect Use this wire to *connect* the VCR to the TV set. We take this plane to Dallas, and then get a *connecting* flight that will take us on to Orlando.

attach He put on his new sweater, not realizing the price tag was still *attached.*

join The Missouri River *joins* the Mississippi River just north of St. Louis.

link The completion of the transcontinental railroad in 1869 *linked* the western United States to the rest of the country.

fasten: He *fastened* the name plate to the door with four heavy screws.

Antonyms: **disconnect, unfasten.**

Mr. Hall asked Rosa to **consider** being the lead in the class play.

She is **pondering** whether she should do it or not.

consider   analyze reflect ponder weigh

VERB: to think about carefully and for some length of time.

consider The jury *considered* all the evidence before reaching its decision. Someone wants to buy their house, and they're seriously *considering* the offer.

analyze The coach watched films of the other team to *analyze* their style of play.

reflect As her plane climbed above the city, she looked down through her window and *reflected* on what had happened on her trip.

ponder Todd isn't sure whether he should transfer to a different high school or not, and he stayed awake all night *pondering* his decision.

weigh While trying to decide which of the two cars to buy, they *weighed* the good and bad points of each one.

considerate   thoughtful attentive concerned solicitous

ADJECTIVE: thinking and caring about the comfort or happiness of others.

considerate Helping the new student find the right classroom was a *considerate* thing for her to do. Mark is a *considerate* person who hates to do anything that might hurt someone's feelings.

thoughtful I dropped the letter somewhere, but Grandma got it anyway—some *thoughtful* person must have found it and mailed it for me.

attentive In that restaurant the waiters are very *attentive* and make sure that all your needs are taken care of right away.

concerned After a story appeared in the paper about the family losing their home, many contributions were sent in for them by *concerned* readers.

solicitous When the salesman saw they were interested in the car, he became *solicitous* and started opening the doors for them and acting very polite.

Antonyms: **inconsiderate, thoughtless.**

contact   touch

VERB: to be in or move into a position directly against some other thing.

contact As the plane came down, we felt a slight bump when the wheels first *contacted* the ground.

touch He is so tall now that he can jump up and *touch* his fingers on the ceiling in his bedroom.

▶ Because **contact** has such a strong connection with its synonym **touch,** some people object to its use in this sense: "Mrs. Maxwell *contacted* all the girls by phone to tell them about the Girl Scout meeting." They say that *contact* should be used only in situations where two things physically come together. But this is too strict a rule; in fact, even *touch* itself is also used in this way: "Mrs. Maxwell got in *touch* with them by phone."

contest   competition rivalry

NOUN: an event in which people or groups compete to win or to gain some advantage.

contest The candy store is having a *contest* to see who can guess the number of jelly beans in a jar. Anton won the spelling *contest;* he was the only one who could spell "pneumatolysis."

competition As part of the summer reading program, the library is sponsoring a *competition* for the best essay on the Fourth of July.

rivalry Stanford University and the University of California have a long *rivalry* in football, and every year in November they play each other in what is known as the "Big Game."

continue last proceed persist endure

VERB: to keep on with some activity or process; go on.

continue The snow began this morning and is expected to *continue* through the night. The news article starts on the front page and *continues* on page 22.

last These special flashlight batteries are supposed to *last* much longer than the regular kind.

proceed Each float in the parade stopped briefly in front of the judges' stand and then *proceeded* up Main Street.

persist The teacher told Kenny to stop bothering the other students, and said that if he *persisted* in doing it he would be sent to the principal's office.

endure The city was hit hard by a hurricane, but the citizens were determined that their town would *endure*.

Antonyms: **stop, cease, end.**

continuous continual constant incessant

ADJECTIVE: going on without a stop; continuing on and on.

continuous The show is a big hit, and there has been a *continuous* line of people buying tickets at the box office all day.

continual When the time is up on the oven timer, it makes a *continual* buzzing noise until it is shut off.

constant The highway had a *constant* flow of traffic in both directions all day.

incessant The Senator said that he was completely fed up with the news reporters' *incessant* questions about his financial dealings.

▶ **Continuous** and **continual** are slightly different. A *continual* thing goes on and on in the same way; a *continuous* thing may have some change or interruption.

control command rule govern dominate

VERB: to have power over; direct the course or actions of.

control This computer has a small device called a "mouse" that *controls* the operation of the machine. The Democrats now *control* the Senate; they have 56 seats and the Republicans have 44.

command General George Washington *commanded* the American army in the Revolutionary War.

rule Ancient kings believed that their right to *rule* came directly from God.

govern The basis of democracy is that people are *governed* by leaders that they themselves elect.

dominate Austria is now a small country, but in earlier times it was the center of a powerful empire that *dominated* central Europe.

cooperate   collaborate unite combine

VERB: to join forces to achieve some goal; work together.

cooperate Cleaning up after the picnic was easy because everyone *cooperated.* He would not *cooperate* with the police and refused to answer their questions.

collaborate John Lennon and Paul McCartney *collaborated* as the writers of most of the Beatles' songs.

unite In the early 1950's, doctors and health officials from all over the world *united* to find a cure for polio.

combine Three different Yankee pitchers *combined* to pitch a shutout against the Red Sox today.

Antonyms: **oppose, compete.**

copy   imitate duplicate mimic

VERB: to make another version that is the same; do or be like something else.

copy Andy wrote the answers on a piece of scrap paper first and then *copied* them over in his workbook.

imitate The comedian Rich Little is known for *imitating* movie stars such as John Wayne and Jimmy Stewart.

duplicate The museum plans to build a ship that will exactly *duplicate* the one in which Columbus sailed to America.

mimic Cathy's older brother sometimes *mimics* her voice to tease her.

Antonyms: **originate, create.**

Sara is **copying** a famous painting of flowers from a book.

Robert is doing his own painting while **imitating** the painter's style.

correct   right accurate exact precise

ADJECTIVE: true to the facts; as it should be; not wrong.

correct In this math book you can check the *correct* answer in the back after you do the problem. Though some people say "He don't," the *correct* way to say it is "He doesn't."

right I thought Dallas was the capital of Texas, but that's not *right*—it's Austin.

accurate The scales that supermarkets use to weigh food have to be checked to make sure that they are *accurate*.

exact He had his camera ready, and at the *exact* moment when the bride kissed her new husband he took a picture.

precise A man's custom-made suit is very expensive, because each part of it has to be specially cut to the customer's *precise* measurements.

<u>Antonyms:</u> **incorrect, wrong, inaccurate.**

Tim told the man the time is "about 2:00." That is **correct,** but 2:04 is the **exact** time.

cost   price charge expense fee

NOUN: the amount paid for something.

cost The *cost* of going to college has become very high in recent years. The movie was filmed on location in Africa, at a *cost* of thirty million dollars.

price The *price* of that magazine is $2.00 per copy at the newsstand, and $74.00 a year for a subscription.

charge The store gives you two prints of each photo, with no extra *charge*.

expense When they fixed up their house, the biggest *expense* was putting on a new roof.

fee Lawyers charge a *fee* to people who use their services.

council   panel cabinet

NOUN: a group of people who meet to give advice or make a decision.

council A *council* of leading educators from around the country met in New York to discuss the future of higher education. Many U.S. cities are governed by a mayor and a city *council.*

panel The governor appointed an advisory *panel* to study the issue of new highway construction.

cabinet If a political leader gets regular advice from a group of old friends, they are often called his "kitchen *cabinet.*"

counsel/council

▶ **Counsel** and **council** have the same sound but do not have the same meaning. **Counsel** is "ideas or opinions about what to do; advice." During the American Revolution, George Washington relied on the *counsel* of his assistant Alexander Hamilton. *Counsel* can also be used as a verb: She wanted to do her paper on Shakespeare, but her teacher *counseled* her to choose a more limited subject.

country   nation state realm

NOUN: an area of land that is under its own government.

country Poland is a *country* whose boundaries have changed considerably over the years.

nation The Basques are an ancient group of people who now live mainly in Spain, but who seek to have their own independent *nation.*

state The Congress of Vienna was a famous meeting at which all the European *state*s that had fought against Napoleon were represented.

realm King Henry VIII of England was a powerful ruler who demanded complete loyalty from every person within his *realm.*

couple   pair duo brace duet

NOUN: two people or things thought of or grouped together.

couple Elizabeth Taylor and Richard Burton were married to each other in real life, and also played a married *couple* in several movies.

pair She wants to get a *pair* of white shoes to wear with her new dress.

duo The comic-strip heroes Batman and Robin were called the "Dynamic *Duo*" because of the way they teamed up to fight crime.

brace The gunfighter wore a *brace* of silver-handled pistols on his hips.

duet In the musical *Annie,* Annie first sings the song "Tomorrow" alone and then later sings it as a *duet* with Daddy Warbucks.

course   way route passage

NOUN: a certain direction in which something moves or goes.

course The control tower told the plane to change its *course* and land at another airfield. The Mississippi River follows a winding *course* in its route to the sea.

way The main road ends here; that dirt road is the only *way* to the lake.

route Let's take the Northern State Parkway; it's the fastest *route* to the city.

passage Early pioneers going West used the Cumberland Gap as a *passage* through the Allegheny Mountains.

crazy   insane mad deranged

ADJECTIVE: not having a healthy mind; not able to think in a sensible way.

crazy The soldier had been on the front line for months, and he felt he'd go *crazy* if he didn't get away from the battlefield.

insane A person who can't tell right from wrong is judged by law to be *insane.*

mad In Edgar Allan Poe's story "The Tell-Tale Heart," a murderer is driven *mad* by his feelings of guilt about his crime.

deranged The man was acting *deranged,* talking loudly to himself and shouting at the people passing by.

Antonyms: **sane, rational.**

crime   offense vice sin

NOUN: something that is wrong and is usually against the law.

crime The man who set fire to the building was charged with the *crime* of arson. A person who is convicted of a *crime* may have to go to prison or pay a fine.

offense Driving with a broken headlight is illegal, but it's not a serious *offense.*

vice The doctor wants my aunt to stop smoking, but she says that's her only *vice* and she just can't give it up.

sin The Bible states that stealing and lying are *sins* against the laws of God.

cross   grouchy cranky irritable

ADJECTIVE: in a bad mood; angry or ill-tempered.

cross Jill was *cross* at dinner because her softball team lost their game today.

grouchy None of Erik's friends were home this weekend, so he just hung around the house in a *grouchy* mood.

cranky The baby hasn't been sleeping well, and he's acting really *cranky.*

irritable The workers never question what the boss does, because he gets very *irritable* if people disagree with him.

The football game drew a huge **crowd** to City Stadium.

A **mob** of fans ran onto the field and tore up the grass.

crowd mob throng horde

NOUN: a number of people gathered together in one place.

crowd Rock music is popular in the U.S., and big *crowds* attend concerts by the top artists. All the trains were late, and a *crowd* of people filled the waiting room.

mob The French Revolution began when an angry *mob* of citizens in Paris attacked a government prison building, the Bastille.

throng After the wedding, the prince and his new bride stepped onto the palace balcony to wave to the *throng* of cheering people.

horde I hate to shop on the day after Thanksgiving; the stores are always filled with *hordes* of people.

cut chop slice carve slit slash

VERB: to make an opening in something with a sharp tool or edge.

cut David *cut* a picture out of a magazine to use in his science report. Don't *cut* the tags off that blouse yet; I'm not sure if I want to keep it.

chop Mom *chopped* some onions to cook in the pan along with the steak.

slice The bakery has a machine that will *slice* a loaf of bread into even pieces.

carve Grandpa always spends Thanksgiving morning sharpening the big knife he's going to use to *carve* the turkey.

slit She carefully *slit* open the envelope with a sharp knife.

slash Low branches were blocking his way along the trail, and he took his axe and angrily *slashed* away at them.

danger threat risk peril hazard

NOUN: a chance that something bad or harmful will happen.

danger The sign at the lake said, "*Danger:* thin ice. No skating today." Cars have to drive very slowly on this mountain highway because of the *danger* of going off the road.

threat Whenever the weather is very dry around here, there is a *threat* of brush fires in the hills.

risk Proper diet and exercise can lower the *risk* of getting certain diseases.

peril The survival of the African elephant is in *peril* because of hunters who kill the animal illegally for its ivory.

hazard Packs of cigarettes have a label that warns of the *hazards* of smoking.

<u>Antonyms</u>: **security, protection, safety.**

dark dim gloomy murky

ADJECTIVE: having little or no light.

dark The night was *dark,* with the moon and stars hidden by clouds. Bobby always leaves a light on at night, because he hates to sleep in a *dark* room.

dim The batteries were almost dead, so the flashlight gave off only a *dim* light.

gloomy It was one of those wet, *gloomy* December days when it seems that the sun has never really come up at all.

murky It was hard to see the bottom through the *murky* waters of the pond.

<u>Antonyms:</u> **light, bright.**

The room was **dark** as we waited for Mom to bring in the birthday cake.

I don't like to walk by that house at night; it always looks so **gloomy.**

date   appointment   engagement   rendezvous

NOUN: an arrangement to meet someone or be somewhere.

date   The two women made a *date* to meet for lunch on Friday. Has your sister set the *date* for her wedding yet?

appointment   He left work early because he had an *appointment* with the doctor.

engagement   My dad has an *engagement* calendar at work where he writes down the day and time of each business meeting.

rendezvous   The two secret agents agreed to have a *rendezvous* at midnight at an old hotel by the waterfront.

dead   deceased   late   extinct   lifeless

ADJECTIVE: without life; no longer alive.

dead   The ocean liner *Titanic* sank in icy waters on its first voyage, leaving over 1,500 people *dead.*

deceased   The *deceased* man had left a will stating that all his money and property should go to his widow.

late   The Beatles singing group consisted of Paul McCartney, Ringo Starr, George Harrison, and the *late* John Lennon.

extinct   The dodo became *extinct* in the 1700's when sailors killed all of these birds for their eggs.

lifeless   The land had been cleared years before, and nothing was left of the forest that had once been there but a few *lifeless* stumps.

<u>Antonym:</u> **alive.**

deal   agreement   transaction   contract   bargain

NOUN: an arrangement that involves paying money or doing business.

deal   The car company is offering really good *deals* on last year's models. She made an offer to buy the house for $95,000, and the owner said, "OK, it's a *deal.*"

agreement   The Walt Disney Company and the government of France made an *agreement* that Disney would build a huge new theme park outside of Paris.

transaction   The bank is now open on Saturdays, for people who are too busy to take care of their *transactions* during the week.

contract   The baseball star signed a *contract* to play for the Yankees for five years.

bargain   I made a *bargain* with my friend that if I took care of his paper route while he was away he'd pay me twenty dollars.

▶ **Deal** is just as correct as its synonyms, but it's not as good a choice for serious writing, such as a school report: In 1803 Thomas Jefferson made an *arrangement* (not a *deal)* to purchase the Louisiana Territory from France for $15 million.

decide   settle resolve determine conclude

VERB: to make up one's mind; come to a decision.

decide   We were going to go to the movies, but because it was such a snowy night we *decided* to stay home. Mom told me to go through my old magazines and *decide* which ones I wanted to keep.

settle   Dad *settled* the question of who would have the TV by saying I could watch my show at 7:00, and my brother could watch at 8:00.

resolve   She was disappointed with her grade on the test, and she *resolved* to study much harder for the next one.

determine   People in the movie industry vote to *determine* which five movies will be nominated for Best Picture of the Year.

conclude   After making a careful study, the company has *concluded* that it would be too expensive to move their business to another city.

Antonyms: **hesitate, waver.**

decorate   trim adorn beautify garnish

VERB: to add something to a thing to make it look better; make more attractive.

decorate   It was Andrew's birthday, and Mom had *decorated* the house with balloons and "Happy Birthday" signs.

trim   Chris went up to the attic to get down the lights and ornaments we use to *trim* our Christmas tree.

adorn   A large bouquet of flowers *adorned* the dinner table.

beautify   The city is going to plant trees and bushes along the downtown sidewalks to *beautify* the area.

garnish   White food such as fish or potatoes is often *garnished* with sprays of bright green parsley to give it some color.

deep   intense extreme profound

ADJECTIVE: great in degree; more than the usual level or amount.

deep   Mom was in a *deep* sleep and didn't hear me come into the room. This book is a very *deep* and detailed study of the Civil War, almost 1000 pages long.

intense   Not many people live in the Sahara Desert, because of the *intense* heat there.

extreme   He has *extreme* views about politics and thinks that our whole system of government should be completely changed.

profound   There was a *profound* silence in the canyon, so that we could hear the calling of birds hundreds of feet above us.

Antonyms: **shallow, light, superficial.**

defend   guard protect shield safeguard

VERB: to resist attack, danger, or harm; keep safe.

defend A small band of Texans *defended* the Alamo against a huge force of attackers. In soccer the fullbacks *defend* their goal against players on the other team who are trying to score.

guard The President was *guarded* by a number of Secret Service men as he walked up the steps to the hotel.

protect Fluoride is put in toothpaste or added to drinking water to *protect* against tooth decay.

shield The sun was very strong, and she raised her hand to *shield* her eyes against the bright glare.

safeguard Senator Smith believes that the United States must always maintain a large army, navy, and air force to *safeguard* the country.

Antonym: **surrender.**

Anna thought the soup was really **delicious.** Linda said that it was **tasty.**

delicious   tasty appetizing savory

ADJECTIVE: very pleasing to the taste or smell.

delicious The strawberries had just been picked and they tasted *delicious*. When my grandmother bakes cookies, a *delicious* smell fills her whole apartment.

tasty After Marty got home from school, he had a *tasty* snack of cheese and crackers.

appetizing I might have the seafood salad—a man at the next table just ordered it and it looks very *appetizing*.

savory She served a *savory* beef stew with chunks of French bread.

Antonym: **distasteful.**

demand   insist require order request

VERB: to ask for something in a strong or forceful way.

demand The radio he bought didn't work, and he *demanded* that the store give him his money back. The striking workers were *demanding* a raise in pay.

insist Even before our state had a law about wearing seat belts, Mom always *insisted* that we wear them in our car.

require At this high school all students are *required* to take four years of English in order to graduate.

order That factory was illegally dumping wastes in the river, and the state government *ordered* them to stop.

request The manager of the movie theater *requested* that all the people waiting to buy tickets form a line along the sidewalk.

The tennis player **demanded** that the umpire change her ruling.

She **requested** that he return to the court and continue play.

democratic   constitutional representative

ADJECTIVE: favoring equal rights or treatment for all people.

democratic The idea that people should vote to choose their own leaders is a basic *democratic* principle.

constitutional The United States has a *constitutional* system in which one body of laws establishes the way the government is run.

representative In a *representative* form of government, the people do not rule directly, but elect leaders who rule for them.

▶ The U.S. can be called both a **democracy** and a **republic**. Either of these words can be used to describe a country in which the people vote for their leaders.

department section bureau

NOUN: a special part or division of some larger group or organization.

department Mr. Tranh is the head of the high school math *department.*

section Supermarkets use the front *section* of the store, near the checkout lines, to display special sale items.

bureau She works for the news *bureau* of Channel 11, a local television station.

deserve earn rate

VERB: to be entitled to have or get; have the right to.

deserve Helen worked hard all weekend on her history report, and she feels she *deserves* to get a good grade on it.

earn At first the boys didn't like having a woman coach, but as the season went on and the team kept winning she *earned* their respect.

rate The critics really like that movie; it *rates* as one of the year's "Ten Best."

differ disagree dissent vary

VERB: to have another opinion or thought.

differ The jury will have a hard time deciding, because the stories of the two main witnesses *differ* widely from each other.

disagree The experts are all picking the Bears to win on Sunday, but I *disagree*—I think the Rams will win.

dissent The local paper called the new school a total success, but parents who struggle with the traffic jams at the entrance might *dissent* from that judgment.

vary The mayor's position on that issue seems to *vary* according to whether he is talking to business people or to senior-citizen groups.

Antonym: **agree.**

different unlike dissimilar diverse

ADJECTIVE: not like someone or something else.

different The main road was closed, so we took a *different* route. The twins look alike, but their personalities are *different*—one's quiet and the other's very lively.

unlike Hawaii is not on the North American mainland, *unlike* the other 49 states.

dissimilar Mike doesn't like his mother to pick out new clothes for him because they have very *dissimilar* taste in clothing.

diverse Karen has many *diverse* interests, such as swimming, playing the piano, making stuffed animals, and playing video games.

Antonyms: **alike, same, identical.**

dig   excavate burrow shovel mine

VERB: to break up, turn over, or remove the earth.

dig When Juan goes to the beach he likes to *dig* holes in the sand. They'll have to *dig* deep to get all the roots of the tree out.

excavate In the science of archaeology, workers *excavate* an area where they believe ancient objects are buried beneath the earth.

burrow We could see marks going back and forth across the lawn where the mole had *burrowed* under it.

shovel Mom *shoveled* up some dirt from along the back fence to put in her flower pots.

mine Coal has been *mined* in the valleys of southern Wales for over 150 years.

dirty   soiled filthy unclean grimy

ADJECTIVE: marked by or covered with dust, mud, grease, or the like; not clean.

dirty While Tim was playing basketball at the school playground, his hands got *dirty* from handling the ball.

soiled After the meal she put the *soiled* tablecloth in the washing machine.

filthy The car had been parked on a busy city street for several weeks, and the outside was really *filthy*.

unclean Some people consider the pig an *unclean* animal because it seems to enjoy lying in mud, but it actually does this to cool its skin.

grimy The ink from the newspaper left a *grimy* mark on his white pants.

<u>Antonym:</u> **clean.**

Brett was **dirty** after he played in the mud.   Kevin was absolutely **filthy.**

disagree   argue   quarrel   differ

VERB: to fail to agree; have a strong difference of opinion.

disagree My dad and his sister *disagree* all the time about politics, because Dad is a strong Democrat and she is a Republican.

argue In big-league baseball, when a runner is called out on a close play he will sometimes *argue* with the umpire about it.

quarrel Mom said that if we couldn't stop *quarreling* about which show to watch, she would shut off the TV for the rest of the night.

differ During the debate, the two candidates for mayor *differed* very sharply over whether or not the city needed a new high school.

Antonym: **agree**.

disappear   vanish   evaporate   dissolve

VERB: to go out of sight; become unable to be seen.

disappear We watched the balloon as it rose higher and higher into the air until it finally *disappeared*.

vanish The deer ran away as soon as it heard us coming, and it seemed to *vanish* into the woods.

evaporate I spilled some water on the hood of the car, but it was so hot from the sun that the water quickly *evaporated*.

dissolve She put a lump of sugar in her tea and stirred it until all the sugar had *dissolved*.

Antonym: **appear**.

disaster   calamity   catastrophe   casualty

NOUN: an event that causes great suffering or loss; a tragedy.

disaster The San Francisco earthquake of 1906 was a great *disaster* in which hundreds of people died.

calamity The defeat of the Spanish Armada was a *calamity* for Spain, because the country never again reached the same level of power.

catastrophe Thinking that the ocean liner *Titanic* was "unsinkable" led to a *catastrophe* in which the ship went down on its first voyage.

casualty Soldiers who are killed or wounded in a war are referred to as battle *casualties*.

▶ Sometimes **disaster** is used in a less serious way, as in: "I got some wet paint on my new jacket. What a *disaster!*" It's better to save *disaster* for very bad things, and to use a weaker word such as **mishap** or **accident** for less serious situations like paint on a jacket.

discouraged   disappointed dejected depressed disheartened

ADJECTIVE: feeling sad or sorry because of something that has happened.

discouraged Jimmy wanted to learn how to ice skate, but after an hour of falling down he got *discouraged* and gave up.

disappointed Michelle is sick with a cold and is *disappointed* that she's going to have to miss her friend's birthday party.

dejected As the fans cheered loudly for the winning home run, the losing pitcher walked off the field with a *dejected* expression.

depressed The man had been out of work for six months and was getting very *depressed* over not being able to find a new job.

disheartened She wants very much to be a movie actress, but she's *disheartened* by how hard it is to get chosen for a part.

discover   realize notice detect ascertain

VERB: to find out about something not known before; learn something.

discover I wondered why no one had called all day, and then I *discovered* that the phone was off the hook.

realize When she saw steam coming out from under the bathroom door, she *realized* she'd left the bath water running.

notice I've *noticed* that there's a lot more traffic in town than there used to be.

detect Josh said that he wanted to go with us, but I could *detect* a lack of interest in his voice.

ascertain Though it is sometimes thought that wolves will attack humans, scientists studying them have *ascertained* that they actually avoid people.

dishonest   crooked deceptive untruthful devious

ADJECTIVE: not according to the truth or the law; not honest or direct.

dishonest It was *dishonest* of the writer to copy an article out of an old book and claim that he'd written it himself.

crooked In the "Black Sox" World Series, some *crooked* players on the White Sox took money from gamblers to lose games on purpose.

deceptive The advertisement was *deceptive;* it said that the land for sale was right on the ocean, when actually it was a mile away from the ocean.

untruthful A witness in court can be charged with the crime of perjury if he says something that he knows is *untruthful.*

devious Teddy had a *devious* reason for offering to go get the mail; he knew his progress report was coming and he wanted to get it before his parents saw it.

Antonym: **honest, straightforward.**

disinterested   neutral impartial unbiased

ADJECTIVE: not favoring one side or the other; not having a personal interest.

disinterested As well as an elected mayor, many towns now have a city manager, a *disinterested* person hired from outside the city to manage its business affairs.

neutral Sweden was *neutral* in World War II and did not fight in the war.

impartial So that the essay contest would be *impartial,* the students' names did not appear on their papers when the judges read them.

unbiased The reporter insisted that his coverage of the election was *unbiased* and that he had not favored either candidate in his stories.

▶ **Disinterested** has another meaning that is very different from the one above: "She is *disinterested* (not interested) in the Super Bowl; she's not a football fan." But **uninterested** is a better choice for that meaning. Save *disinterested* for the idea of "fair:" The Super Bowl referee watches the game in a *disinterested* way.

A judge should be **disinterested** when he hears a case in court.

One man on the jury seemed to be **uninterested** in the case.

do   perform accomplish achieve

VERB: to cause a certain thing to happen; carry out some action.

do David couldn't go to the movies with us; he had to help his father *do* some yard work. She only got a C on the first test and hopes to *do* better this time.

perform The football player's knee was badly injured in a game, and the team doctor had to *perform* an operation to repair it.

accomplish In his State of the Union address, the President stated what he hopes to *accomplish* during the coming year.

achieve Though he became famous for discovering the New World, Christopher Columbus never *achieved* his lifelong goal of finding a sea route to India.

doctor/physician

▶ Either the word **doctor** or the word **physician** can be used to describe a person who is specially trained and licensed to treat sickness or injury. However, *doctor* also has a second meaning. A *doctor of philosophy* is a person who has earned an advanced degree from a university—for example, the former secretary of state, Doctor Henry Kissinger, or the well-known psychologist, Doctor Joyce Brothers. To make it clear that the "doctor" being referred to is a medical doctor (M.D.) rather than a doctor of philosophy (Ph.D.), people often use the term **physician** instead. *Physician* always means a medical doctor.

done   over through finished completed

ADJECTIVE: brought to or at an end; no longer going on.

done The new school was supposed to open in September, but now they say the work won't be *done* until December. Grandma put the roast back in the oven, because it wasn't quite *done* yet.

over When the team at bat in baseball has made three outs, the inning is *over* and the other team comes to bat.

through After you're *through* reading the newspaper, I'd like to take a look at the sports section.

finished Teachers of writing say that it is better for students to think about what they want to write first, instead of trying to write a *finished* paper right away.

completed If you want to go to summer camp this year, you have to send in a *completed* application form before May 1st.

door   doorway entrance entry gateway portal

NOUN: a way into or out of a room, building, or other such place.

door To get to the principal's office, walk down that hall and go in the last *door* on the right. Andrew knew he had to be home by six, and just before the hour he came rushing through the *door.*

doorway As we drove away from her house, Grandma stood in the *doorway* waving goodbye to us.

entrance People who work in the store go in and out by a separate *entrance* at the back of the building.

entry That factory has a fence all around it, and the only *entry* is a gate where there is always a guard on duty.

gateway Because many early settlers going west left from St. Louis, Missouri, the city became known as "The *Gateway* to the West."

portal As you walk into the restaurant you go under a big sign that says, "Through these *portals* pass the people with the best taste in town."

doubt   suspect question distrust

VERB: to not believe or trust; feel uncertain about.

doubt He says his uncle played big-league baseball, but I *doubt* it because his name isn't in the record book. The ancient Greeks believed in a "lost continent" called Atlantis, but today most people *doubt* that such a place ever existed.

suspect The man seems to have much more money than he could actually earn from his job, and the police *suspect* he is getting it from illegal gambling.

question The famous businessman referred to himself as a billionaire, but many people *questioned* whether he really had that much money.

distrust Dad says he *distrusts* those television ads that say you can earn millions of dollars by buying houses without using your own money.

<u>Antonyms:</u> **believe, trust.**

I **doubt** Uncle Buddy is sticking to his diet. Mom **suspects** that he ate all the snack food.

draw   sketch illustrate paint trace

VERB: to create a certain picture or image on paper or other such material.

draw Kelly uses colored pencils to *draw* her favorite kinds of animals.

sketch While the witness sat answering questions, a courtroom artist quickly *sketched* her picture for a newspaper story about the trial.

illustrate N. C. Wyeth *illustrated* such books as *Treasure Island* and *Robin Hood* by showing well-known characters and action from the books.

paint Artists of the Middle Ages often *painted* scenes from the Bible.

trace Spencer *traced* a picture of an F-14 jet fighter from a photograph of one in a magazine.

drug   medicine cure remedy

NOUN: a substance that is taken into the body to relieve or prevent disease.

drug Aspirin is a *drug* that is used to relieve headaches and other pains. People with high blood pressure may be given *drugs* to bring the pressure down.

medicine Mom took some *medicine* to get rid of the cough she's had all week.

cure His bathroom cabinet is filled with pill bottles, *cures* for all the various ills he has or claims to have.

remedy My grandmother says that chicken soup is a good *remedy* for a cold.

▶ **Drugs** such as aspirin are intended to help people's health, but there are also certain harmful drugs that are against the law to use. This second meaning is the one used in phrases like "Say 'No' to Drugs." Both meanings are correct.

dry   arid parched dehydrated rainless

ADJECTIVE: having little or no water; not wet or moist.

dry Southern California is known for its warm, *dry* weather. Cathy always drinks water during her soccer games, because her throat gets really *dry.*

arid Because olive trees have long roots that reach far below the ground, they will grow well even in *arid* climates.

parched We haven't had any rain all summer, and that place where the flowers grew this spring is just hard, *parched* earth.

dehydrated This soup comes in the form of a *dehydrated* powder; you add water to it to make the soup.

rainless Certain small animals are able to live in *rainless* desert areas by getting moisture from the plants they eat.

Lake Hodges is completely **dry.** What was once the lake bottom is now **parched** ground.

duck   dodge evade sidestep

VERB: to move quickly down or away to avoid something.

duck When the jet plane flew low over the grandstand, everyone in the crowd *ducked*. The gopher *ducked* out of sight in his hole when he saw me coming.

dodge In this game, the idea is to *dodge* the ball when it is thrown at you.

evade Pro football's Gale Sayers was a tricky runner, good at *evading* tacklers.

sidestep The man was walking straight ahead without looking, and I had to *sidestep* to keep from bumping into him.

due   owed unpaid outstanding

ADJECTIVE: to be paid to someone as a debt or right.

due This library book was supposed to be returned last Saturday, and there is a fine of twenty cents *due* on it. The money for our team pictures is *due* today.

owed Danny is *owed* $10 for the yard work he did for his father this weekend.

unpaid Mom's desk was piled high with a stack of *unpaid* bills that she had to take care of by the end of the month.

outstanding They've paid $2,000 on their loan, and $1,500 is still *outstanding*.

dumb   speechless silent mute

ADJECTIVE: not speaking; not making a sound.

dumb The boy tried to scream for help, but he was struck *dumb* by fear.

speechless She never expected to win the prize, and she was *speechless* with surprise when her name was announced.

silent Dad gave us his *silent* approval with a quick nod of his head.

mute The police asked their prisoner one question after another, but he remained *mute* as if he didn't even understand their language.

▶ The use of **dumb** to mean "not intelligent; stupid" is correct, but it is not a good choice for serious writing. However, because of this meaning the use of *dumb* to mean "not able to speak" is now considered impolite. Use *mute* instead.

duty   responsibility obligation

NOUN: something that one ought to do or has to do.

duty When a soldier is on guard, it's his *duty* to stay at his post and keep alert. In a democracy, voting in elections is considered to be both a right and a *duty*.

responsibility Mom will help me with my homework, but she says it's my own *responsibility* to keep track of when it has to be done.

obligation The money was a gift, not a loan—I have no *obligation* to pay it back.

each   every apiece respectively

ADJECTIVE: for or to all the members of a group.

each *Each* child in the class has his or her own textbook, but they share one set of encyclopedias. Winter is coming, and *each* day it gets dark a little earlier.

every *Every* person who went to the new shopping center on opening day was given a $5.00 gift certificate.

apiece In batting practice, the coach has all the players take ten swings *apiece.*

respectively Dave, Kyle, and Sarah all got high marks on the test; they got 90, 92, and 95, *respectively.*

Tara and Biff were **eager** to get out of the house for a walk.

It was getting late, and Tara was **anxious** to get home for dinner.

eager   anxious keen enthusiastic avid

ADJECTIVE: wanting to do or have something very much.

eager The children enjoyed their day at the beach and are *eager* to go back again. He's *eager* for a home-cooked meal after eating cafeteria food at college all fall.

anxious Kerry checks the mail as soon as she gets home every day, because she's *anxious* to get her grade report from school.

keen Christina wasn't very *keen* about having to stay home to babysit for her little sister.

enthusiastic The movie producers are very *enthusiastic* about her script and want to start filming it right away.

avid Since he retired from his job, he's become an *avid* golfer who plays as often as he can.

Antonyms: **indifferent, unenthusiastic.**

early   soon beforehand prematurely

ADVERB: before the usual or expected time.

early He usually leaves work *early* on Fridays so that he can beat the rush-hour traffic out of the city. The first snowfall was *early* this year; it came the last week in October.

soon At the start of the race one swimmer dove into the water too *soon,* before the starter gave the signal to go.

beforehand Mom wanted to be sure we didn't miss our flight, so she had us get to the airport an hour *beforehand.*

prematurely Mr. Lewis is still a young man, but his hair has gotten *prematurely* gray.

Antonym: **late.**

earth   world globe

NOUN: the planet that is inhabited by the human race.

earth It's often said that the voyage of Columbus proved that the *earth* was round, but actually scientists knew this long before his time. Recent studies seem to indicate that the *earth's* weather is gradually getting warmer.

world The elephant is the largest animal that lives on land, but the blue whale is the largest animal in the *world.*

globe In the late 1800's the British Empire was at its height, and the British flag could be seen in all the corners of the *globe.*

easy   simple effortless manageable

ADJECTIVE: not hard to do or understand; needing little effort or work.

easy Jerry thinks the math test was really *easy* and is sure he got an 'A' on it. Riding a bike is *easy* once you have learned how to do it.

simple A dog can be trained to do *simple* tasks, like catching a tennis ball in the air or bringing in the newspaper.

effortless The ballet dancer was so graceful that she made even the most difficult steps look *effortless.*

manageable Having a paper route takes up a lot of his time, but it's a fairly *manageable* job.

Antonyms: **hard, difficult.**

▶ **Easy** is also used as an adverb, in expressions such as "Take it *easy* on her" or "Go *easy* with the salt." But in school writing it's better to use **easily** when an adverb is needed: "I pushed against the door, and it opened *easily*" (not "it opened easy").

eat   feed dine feast consume devour

VERB: to chew and swallow food.

eat   Dad wants to lose some weight, and he's trying not to *eat* as much snack food.

feed   Although gorillas have a ferocious appearance, they are actually shy, gentle animals that *feed* on leaves and fruit.

dine   She hopes to visit France to *dine* in some of the famous restaurants there.

feast   After the wedding, there was a big party at which the guests *feasted* on shrimp, lobster, and roast beef.

consume   When Eric went to stay with his grandparents, they were amazed to see how much food a teenage boy could *consume.*

devour   I always find it funny that my dog waits all day for his dinner and then *devours* the whole thing as soon as he gets it.

Mrs. Allen had a busy day and had to **eat** lunch at her desk.

She met her husband after work and they **dined** out together.

economical   thrifty frugal prudent

ADJECTIVE: careful and sparing in the use of money, goods, or other resources.

economical   It's usually more *economical* to buy a large box of cereal than to buy the small individual boxes.

thrifty   She's a very *thrifty* cook, and when she buys a cut of meat she always uses up all the leftovers in soups and stews.

frugal   When he was a college student he had almost no extra spending money, so he lived a rather *frugal* existence.

prudent   This magazine appeals to *prudent* car buyers because it analyzes just how much it costs to own each type of car.

Antonyms: **extravagant, wasteful.**

edge border rim margin brink

NOUN: the line or place where something ends.

edge The back yard has grass in the middle and bushes along the *edges.* After swimming a few laps, he got tired and held on to the *edge* of the pool to rest.

border The Mississippi River forms the eastern *border* of the state of Iowa.

rim Their house is right on the *rim* of the canyon and has a view of the whole valley below.

margin When you write a letter, you should leave a *margin* of an inch or so on either side, instead of writing all the way across the page.

brink I watched the log go over the waterfall—it seemed to stop for a moment at the *brink,* then it disappeared below.

education schooling training instruction

NOUN: the development of the mind through some kind of teaching and study.

education My dad went to the University of Michigan, and he says he got a very good *education* there.

schooling In some countries, the children of wealthy families are sent away from home for their *schooling.*

training Mrs. Hall received her *training* as a nurse at New York Medical Center.

instruction For people who buy the new computer system, the company will provide ten hours of free *instruction* in how to use it.

effect result outcome consequence upshot

NOUN: something that happens because of something else.

effect One *effect* of the personal computer has been that more people now do office work at home. The medicine had an immediate *effect,* and his skin rash is almost gone.

result The theater put the remaining tickets on sale at half price, and as a *result* they were able to sell them all.

outcome Both labor and management are working hard to settle the strike, but no one knows yet what the *outcome* of their negotiations will be.

consequence The big increase in our city's population has had some negative *consequences,* like heavy traffic on the roads and overcrowding in the schools.

upshot Many people wrote in to complain when that TV show was taken off the air; the *upshot* of this is that it will be put back on next year.

▶ Remember that **affect** is not a synonym for **effect**. Though the two words have similar meanings, *affect* is a verb and *effect* is a noun: The food that we eat *affects* our health. (verb) This food has an *effect* on our health. (noun)

elegant refined tasteful stylish

ADJECTIVE: having such qualities as richness, grace, and good taste.

elegant The movies of Fred Astaire and Ginger Rogers were known for their lively dancing, witty dialogue, and *elegant* settings. The meal was served on simple but *elegant* dishes, of plain white china with a gold band.

refined "The Odd Couple" was a popular TV show about two roommates, the sloppy Oscar Madison and his neater, more *refined* friend Felix Unger.

tasteful I want to send Grandma a get-well card, and Mom said not to get a funny card, but to look for one that's attractive and *tasteful.*

stylish Ads for expensive cars often show well-dressed, *stylish*-looking models posing next to the car.

Antonyms: **crude, vulgar.**

elementary basic fundamental primary

ADJECTIVE: having to do with the first or simplest part of something.

elementary *Elementary* school comes before junior high and high school. In this *elementary* science course, you learn things that are needed to go on to more advanced courses, such as biology and physics.

basic *Basic* English is a form of the language that uses only 850 short, common words, such as "and" or "the."

fundamental At the first day of basketball practice the coach had us work on *fundamental* skills—dribbling and passing the ball.

primary Kindergarten, first grade, and second grade are often called the *primary* grades, because they are the beginning of a student's education.

Antonym: **advanced.**

embarrassed ashamed flustered uneasy mortified

VERB: feeling upset, nervous, or uncomfortable about something.

embarrassed Heather was *embarrassed* at her birthday party when her father insisted on doing his card tricks for her friends.

ashamed Aunt Carol asked how I liked the game she got me, and I was *ashamed* to tell her I had given it away to a friend without playing it.

flustered When Kirk couldn't think of his next line in the class play, he got really *flustered* and called out to the teacher, "Help! What do I say now?"

uneasy Cathy is willing to stay home alone now, but she's still *uneasy* about it and keeps everything locked up tight.

mortified Everyone was watching as Tricia went to kick the ball, and she was absolutely *mortified* when she slipped on the mud and fell down.

The movie theater was half **empty,** so we were easily able to find two **vacant** seats.

empty   vacant uninhabited unoccupied

ADJECTIVE: lacking what could or should be present; without the usual contents.

empty In this car a light goes on to warn when the gas tank is almost *empty.* It was a bitter cold night, and the streets were nearly *empty* when I walked home.

vacant There's a *vacant* apartment on this floor; the people in 5-A moved out.

uninhabited The Sahara Desert gets very little rainfall, and large parts of it are completely *uninhabited.*

unoccupied We wanted to park near the library, but there wasn't one *unoccupied* space in the whole parking lot.

Antonyms: **full, occupied.**

encourage   inspire cheer reassure

VERB: to give courage or hope to someone.

encourage Tim is very interested in ancient history, and his teacher *encouraged* him to do some outside reading on the subject. Sharon hasn't won a race yet, but she is *encouraged* by the fact that her time keeps improving.

inspire The first black player in major-league baseball, Jackie Robinson, *inspired* younger blacks to make their way to the big leagues.

cheer Bruce was afraid he'd need an operation on his shoulder, so he was greatly *cheered* when the doctor said it would heal without one.

reassure Whenever Cara is working on a paper she's afraid it won't be any good, and her mom has to *reassure* her that she's a good writer.

Antonyms: **discourage, depress.**

end   finish   conclusion   completion

NOUN: the part that comes after all others; the last part.

end Labor Day is a holiday at the *end* of the summer. She opened the book to the back and read the *end* of the story first, so she'd know how it came out.

finish Even though all the polls said the mayor had no chance to be re-elected, he campaigned hard right up to the *finish*.

conclusion The movie is a four-part series, with the first three parts on this week and the *conclusion* shown next Monday.

completion The *completion* of the new baseball stadium is set for April 1st.

<u>Antonyms:</u> **beginning, start.**

Our team scored at the **end** of the fourth quarter. It was a thrilling **finish** to the game.

enemy   opponent   rival   foe   adversary

NOUN: someone who fights or acts against another.

enemy Shakespeare's play *Macbeth* tells how King Duncan is murdered by his *enemy* Macbeth. The United States and Japan were *enemies* in World War II.

opponent A famous chess champion came to our city and put on an exhibition in which he played ten different *opponents* at the same time.

rival Chris Evert and Martina Navratilova were *rivals* for many years in women's professional tennis.

foe In his first speech as President, John F. Kennedy said that the U.S. would be willing to oppose any *foe* for the sake of liberty in the world.

adversary Abraham Lincoln had a famous series of debates with his political *adversary,* Stephen A. Douglas.

<u>Antonyms:</u> **friend, ally.**

energy   vigor vitality liveliness pep

NOUN: the strength or will to do something; the power to move or act.

energy My baby brother has a lot of *energy;* he's always crawling on the floor or climbing up on the furniture. The coach told us not to run around too much before the game, to save our *energy* for the game itself.

vigor Theodore Roosevelt was still a young man when he became President, and he took on his duties with enthusiasm and *vigor.*

vitality My grandfather has a lot of *vitality* for a man his age, and he gets out of the house for a long walk every day.

liveliness Monkeys are known for their *liveliness,* and even when they are confined in zoos they constantly move about.

pep She's back in school after being sick with the flu all last week, but she still doesn't have much *pep.*

enough   sufficient ample adequate plenty

ADJECTIVE: as much as is needed; the right amount.

enough I'm going to wait to work on my paper this weekend; I'll have *enough* time to do a good job on it then. The bill didn't get *enough* votes to become a law.

sufficient She wasn't sure how much cash to bring on her trip, but she decided $200 would be *sufficient.*

ample The house has a big back yard, with *ample* room for the boys to play ball.

adequate Because the Western plains can be very dry, early settlers had to be careful to find a spot with *adequate* water.

plenty Take as many pieces of paper as you need; I've got *plenty* more in my desk.

Antonyms: **inadequate, insufficient.**

ensure   insure assure secure

VERB: to make a person or thing sure or safe; make certain.

ensure The bank asked her for some identification to *ensure* that it was really her check. Having a plane ticket does not *ensure* that you will get on a flight, because the airlines often sell more tickets than there are seats available.

insure People *insure* their house so that if it is damaged in some way they will receive money to pay for repairing it.

assure I know my car looks old and beat-up, but I can *assure* you that it runs well and has never had any major problems.

secure When they moved into the apartment, they *secured* the front door by installing a special double lock.

enter   penetrate invade intrude

VERB: to move to a place so as to pass through to the inside; come or go in.

enter In some countries, it is the custom to take off your shoes before you *enter* a house. An actor waiting to go on stage listens for the cue that will tell him when to *enter*.

penetrate He accidentally stepped on a nail, but he was wearing thick-soled shoes and it didn't *penetrate* his skin.

invade World War II began after Nazi Germany sent tanks and troops across its eastern border to *invade* Poland.

intrude She waited outside the boss's office, because she didn't want to *intrude* while he was having a private conversation on the phone.

Antonym: **exit, leave.**

entertain   amuse divert absorb regale

VERB: to keep interested and pleased; hold the attention in a pleasant way.

entertain For many years Bob Hope took groups of singers and dancers overseas to *entertain* American troops. When we take a long car trip, Dad tries to *entertain* us with a game of "Initials" or "20 Questions."

amuse When the baby's in her crib, she likes to *amuse* herself by playing with the spinning toy that hangs overhead.

divert The stewardess could see that the boy was very nervous about flying, so she told him a joke to *divert* his attention while the plane was taking off.

absorb I got really excited when the winning run scored, but Mom was *absorbed* in her book and didn't even look up at the TV.

regale The movie director Orson Welles often appeared on talk shows to *regale* the audience with stories of his days in Hollywood.

Antonym: **bore.**

envy   begrudge covet resent

VERB: to have a selfish interest in something that someone else has; be jealous.

envy He had been driving the same old car for twelve years, and he *envied* his neighbor who bought a fancy new car every couple of years.

begrudge My sister gets straight A's and I don't, but I don't *begrudge* her those good grades because I know she studies much harder than I do.

covet A lot of developers *covet* that piece of property because it's right on the lakefront, but the owner says she will never sell.

resent The actress *resented* the fact that the two other stars of the movie were both nominated for acting awards, but she was not.

erase   delete obliterate eradicate

VERB: to remove completely, as if by rubbing out.

erase   Ricky saw he'd written the wrong date, so he *erased* the 4 and wrote a 5. If you record on a videotape, you *erase* any program that was on the tape before.

delete   Laura realized that the last paragraph did not fit with the rest of her topic, so she *deleted* it from her paper.

obliterate   When Joseph Stalin removed Leon Trotsky from power, he had the history books changed to *obliterate* any mention of his former rival.

eradicate   After the English defeated the Scottish clans, they tried to *eradicate* their culture, and it was forbidden to play the bagpipes or wear the clan colors.

Antonyms: **record, preserve.**

escape   elude avoid shun evade

VERB: to get away from someone or something; move away.

escape   Bank robber Willie Sutton was known for the clever ways he was able to *escape* from prison. The bird got out of its cage and *escaped* through a window.

elude   To *elude* the detective who was following him, the man hid in a doorway.

avoid   Tracy is mad at Jennifer, and when she saw her coming in the mall she walked the other way to *avoid* her.

shun   After the other prisoners in the camp found out that he was secretly passing information to the guards, they completely *shunned* him.

evade   Billy got embarrassed when his aunt wanted to give him a big hug, and he tried to *evade* it by ducking away.

Ellen left the door open, and the puppy **escaped** into the yard.

Every time they tried to grab him, he would **elude** them.

especially   particularly specifically primarily expressly

ADVERB: in a way more than others; more than the usual.

especially Everyone in our family likes to watch that TV show, *especially* Dad. We've had good weather all week, and today was *especially* nice.

particularly Watch out that you don't break anything, and be *particularly* careful with those crystal glasses.

specifically The first people to fly faster than the speed of sound were American test pilots, *specifically* Chuck Yeager and Scott Crossfield.

primarily The Farm Stand sells all kinds of fresh vegetables, which are grown *primarily* by farmers right in the area.

expressly This armored limousine was built *expressly* for use by the President.

▶ **Especial**ly and **specially** are very close in form but are usually not used the same way. *Especially* usually goes with an adjective, and *specially* with a verb: Many pro basketball players are *especially* tall and must have their clothes made *specially* for them, because ordinary sizes are too small.

establish   organize found institute

VERB: to create or begin; set up.

establish After the American colonists won their freedom from Great Britain, they *established* the separate government of the United States.

organize Concerned that British youth did not have enough outdoor training, Sir Robert Baden-Powell *organized* the Boy Scout movement in 1908.

found Harvard, the oldest college in the United States, was *founded* in 1636.

institute New Zealand was the first country to *institute* the right to vote for women.

Antonyms: **abolish, disband.**

event   incident adventure happening occurrence

NOUN: something that happens, especially something important or unusual.

event The writing of the Constitution was a major *event* in American history. The County Fair is a very popular summertime *event* in our town.

incident Several demonstrators were arrested after the President's speech, and this morning's paper had a story on the *incident*.

adventure When we have a power blackout, my dad always treats it as a big *adventure* and gets out all kinds of candles and flashlights.

happening *Alice in Wonderland* tells of the strange *happenings* that take place after Alice falls down a rabbit hole.

occurrence Route 15 is really busy, and traffic jams are a common *occurrence*.

evidence   proof   grounds   testimony

NOUN: anything that shows or makes clear.

evidence In order for someone to be found guilty of a crime, the state has to present *evidence* that the person did it. There is now clear *evidence* that smoking is harmful to health.

proof The clerk told her to keep the sales slip as *proof* that she had bought the sweater in that store.

grounds The author argues that Shakespeare did not write his own plays, but even after I read her book I couldn't see any *grounds* for thinking that.

testimony The witness's *testimony* was that he had seen the accused man running away from the bank just after the robbery.

I think Jason is **exaggerating** about the fish he caught. He **overstated** how big it was.

exaggerate   magnify   overstate   embroider

VERB: to make something seem more than it really is.

exaggerate He's really five-six, but he always *exaggerates* and says he's five-nine. She shouted and cried as if her leg were broken, but she was just *exaggerating*.

magnify Because so many news organizations are centered in New York City, events that happen there are sometimes *magnified* beyond their true importance.

overstate He *overstated* his role in the making of that movie; he was not really the assistant director, but just someone who ran errands for the director.

embroider When she told what happened, Mindy tried to make her story more interesting by *embroidering* the details a little.

Mr. Lane wrote an **example** sentence on the chalkboard.

He explained how a jet plane works by showing the class a **model** of one.

example   sample illustration model instance

NOUN: a thing that is typical of its kind or that shows what others are like.

example To add means to put one number with another: for *example,* 12+8=20. Air conditioning made it possible for large cities to grow up in very hot areas—Phoenix, Arizona is a good *example.*

sample She needed new wallpaper for her kitchen, so she went through a book of *samples* to pick out the style she wanted.

illustration Smoke moving upward from a fire is an *illustration* of the fact that hot air rises.

model When a group of houses is being built, the builder will often furnish and decorate one home as a *model* for buyers to look at.

instance Miss Keith spent an hour after school helping Todd with his speech; that's just one of the many *instances* of her giving extra time to help a student.

except   save excluding barring

PREPOSITION: not including; leaving out.

except Soccer players are not allowed to use their hands, *except* for the goalie. No President has served more than two terms *except* Franklin D. Roosevelt.

save All the birds at the pond are gone until spring, *save* for a few Canada geese.

excluding The car has a list price of about $15,000; that's *excluding* state sales tax and license fees.

barring The trip should take you about five hours, *barring* any heavy traffic.

excuse justification defense alibi plea

NOUN: a reason that explains some fault or failure.

excuse When a student is absent from school, he or she needs a written *excuse* to explain the absence. His *excuse* for missing practice was that his mother couldn't get her car started, but I think he just didn't want to go.

justification I know that Suzie gets a lot of homework, but that's no *justification* for her spending the whole dinner hour complaining about it.

defense The President's new policy on Latin America is very unpopular in the area, so he sent the Vice President there to speak in *defense* of the policy.

alibi He told the police he had nothing to do with robbing the jewelry store; his *alibi* is that he was home watching TV all night.

plea The mayor told the reporters he would have to offer a *plea* of ignorance; he had not read the article yet and therefore couldn't comment on it.

expect await anticipate foresee

VERB: to think something will probably come or happen.

expect I thought I just heard the doorbell—are you *expecting* a visitor? The studio *expects* this movie to be very popular, and they're spending a lot of money to advertise it.

await The plane had landed, and a group of people stood outside the gate *awaiting* the arrival of friends and relatives.

anticipate The school board hadn't *anticipated* that so many people would come, and the meeting room was much too small for the crowd.

foresee More and more people are moving to our town; I can *foresee* a day when all the land between here and the highway will be built up with houses.

experience background skill practice training

NOUN: knowledge or ability that is gained by doing something.

experience When the publishing company hires people to sell school textbooks, they look for people who have had *experience* as teachers.

background In writing his "James Bond" spy novels, Ian Fleming drew on his own *background* as a secret agent in World War II.

skill The American Indians were known for their great *skill* at tracking wild animals.

practice He worked at a newsstand right next to the railroad station, so he's had a lot of *practice* dealing with customers who are in a big hurry.

training The history teacher makes his students work hard on their reports, but it's good *training* for the reports they'll have to do in college.

expert   authority specialist wizard

NOUN: a person who knows a lot about something or is very good at it.

expert I couldn't tell you if that is a rare coin or not; you'd have to show it to an *expert.* At the ski resort they have easy trails for beginners and steeper, more difficult ones for *experts.*

authority The critic H. L. Mencken was an *authority* on the American language and wrote several famous books on this subject.

specialist When she hurt her ankle she went to her family doctor, who sent her to another doctor, a *specialist* who deals with bone injuries.

wizard My Uncle Dan is a real *wizard* at fixing cars, and my mom always brings her car to him when she has a problem.

Antonyms: **beginner, novice, amateur.**

explain   demonstrate clarify interpret justify

VERB: to make something clear or easy to understand.

explain I didn't understand how a heavy steel ship could float on water, and Mom *explained* that it's because there is air trapped inside. That book has a glossary in the back to *explain* hard words used in the text.

demonstrate When the salesman took us for a test drive in the new car, he *demonstrated* how all the various controls and instruments worked.

clarify The lawyer didn't understand what the witness meant by "I might have seen him that day," and she asked him to *clarify* his answer.

interpret As the President spoke in English, a woman in the TV studio *interpreted* his remarks for the Russian-speaking audience.

justify They asked the coach why he always used his own son Tim as the pitcher, and he tried to *justify* it by saying Tim had the most experience.

Antonyms: **obscure, complicate.**

explode   erupt blast detonate

VERB: to burst suddenly with a loud noise; blow up.

explode When an atomic bomb *explodes,* it produces a huge mushroom-shaped cloud. The little boy stuck a pin in the balloon and it *exploded* with a loud bang.

erupt The ancient Roman cities of Pompeii and Herculaneum were completely buried in 79 A.D. when a large volcano *erupted* nearby.

blast When the workers dug the hole for the swimming pool, they had to use dynamite to *blast* away a large boulder that was in the way.

detonate A land mine is a type of weapon used in warfare, in which a charge is *detonated* by a person stepping on the mine.

extra   spare surplus excess supplementary additional

ADJECTIVE: more than what is usual or needed; more.

extra Some of the guests didn't eat anything, and there was a lot of *extra* food left over. During leap year, the month of February has one *extra* day.

spare Dad always keeps a *spare* set of car keys in the kitchen drawer, in case he can't find the ones he usually uses.

surplus After World War II ended, millions of men were released from the service, and the Army had a huge supply of *surplus* uniforms.

excess Before you cook the meat, cut away all the *excess* fat around the edges.

supplementary For students who are having trouble with the regular math book, there's a *supplementary* workbook that gives more practice.

additional We get to drive the rental car for 100 free miles per day; then any *additional* miles cost 15 cents a mile.

This station wagon has an **extra** seat in back.

They carry a **spare** tire to put on if a tire gets flat.

eye   inspect scan regard

VERB: to watch carefully or closely.

eye Gary *eyed* the last cookie on the plate, hoping no one else would want it.

inspect Once a year this elevator has to be *inspected* to make sure it is working properly.

scan The sailor thought he heard the sound of thunder, and he *scanned* the horizon looking for signs of a storm.

regard The magician clapped his hands and the two birds seemed to disappear, as the children *regarded* him with amazement.

fact   truth reality actuality certainty

NOUN: something known to be real; something that exists or that has happened.

fact It's a matter of opinion who is Hollywood's greatest actress, but it's a *fact* that Katherine Hepburn has won the most Oscars for Best Actress.

truth Witnesses in court are supposed to tell only the *truth* about what they know, not make guesses about what might have happened.

reality Though he says his new book is coming along well, the *reality* is that he has only written one chapter.

actuality The expression "lone wolf" comes from the idea that wolves live and hunt alone, but in *actuality* they live in packs of eight animals or more.

certainty Investing money in the stock market is always a risk, because there is no *certainty* that the value of a stock will go up.

Antonyms: **fiction, opinion.**

It's a **fact** that if you mix blue and yellow paint, you get green.

Jimmy told the **truth** about how paint got on the wall.

fad   fashion trend rage mania

NOUN: something that is very popular at a certain time.

fad While "Davy Crockett" was a top-rated TV show in the 1950's, wearing a Crockett-style coonskin cap was a big *fad* among young boys.

fashion The magazine showed models wearing the latest *fashions* from Paris.

trend The newest *trend* in home building is to allow space for an at-home office with computer facilities.

rage A short, flat haircut known as a "bob" was the *rage* for women in the 1920's.

mania "Beatle *mania*" was the name for the great excitement created by this English rock group on their first visit to the U.S. in 1964.

fade   pale dim bleach blanch

VERB: to lose or cause to lose color or brightness.

fade The sun had *faded* the bright print of the sofa cover. This shirt was bright red when I bought it, but now it has *faded* to a dull pink.

pale When he saw the bear coming toward the tent, Jeff's face *paled* with fear.

dim The lights in the theater were kept on while people were being seated and then *dimmed* as the play was about to begin.

bleach Maria got a pair of dark-blue jeans as a present, and she wants to *bleach* them so that they'll be a lighter color.

blanch According to the recipe, we should *blanch* the celery by boiling it quickly before we add it to the stew.

fail   miscarry flop misfire flunk

VERB: to not have the desired or expected result; not succeed.

fail William Jennings Bryan ran three times for President but *failed* each time. The high jumper *failed* to clear the bar; his foot knocked it off as he went over.

miscarry In 1961, U.S.-backed rebel forces tried to overthrow the government of Cuba, but the plan *miscarried* and their attack was defeated.

flop Although the movie *Ishtar* had two famous actors as stars and opened with lots of publicity, it *flopped* completely and lost millions of dollars.

misfire The comedian told what he thought was a very funny joke about Queen Elizabeth, but it *misfired* because the audience thought he was being cruel to her.

flunk Danny said to his older sister, "You've got to help me study for my algebra test! If you don't I'll *flunk* for sure!"

Antonym: **succeed.**

fair   just impartial equal

ADJECTIVE: not choosing or favoring one side over another.

fair The race wasn't *fair* because Bobby started running before the coach said "Go." To be *fair,* she divided the cookies so that each child would get the same number.

just The judge listened carefully to both sides in the dispute as she tried to reach a *just* decision.

impartial A baseball umpire is supposed to be *impartial* and not call plays to favor either team.

equal Martin Luther King worked to help black people gain civil rights *equal* to the rights held by white people.

Antonyms: **unfair, partial, biased.**

faithful loyal true devoted steadfast

ADJECTIVE: holding to some cause, duty, or promise.

faithful *Old Yeller* is the story of a boy and his *faithful* dog who stays by his side wherever he goes. When people get married, they promise to be *faithful* to one another.

loyal When the Civil War began, Robert E. Lee was offered command of the Union Army, but he felt more *loyal* to his home state of Virginia and refused.

true He was *true* to his word and paid me back all the money he had borrowed.

devoted In the Sherlock Holmes detective stories, Holmes is helped in his work by his *devoted* friend, Dr. Watson.

steadfast The emperor Napoleon had a special body of troops, the "Old Guard," who remained *steadfast* in their support of him until the end of his career.

Antonyms: **unfaithful, disloyal.**

fake false imitation counterfeit phony

ADJECTIVE: not authentic or genuine; not real.

fake Except for the price, it was hard to tell the real pearl necklace from the *fake* one. The spy had obtained a *fake* passport to use in traveling out of the country.

false She has trouble getting her real fingernails to grow as long as she wants, so she wears *false* ones.

imitation The *imitation* crab in the seafood salad is actually smoked fish that is colored and shaped to look like real crab.

counterfeit Police reported that a number of *counterfeit* twenty-dollar bills had been passed at local department stores.

phony The rock concert was completely sold out, and some people tried to get in by using *phony* tickets they had printed up themselves.

Antonyms: **real, genuine, authentic.**

fall drop sink collapse

VERB: to move or go down from a higher place or level.

fall Be careful on the steps there—you might slip and *fall* on the ice. The sky above the lake turned gray, and a cold rain began to *fall*.

drop Even though it's just the beginning of October, the temperature has *dropped* below freezing the last few nights.

sink I tossed a penny into the pond and watched it *sink* slowly to the bottom.

collapse They kept loading more and more books onto the old table, until finally the legs just *collapsed*.

Antonym: **rise.**

family   relatives kin clan

NOUN: a group of people who are related to each other.

family I grew up in a big *family;* there were eight of us—my mom and dad, my four sisters, my brother, and myself.

relatives He was born in Italy, and he still has a lot of *relatives* living over there.

kin Yes, I know we have the same last name, but she's no *kin* of mine.

clan I remember the Thanksgiving holidays when I was a kid—our whole *clan* would get together for dinner at my Uncle Michael's house.

famous   noted prominent famed

ADJECTIVE: known to many people.

famous Mickey Mouse and Donald Duck are *famous* characters created by Walt Disney. Irving Berlin wrote many *famous* songs, such as "White Christmas."

noted The chef at this restaurant comes from the Burgundy region of France, an area *noted* for its fine food and wine.

prominent In her book on acid rain, the author interviews several *prominent* scientists who warn that it is a serious problem.

famed Miramar Naval Air Station in California is the site of the *famed* "Top Gun" training school for fighter pilots.

Antonyms: **unknown, obscure.**

▶ **Famous** and **notorious** are not quite the same. Both mean "well-known," but *notorious* carries a negative sense, "well-known for something that is bad."

The actor Red Rodney is **famous** for his roles in Western movies.

He is **notorious** for being hard to get along with on the set of a movie.

fan   supporter follower booster

NOUN: someone who admires or gives support to a certain person or thing.

fan When the popular rock group arrived in town for their concert, hundreds of their *fans* came out to the airport to meet them. My dad is a real baseball *fan* and always watches the games on TV.

supporter Dr. Ruiz is a strong *supporter* of the local drama group; he has given a large sum of money to build a new theater.

follower Mahatma Gandhi was a famous religious leader of India who had many *followers* throughout the nation.

booster The high school has a *Booster* Club made up of parents who do things to help the school's sports teams.

far   distant remote faraway far-off

ADJECTIVE: at or in a place that is some distance away; not near or close.

far The island state of Hawaii is *far* from the mainland of North America. The mall was very busy and the only spaces left were at the *far* end of the parking lot.

distant She looked out across the lake and could just make out a few faint lights shining on the *distant* shoreline.

remote He wants to be alone to write a book, and he's thinking of moving from the city to a *remote* cabin in the mountains somewhere.

faraway On Sundays she likes to read the travel section of the newspaper and imagine herself taking trips to exciting, *faraway* places.

far-off As I was lying in bed trying to sleep, I heard the *far-off* sound of a train going by in the night.

Antonyms: **near, close.**

Their house is **far** back from the main road. It is in a **remote** area away from any town.

fast quick rapid speedy swift

ADJECTIVE: moving or acting with speed; not slow.

fast No other animal is as *fast* as the cheetah, which can chase its prey at over 60 miles an hour. The *fastest* way to travel across the United States is by jet airplane.

quick When the rabbit heard me coming, it ran under the fence and made a *quick* escape into the bushes.

rapid The fire department now uses a special computer system so that it can make a very *rapid* response to fire alarms.

speedy The San Francisco Super Bowl teams featured quarterback Joe Montana throwing passes to the *speedy* wide receiver Jerry Rice.

swift The Cheyenne Indians of the Great Plains were noted for the skill with which they rode their small, *swift* horses.

Antonym: **slow.**

fat chubby stout overweight portly

NOUN: weighing a lot or weighing too much.

fat Rachel always drinks diet soda instead of regular soda; she says she does it because she doesn't want to get *fat*.

chubby My baby brother looks so cute with his round, *chubby* little face.

stout The great British statesman Winston Churchill was often said to look like a bulldog, because of his determined expression and short, *stout* body.

overweight The doctor told Mr. Ross that he is twenty pounds *overweight* and that he should eat less and get more exercise.

portly A famous comedy team in movies was made up of the thin, nervous Stan Laurel and his *portly*, dignified friend Oliver Hardy.

Antonyms: **thin, slender, skinny.**

fault blame guilt responsibility

NOUN: the fact of being the one who did or caused something wrong.

fault The accident was her *fault* because she went through a red light. Bobby didn't let the dog out on purpose, but he was still at *fault* for not closing the door.

blame The coach took the *blame* for the team's loss by saying he had called the wrong plays from the bench.

guilt In a court of law, the jury considers all the evidence to decide if there are enough facts to prove the *guilt* of the defendant.

responsibility The judge ruled that the factory had *responsibility* for polluting the river, and he ordered the company to take immediate steps to clean it up.

Antonym: **credit.**

favorite   preferred choice prized pet

ADJECTIVE: liked the most or thought of in the best way.

favorite My dad is from Detroit, and the Tigers are his *favorite* baseball team. It's Andy's birthday, so we're having his *favorite* dinner, chicken with rice and corn.

preferred In the company parking lot, the top executives get *preferred* parking spaces right next to the door.

choice When the developer put up these houses, he kept the *choice* lot on top of the hill for his own house.

prized Mario's new racing bike is his *prized* possession.

pet At every council meeting she suggests that the town should build a public golf course; that's her *pet* project.

Taking swimming lessons has helped Greg overcome his **fear** of the water.

Jeff has an absolute **terror** of snakes and doesn't want to be near them.

fear   fright alarm terror dread

NOUN: a bad feeling that pain, harm, or something dangerous will happen.

fear He has a great *fear* of flying and always takes the train when he has to travel. Because of their huge size, elephants show little *fear* of other wild animals.

fright A car went through a red light and just missed us—it gave me a real *fright*.

alarm The passengers were filled with *alarm* by the report that their ship was in the path of an oncoming hurricane.

terror In early times, the fierce Viking warriors of Scandinavia brought *terror* to northern Europe with their sudden attacks from the sea.

dread In this book the author expresses his *dread* of an all-out nuclear war.

<u>Antonyms:</u> **bravery, courage.**

feel   touch handle finger probe

VERB: to find out about by contacting with the hand or hands.

feel He put down his packages on the doorstep and *felt* around in his pockets for the front door key. Karen *felt* the tires on her bicycle to see if they needed air.

touch Mom told us not to *touch* the kitchen walls because the paint on them was still wet.

handle As she picked up the package, she *handled* it carefully to avoid damaging the expensive crystal vase inside.

finger While he sat waiting for his job interview to begin, the man nervously *fingered* his necktie, tightening and then loosening it again and again.

probe The doctor *probed* the cut on Darryl's leg to see if there was broken glass under the skin.

feeling   sensation perception impression awareness

NOUN: a certain sense that the body or mind experiences.

feeling As he watched his daughter receive the award, he had a *feeling* of pride. She had an odd *feeling* that someone was following her and turned around to check.

sensation Sometimes I have a dream that I'm looking down from a tall building, and then I wake up with the *sensation* that I'm falling.

perception Dogs do not have very sharp eyesight; their *perception* of things is based much more on sound and smell.

impression I was surprised when Brian told me he was born in Chicago; I had the *impression* he'd lived in this town all his life.

awareness Even though we were watching the deer with binoculars from across the ridge, they seemed to have an *awareness* that we were there and moved off.

few   rare scarce meager

ADJECTIVE: not large in number; not many.

few The mall had just opened for the day, and there were just a *few* shoppers in the stores. He didn't bring his wallet with him and he had only a *few* dollars in change.

rare Wolves are very *rare* in the United States, and not many people have ever seen one in the wild.

scarce Fresh strawberries are *scarce* in the stores at this time of year, though there will be a lot later in the spring.

meager When they were rescued, the lost campers told how they'd existed for a week on a *meager* diet of wild berries and nuts.

field   range   scope   sphere   realm

NOUN: an area of learning, activity, or interest.

field   Each year Nobel Prizes are awarded in such *fields* as literature, medicine, chemistry, and physics.

range   She had been in education for many years and had a wide *range* of experience as a teacher, principal, and reading specialist.

scope   The *scope* of Leonardo da Vinci's talent was very great.

sphere   He has a limited *sphere* of interest and pays little attention to anything other than his work in the laboratory.

realm   Because psychology is the study of the mind, some people argue that it cannot be properly included within the *realm* of science.

fight   battle   struggle   conflict   feud

NOUN: a contest or effort to defeat or overcome some opposing force.

fight   During the hockey game a *fight* broke out between the two teams when one player knocked over the other team's goalie.

battle   The British forces in North America surrendered to the American colonists after being defeated at the *Battle* of Yorktown.

struggle   There was a *struggle* outside the courtroom as friends of the accused man clashed with members of the victim's family.

conflict   Israel has often been the site of armed *conflict* between Israelis and Arabs.

feud   The movie actor was having a *feud* with his co-star, and they never spoke to each other on the set.

fill   stuff   pack   load   cram

VERB: to put as much into something as it will hold.

fill   She *filled* the water glass too full, and water began to spill over the sides. The large crowd *filled* every available seat in the theater.

stuff   He ate as if he hadn't had a meal in a week, *stuffing* his mouth with food and gulping down his milk.

pack   During the afternoon rush hour all the roads leading out of the city were *packed* with cars.

load   Dad was getting ready to drive Chris to college, and they had *loaded* the station wagon with suitcases and boxes.

cram   Brad was supposed to throw away all his old school papers, but he just *crammed* them into one of his desk drawers instead.

Antonyms: **empty, drain.**

finance   economics accounting banking investment

NOUN: the control or management of money.

finance The American dollar, the German mark, and the Japanese yen are important units of money in international *finance*.

economics Professor Milton Friedman won the Nobel Prize in *economics* for his theory that the supply of money in a country affects business conditions there.

accounting Many Americans go to *accounting* firms each year for help in filling out their income tax forms.

banking Security Federal offers a full range of *banking* services, such as savings and checking accounts, credit cards, and loans for buying homes and cars.

investment Because their value is guaranteed by the government, U.S. Savings Bonds are considered to be a safe *investment*.

find   discover locate detect uncover

VERB: to come upon something that was lost or not known of before.

find When Mom was cleaning under the car seat she *found* the watch I lost last week. The diving expedition hopes to *find* sunken ships with cargoes of treasure.

discover The planet Uranus was *discovered* in 1781 by Sir William Herschel.

locate The police searched for the stolen car and finally *located* it in a waterfront parking lot.

detect At airports all passengers have to pass by a machine that is able to *detect* metal objects inside clothing or luggage.

uncover The FBI *uncovered* a spy ring that sold military secrets to the USSR.

Antonym: **lose.**

Marcy looked in the tall grass to **find** the golf ball she had lost.

In the grass, she **discovered** an old road sign from the 1800's.

fine

ADJECTIVE: better than the usual; very good.

▶ **Fine** is a widely used general word for positive statements: It was a *fine* day. They did a *fine* job. That is a *fine* book. These uses of *fine* are completely correct, but some writers rely too much on this word. It's easy to let a single adjective like *good* or *fine* do the work of describing something. But your writing will be more interesting if you don't just say something is *fine* and leave it at that. Instead, give details to show the reader why it is a fine day or a fine book.

fine   penalty   damages

NOUN: an amount paid for breaking a law or rule.

fine   A *fine* of ten cents per day is charged on overdue library books. My older brother got a speeding ticket last month and had to pay a $35 *fine.*

penalty   If you don't pay the tax on time, you are charged a *penalty* of 10 percent of the amount due.

damages   The chemical company was convicted of polluting the river and had to pay $100,000 in *damages* to the state.

finish   shine   polish   glaze

NOUN: the smooth outer surface of something.

finish   The *finish* on that chair makes it look like an antique. The car had been given more than twenty coats of paint, so that it had a beautiful *finish.*

shine   Their house was kept so clean that you could see your reflection in the *shine* on top of the dining room table.

polish   Jennifer's mother told her not to put that bright red *polish* on her nails.

glaze   The pottery maker applied a bright blue *glaze* to the surface of the vase.

fire   dismiss   discharge   terminate

VERB: to remove from a job or position.

fire   The other workers in the mail room keep telling Stuart that he's going to get *fired* for coming in late to work every day.

dismiss   The movie studio decided to *dismiss* the director of the film because the project was way over budget and out of control.

discharge   Business is so slow at the restaurant that the owner had to *discharge* all his waiters, and now he and his wife wait on tables themselves.

terminate   The department store has the right to *terminate* any worker who is caught stealing store merchandise.

fit   alter adjust conform

VERB: to be or make the right size and shape.

fit   Mike has grown a lot since last year and his old winter jacket doesn't *fit* him any more. On this car, the spare tire *fits* into a compartment inside the trunk.

alter   He had to have the trousers of his new suit *altered;* they were too tight at the waist.

adjust   When Chrissie borrowed her big sister's bicycle, she had to *adjust* the seat so that she could reach the pedals.

conform   All telephone receivers look somewhat the same because they are made to *conform* to the average distance between a person's mouth and ear.

Uncle Leo tried to
fix my bicycle chain.

My mom had to **mend**
the rip in his pants.

fix   repair mend patch rebuild

VERB: to cause something that is not working properly to act in the proper way.

fix   The plumber *fixed* the kitchen faucet so that it wouldn't leak any more. Can you *fix* this stapler so that the staples don't come out crooked?

repair   My new watch wasn't working right, and I took it back to the store to have it *repaired.*

mend   She *mended* her sweater where it had worn out at the elbow.

patch   Terry tore a hole in the knee of his baseball pants, so his mother had to *patch* it.

rebuild   The mechanic said that the problem was much worse than he thought, and now he'll have to completely *rebuild* the engine.

flash   shine gleam sparkle glisten glitter

VERB: to give off a strong, bright light.

flash The truck driver *flashed* his headlights at our car as a signal that it was all right to pass him.

shine Coal miners wear helmets with lamps that *shine* into the darkness of the mine.

gleam As she looked out the window of the plane she saw the lights of the desert city far below, *gleaming* in the dark night.

sparkle Behind the house it was dark and quiet, with no light except from the fireflies *sparkling* here and there among the trees.

glisten A big fish jumped out of the water right in front of the boat, its back *glistening* in the sunlight.

glitter In the window of the jewelry store there was a beautiful diamond necklace, *glittering* against a black velvet background.

flat   even level smooth

ADJECTIVE: having a straight, horizontal surface.

flat The game of pool is played on a *flat* table with six pockets for the balls. California's Central Valley is very *flat,* and you can see for miles in any direction.

even The lawnmower is set so that it cuts the grass to be very *even,* at a height of exactly two inches.

level When the house was being built, the workers checked to make sure that all the floors and counter tops were completely *level.*

smooth At the ice-skating rink they have a special machine that goes over and over the ice to make it *smooth.*

Antonyms: **uneven, rough.**

floor   bottom bed base foot

NOUN: the lower part or surface of something.

floor I knocked the glass off the kitchen table and it fell to the *floor* and broke. There is always a lot of activity on the *floor* of the New York Stock Exchange.

bottom The water was so clear that day that we could see all the way down to the *bottom* of the lake.

bed The dam now blocks the stream that used to flow along here, and trees have grown up all along the dry river *bed.*

base The Statue of Liberty rests on a huge concrete *base* over 150 feet high.

foot Mark told me to meet him in front of the public library, at the *foot* of the main staircase.

I found this dog when he **followed** me home one day.

He thinks that he can **track** rabbits, but I'm not so sure.

follow   chase pursue trail track stalk

VERB: to go after or behind someone or something.

follow The police think that the man will lead them to the stolen money, and they are *following* him wherever he goes.

chase Shawn *chased* after the ball as it rolled past him toward the outfield fence.

pursue The rock star jumped into his limousine and drove off, *pursued* by a group of shouting teenagers calling for his autograph.

trail The duck walked along beside the pond, her four ducklings *trailing* her.

track The photographer *tracked* the snow leopard for miles over the mountains, hoping to get a picture of this rare and beautiful beast.

stalk American Indian hunters trained themselves to move silently as they *stalked* their prey.

fool   trick deceive bluff

VERB: to act toward someone in a dishonest way.

fool In *Huckleberry Finn,* the "Duke" and the "King" try to *fool* people by claiming to be European royalty, when actually they are just two traveling actors.

trick The thief knew that the police had a description of him, so he put on false glasses and a fake beard to try to *trick* them.

deceive When you sell a house, it is against the law to *deceive* the buyer by not telling him about things that you know are wrong with the house.

bluff The dictator threatened to invade a neighboring country, but he was only *bluffing*—as soon as their troops moved up to the border, his army retreated.

forbid   prohibit   prevent   ban

VERB: to order not to do; rule against.

forbid   Many states have laws that *forbid* the sale of alcohol to people under the age of 21. In Nazi Germany it was *forbidden* for anyone to criticize Adolf Hitler.

prohibit   In order to limit the amount of noise at the airport at night, planes are *prohibited* from landing after 11:30 P.M.

prevent   Our school has speed bumps in the parking lot to *prevent* people from driving fast there.

ban   Because their fans caused so much trouble, English soccer teams were recently *banned* for two years from playing any games in Europe.

Antonyms: **permit, allow.**

force   compel   drive   impose

VERB: to make someone do something one does not want to do.

force   The robbers threatened the bank manger with a gun and *forced* him to open the safe. Grain prices were so low this year that many farmers were *forced* to sell their crops at a loss.

compel   George Orwell's book *1984* tells of a nightmare world in which citizens are *compelled* to obey the mysterious ruler "Big Brother."

drive   The marshal brought peace to the wild frontier town and *drove* all the outlaws out of town.

impose   One cause of the American Revolution was the heavy taxes that the British *imposed* on the American colonists.

foreign   imported   alien   external   exotic

ADJECTIVE: not part of one's own land and culture; not belonging naturally.

foreign   The coin machine only works with U.S. money; it will not take *foreign* coins. Until recently Africa had few independent nations; the continent was ruled by *foreign* powers.

imported   Japan does not have its own oil industry and must rely on *imported* oil for its energy.

alien   In the Arab world a woman who goes out in public often has her face covered by a veil, a custom that is *alien* to most Westerners.

external   President George Washington warned the new country of the United States to concentrate on its own affairs and stay free of *external* conflicts.

exotic   Early Southern California had almost no trees, and many *exotic* plants were brought in from places such as Australia, North Africa, and Hawaii.

Antonym: **native, domestic.**

forget   neglect overlook ignore disregard

VERB: to not remember; pay no attention to something.

forget Tommy *forgot* to close the back door when he ran outside. Tania brought her raincoat, but she *forgot* her umbrella.

neglect After we *neglected* to water the plants, the leaves began to turn brown.

overlook Vic cleaned his room, but he *overlooked* the pile of papers by the door.

ignore It began pouring rain in the middle of their tennis game, but they *ignored* the rain and kept on playing.

disregard The judge told the jury to *disregard* the witness's last remark.

Antonyms: **remember, notice.**

Bucky **forgot** to put
the top up last night.

He **ignored** the "No Parking"
sign and parked right beside it.

forgive   excuse pardon condone absolve

VERB: to stop giving blame to; no longer want to accuse or punish.

forgive The teacher told the two boys to *forgive* each other for their fight, and to shake hands and be friends again.

excuse The delivery man asked us to *excuse* him for being so late, saying he'd been caught in a huge traffic jam.

pardon In 1979 President Jimmy Carter *pardoned* all those who had refused to serve in the Vietnam War, so that this would no longer be considered a crime.

condone The coaches said that even though Jim is the team's star pitcher, they can't *condone* the fact that he misses practice all the time.

absolve The accident was completely the fault of the first driver, and the other driver was *absolved* of any blame.

form   shape mold fashion

VERB: to make so as to have a certain figure or design.

form I looked down at the marks the skater had made on the ice and saw that she had *formed* a perfect circle. The teacher told the students to *form* a line outside the door.

shape Children build a snowman by *shaping* large balls of snow to look like a human figure.

mold As an art project Timmy *molded* some clay to look like the walls of a castle.

fashion Beavers block up water in a stream by *fashioning* a dam out of sticks, leaves, and mud.

former   previous preceding prior

ADJECTIVE: during the past; at some earlier time.

former Grandma lives on Redfield Street now; Park Terrace West is her *former* address. Siam is the *former* name of the country that is now known as Thailand.

previous Marty woke up feeling sick; he blamed it on something he had eaten the *previous* night.

preceding On the first day of each new month, she sits down and pays all the bills that have come in during the *preceding* month.

prior The video store said I couldn't reserve the tape I wanted, because someone else had made a *prior* request for it.

Antonyms: **future, later, subsequent.**

Philip's dad is a **former** pro basketball player. He has photos from his **previous** career.

forward   advance promote further

VERB: to help onward or toward some goal or destination.

forward The letter was sent to his old address and the post office had to *forward* it to the new address. The Senator said that he hoped that removing the Berlin Wall would *forward* the cause of world peace.

advance The invention of the telescope greatly *advanced* our knowledge of the solar system.

promote The author is going to *promote* his new book by going on television interview shows to talk about it.

further The Rotary Club awards scholarship money to high school students so that they can *further* their education in college.

Antonyms: **hinder, block, impede.**

free   independent autonomous self-governing

ADJECTIVE: not under the control or power of another.

free After the American Revolution the colonists set up the *free* country of the United States. *Free* speech means that the government cannot make laws to stop a person from saying certain things.

independent For hundreds of years Norway was controlled by either Denmark or Sweden, until it became *independent* in 1905.

autonomous Though it has only the size and population of a small city, Liechtenstein is actually an *autonomous* nation with its own government.

self-governing After World War II, many former British colonies in Africa and Asia became *self-governing.*

friend   companion pal buddy comrade

NOUN: someone other than a family member that a person knows and likes.

friend On the Fourth of July, my family got together with a group of our *friends* for a picnic in the park.

companion If you win that contest, you get a free trip to London for yourself and a *companion.*

pal Nick likes his new neighborhood, but he still misses his *pals* from the street where he used to live.

buddy My dad got a surprise visit from an old *buddy* of his who served with him in the Army.

comrade The novel *The Three Musketeers* tells of the daring young swordsman D'Artagnan and his loyal *comrades,* Athos, Porthos, and Aramis.

Antonyms: **enemy, foe.**

front face head facade fore

NOUN: the forward part of something; the part away from the back.

front The title of the book was printed on the *front* in large letters. The area of a war where soldiers are actually fighting with the enemy is called the *front.*

face The climbers slowly and carefully made their way up the *face* of the steep cliff.

head The Girl Scout troop marched by in a line, with the two troop leaders walking at the *head.*

facade As you walk toward Grand Central Station you notice the figures of ancient Greek gods carved into the *facade* of the building.

fore When spring practice started, all three quarterbacks were rated equal, but Jones soon came to the *fore* and took over the starting position.

Antonyms: **back, rear.**

frown pout scowl glare glower

VERB: to put on an angry or unhappy expression; show negative feelings.

frown Susie *frowned* as she opened her report card, so I knew she hadn't gotten the grades she'd hoped for. Seeing Billy's messy room made his father *frown.*

pout Lisa *pouted* when Mom made her turn off the TV and do her homework.

scowl The pitcher stood tall on the mound and *scowled* at the batter, in an effort to make him nervous.

glare Two boys sitting behind her in the theater were making a lot of noise, and the woman turned and *glared* at them.

glower Instead of answering the question, the prisoner just sat on the bench with his arms folded, *glowering* at the officer.

full filled loaded packed abundant

ADJECTIVE: holding or having as much as possible, or a great amount.

full This suitcase is *full;* if you want to bring more clothes you'll need another one. The ship was carrying a *full* cargo of grain from the United States to Europe.

filled She made sure the car's tires were *filled* with air before she started on her trip upstate.

loaded The farmer drove to the market with a truck *loaded* with fresh vegetables.

packed Midvale East High and Midvale West are big rivals in football, so the stands are always *packed* when they play each other.

abundant In early times, cities tended to grow up only in places where there was already an *abundant* supply of water.

Antonyms: **empty, vacant.**

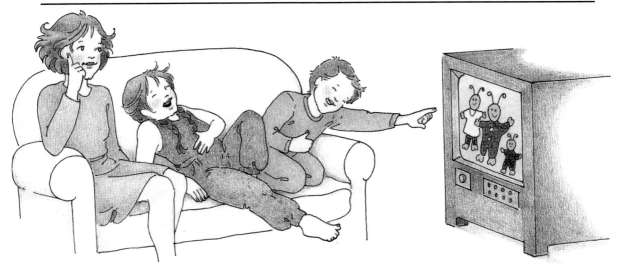

Mom thinks "The Moon Family" is a **funny** TV show. My brother and I think it's **hilarious.**

funny   amusing hilarious humorous comical comic

ADJECTIVE: causing people to laugh; bringing laughter.

funny Johnny Carson always opens his "Tonight Show" with some *funny* jokes to get the audience relaxed and laughing.

amusing The movie is *amusing,* but it certainly didn't make me laugh out loud.

hilarious The audience thought the new play was *hilarious,* and the theater was filled with roars of laughter.

humorous The book *Tom Sawyer* has several *humorous* episodes, such as the time when Tom fools his friends into painting his fence.

comical The Keystone Studio made many silent movies in which the characters chased each other wildly, fell in vats of paint, and had other *comical* adventures.

comic Amelia Bedelia is a *comic* character who always gets into trouble because she misunderstands what people say to her.

Antonyms: **serious, sober.**

future   coming impending eventual

ADJECTIVE: happening in a time yet to come.

future The game was rained out and will be played at a *future* date. In choosing their high school courses, students should consider what their *future* plans are.

coming Many Sunday newspapers publish TV magazines listing the programs that will be on the air in the *coming* week.

impending This article warns that current conditions in the stock market may indicate an *impending* financial crisis.

eventual It's too early to tell what the *eventual* outcome of the election will be.

Antonyms: **past, previous, former.**

gadget   device gimmick contraption

NOUN: a name for any small tool or machine.

gadget My dad's hobby is cooking, and he has all kinds of kitchen *gadgets* to cut up or process food.

device The bakery has an automatic *device* that cores and peels apples for pies.

gimmick Grandma just bought some *gimmick* that will turn off the lights in her bedroom when she claps her hands in the air.

contraption He cuts a lot of wood for his fireplace, and he has put together a *contraption* that saws the wood into logs exactly two feet long.

The man was selling a new **gadget** that is supposed to cut food easily.

The store has a computer **device** that automatically reads the price of an item.

game   sport recreation pastime amusement entertainment

NOUN: something that is done to have fun or as a way of playing.

game When my uncle comes over he likes to play a *game* of cards with my sister and me. In the *game* of "Initials" you try to guess the name of a famous person.

sport Pro football is a *sport* that many Americans watch on TV.

recreation New England has long winters, so activities such as skiing, ice-skating, and hockey are popular forms of *recreation* there.

pastime Because fishing involves waiting patiently for a fish to bite, many people find it to be a relaxing *pastime*.

amusement The town is very small and has few *amusements* for young people.

entertainment I know that you study a lot during the week, but what do you do on weekends, for *entertainment*?

gap   opening space crack crevice

NOUN: an open space; a hole.

gap Melanie has to get braces to close up the *gap* between her two front teeth. The ball was hit into the *gap* between the centerfielder and rightfielder.

opening The moon could be seen overhead through an *opening* in the clouds.

space So many people were crowded onto the beach that we had a hard time finding enough *space* to put down our blanket.

crack There are *cracks* in the surface of the driveway where the heavy moving van was parked.

crevice The mountain climber found a small *crevice* in the rock and was able to get a foothold there.

gas   vapor fumes

NOUN: one of the three basic forms of matter, along with a liquid and a solid.

gas A *gas* does not have a fixed shape the way a solid does, and it does not fill a fixed amount of space the way a liquid does. Many *gases*, such as oxygen, have no color or odor.

vapor If a solid or liquid is heated to a certain point, it will become a *vapor*.

fumes When the bus passed by, I could smell exhaust *fumes* from the engine.

▶ **Gas** is also used as a shortened form for **gasoline,** which is not a gas but a liquid fuel used to run cars, trucks, airplanes, and other such vehicles. It was once said that this use of the word was not as correct as the first meaning, but today it is completely accepted.

generous   unselfish charitable thoughtful liberal

ADJECTIVE: willing and happy to give to others; not selfish.

generous Carla is very *generous* with her money and is always buying nice gifts for her family and friends. Many public libraries were built in the U.S. through *generous* donations by the businessman Andrew Carnegie.

unselfish Lennie is an *unselfish* basketball player who passes the ball to other players instead of always trying to take the shot himself.

charitable People who lost their homes in the big flood were aided by *charitable* organizations such as the Red Cross.

thoughtful My mom is feeling much better now; it was *thoughtful* of you to send her that get-well card.

liberal The professor wants to finish his book soon, and the college is giving him a *liberal* amount of time off to work on it.

Antonym: **stingy.**

gentle   mild soft bland

ADJECTIVE: not harsh, rough, or wild.

gentle Be *gentle* when you play with the baby, so that you don't hurt him. A *gentle* breeze blew through the trees, and the leaves stirred lightly back and forth.

mild San Diego is cooled by the nearby Pacific Ocean and is famous for its year-round *mild* weather.

soft The mother spoke in a *soft* voice to the frightened child.

bland He is supposed to eat a *bland* diet and avoid hot, spicy foods such as chili, salsa, or Tabasco sauce.

Antonyms: **cruel, hard.**

get   receive gain obtain acquire

VERB: to come to have for oneself.

get I need to *get* some books from the library for my report on sharks. The batter broke his bat and went back to the bench to *get* another one.

receive You can order tickets for the show by phone, and you will *receive* them in the mail in about two weeks.

gain She is hoping that her good grades in law school will *gain* her a position with a top law firm.

obtain Before American citizens can travel to foreign countries, they have to *obtain* a passport from the U.S. government.

acquire In the 1980's several American publishing companies were *acquired* by larger companies from Europe.

Antonym: **lose.**

gift   present favor donation grant

NOUN: something that is given.

gift Children often receive *gifts* from family members and friends on their birthday. After the Duke of Marlborough won many battles for England, a palace was built for him as a *gift* from Queen Anne.

present I want to get Barry a *present* for his birthday—do you think he'd like this book?

favor Mom tried to pay Mrs. Lee for watching our dog while we were away, but she said she just did it as a *favor.*

donation Stanford University came into being after the Stanford family *donated* $20 million for the land and buildings.

grant Professor Jones was awarded a *grant* of $50,000 from the Ford Foundation to continue her research on reading education.

girl   miss lass maiden

NOUN: a female child who is not yet a woman or adult.

girl My mom still keeps an old teddy bear that she had when she was a little *girl.*

miss In former times young *misses* were often sent to finishing school to learn how to act in polite society.

lass In Scotland a young man can be called a lad and a young woman a *lass.*

maiden Many old folk tales tell of a poor but brave young man who sets out to rescue a beautiful *maiden* from danger.

▶ The other words given above are not really synonyms for **girl,** but special words that can be used in certain ways to describe a girl. *Girl,* like *boy,* is such a basic word that it has no true synonym.

give   present donate grant bestow

VERB: to take something that one has and pass it to another as a gift.

give My brother says he doesn't like rock music any more and he's going to *give* me all his old tapes. Aunt Peggy *gave* me ten dollars for my birthday.

present The famous star Elizabeth Taylor will *present* the award for Best Actress.

donate The land used for UN headquarters was *donated* by the Rockefellers.

grant He asked the company if he could take some time off to write a book, and they *granted* him a six-month leave of absence.

bestow If a British citizen has given great service to his country, the Queen may *bestow* on him the title of "Sir."

Antonyms: **take, receive.**

Jim's parents **gave** him a new tennis racket for his birthday.

The Tennis Club **presented** a trophy to Jim for winning the tournament.

glass   cup beaker tumbler goblet

NOUN: a small container that is used for holding liquid.

glass Ben filled his *glass* with milk and sat down to eat his lunch.

cup My mom always drinks her breakfast coffee from an old blue *cup* that she's had for years.

beaker Our science teacher measured off the amount of water we needed for the experiment and poured it into a large *beaker*.

tumbler She brought in a pitcher of orange juice and four blue plastic *tumblers* to serve it in.

goblet The host served the wine to his guests in expensive crystal *goblets*.

Every day Ms. Jones **goes** to work in New York City.

Last summer our family **traveled** to New York City for our vacation.

go   travel advance proceed progress

VERB: to move from one place to another; move along.

go We have to *go* to the mall to buy some clothes for school. Mom told me to *go* around the house and pick up any newspapers that are lying on the floor.

travel She loves the theater, and she often *travels* to London to see shows there.

advance The Korean War began when troops from North Korea *advanced* across the border into South Korea.

proceed The Vice President's speech will be over at 4:30, and he will *proceed* immediately to the airport for a flight back to Washington.

progress They'd hoped to ride more than 100 miles a day on their cross-country bike trip, but after the first two days they had only *progressed* about 150 miles.
Antonym: **stay.**

good   fine first-rate worthy respectable

ADJECTIVE: having the right properties; proper or correct.

good That is a *good* book; the story is really exciting. This is a *good* place to plant the flowers, because it gets a lot of sunlight.

fine "Looks like a *fine* morning for fishing," Dad said as we reached the lake.

first-rate Because many people from Italy have settled here, this town has a number of *first-rate* Italian restaurants.

worthy That actress is interested in giving money to help people, and she's always looking for a *worthy* cause that she can support.

respectable I wouldn't say he pitched a great game, but he did a *respectable* job, considering it was his first time.

Antonyms: **bad, poor.**

▶ The word **good** can be replaced by **excellent** in many sentences, but *excellent* is a stronger word, rather than a true synonym. C- would be a *fair* grade in school, B is a *good* grade, and A$^+$ is *excellent*. Something that is excellent is really "better than good."

gossip   rumor scandal hearsay

NOUN: talk or news about the lives of others that is negative and often harmful.

gossip Supermarkets sell brightly colored newspapers that offer *gossip* about the love affairs and career problems of Hollywood stars.

rumor There is a *rumor* going around school that the principal is about to resign from his job.

scandal Teapot Dome, a famous *scandal* of the 1920's, involved a government official who was secretly paid to allow oil drilling on Federal land.

hearsay The witness said that someone told him the defendant was guilty, but the judge said that was *hearsay* and told the jury to ignore the statement.

government   authority administration regime

NOUN: the group of people who manage or rule a certain place.

government Our town just built a new City Hall to house the city *government*. In Great Britain the Prime Minister is the head of the *government*.

authority Robert Moses built many bridges and highways in the New York area in his role as head of the New York Port *Authority*.

administration At present the college is for women only, but the *administration* wants to start admitting male students next year.

regime In 1949 the Communists took over control of China, bringing to an end the *regime* of General Chiang Kai-shek.

I **grabbed** my little brother so he wouldn't run into the water.

A seagull came down and **snatched** my sandwich and flew away with it.

grab   catch snatch grip grasp clutch

VERB: to take a tight hold on something.

grab Jeff *grabbed* his lunch bag off the table as he rushed out the door to catch the school bus. The dog tried to get out, but I *grabbed* him by the collar.

catch Our coach told us we should use both hands when we *catch* a fly ball.

snatch I was just starting to read the magazine when my brother *snatched* it out of my hands.

grip The tennis player *gripped* her racket tightly as she swung at the ball.

grasp When you chin yourself, you *grasp* the bar with both hands and pull up until your chin is over the bar.

clutch The little boy started to cross the street, *clutching* his mother's hand.

grateful   thankful pleased indebted

ADJECTIVE: feeling thanks for a favor or for something good that has happened.

grateful Mr. Riley was *grateful* to us for doing his errands for him while he was sick. She let the other driver pull ahead of her, and he gave her a *grateful* wave.

thankful One of their trees blew down during the storm, but they were *thankful* that the damage was not much worse.

pleased Mom was *pleased* to see that Cathy had already set the table for dinner.

indebted In the introduction to his book, the author said that he was *indebted* to his wife for all the help she had given him on the project.

Antonym: **ungrateful.**

great wonderful outstanding superb remarkable magnificent

ADJECTIVE: much better than is usual; of very high quality; very good.

great Italy has produced *great* artists, such as Michelangelo and Leonardo. The discovery of a way to cure cancer would be a *great* advance in science.

wonderful Their house is right on the beach, with a *wonderful* view of the ocean.

outstanding In women's tennis Chris Evert and Billie Jean King are usually rated as the *outstanding* American players of recent times.

superb The Burgundy region of France is known for its *superb* food and wine.

remarkable Margaret Mitchell's *Gone with the Wind* is the best-selling novel of all time, a *remarkable* achievement since it was her only book.

magnificent One of the most famous buildings in the world is the Taj Majal, a *magnificent* palace built in India in the 1600's.

▶ **Great** is a powerful word and should be used carefully. Save it for things that really deserve this high praise, and use milder words such as *good* for other situations.

greedy selfish acquisitive grasping

ADJECTIVE: wanting very much to have more than one needs or should have.

greedy The story of King Midas tells of a man who is so *greedy* that he asks the gods for the power to turn everything he touches into gold.

selfish Tina is *selfish* about her bike and never lets anyone else ride it.

acquisitive She was very *acquisitive* in collecting art and kept buying more and more paintings even though she had no place to put them.

grasping He's a *grasping* man, with no real interests except earning more money.

Antonyms: **generous, unselfish.**

gross vulgar crude coarse obscene

ADJECTIVE: obviously wrong or bad; not polite or proper.

gross The horse almost starved to death because of its owner's *gross* neglect. His *gross* comments greatly embarrassed the other dinner guests.

vulgar Talking with your mouth full of food is a *vulgar* thing to do.

crude As the "bad guy" wrestler entered, the fans shouted *crude* remarks at him.

coarse *My Fair Lady* is the story of how a cultured professor teaches a poor, uneducated girl to improve her *coarse* speech.

obscene Children are not admitted to films that contain *obscene* subject matter.

▶ **Gross** is properly used only of things that are very wrong or bad. In writing you should avoid using it just to describe something you don't like, as in "The lunch at school today was so gross."

group   bunch gang pack company band

NOUN: a number of persons, animals, or things together.

group She sorted the dirty clothes for the wash into two *groups,* light and dark. The Ivy League is a *group* of old and famous colleges in the Northeast.

bunch On Joey's birthday he and a *bunch* of his friends went roller skating.

gang In the 1920's John Dillinger was the leader of a notorious *gang* of criminals who roamed up and down the Midwest robbing banks.

pack Wolves usually live together in *packs* of eight animals or more.

company In the novel *Oliver Twist,* Oliver falls in with bad *company* when he is taken up by the evil Fagin and his gang of thieves.

band At the Alamo a small *band* of Texans fought against a huge Mexican army.
Antonym: **individual.**

grow   expand increase develop

VERB: to become larger, higher, or greater.

grow Grass needs a lot of water in order to *grow.* The population of India is one of the largest in the world and is still *growing.*

expand She's going to *expand* her business and open two more stores.

increase The sale of videocassette recorders *increased* greatly during the 1980's.

develop The football coach told Josh he should take up weightlifting to *develop* more upper-body strength.
Antonyms: **shrink, decrease.**

Carlos has **grown** so much that his jacket is too small for him.

When he took a breath, his chest **expanded** and popped a button.

guarantee   assure promise pledge

VERB: to make a definite statement that one will do something.

guarantee When asked if he thought his Jets could beat the Colts in the Super Bowl, quarterback Joe Namath said, "I don't just think so, I *guarantee* it." The company *guarantees* that if this toaster breaks at any time within one year, they will replace it for free.

assure The magazine editor called the writer to ask why he hadn't sent in his article, and he *assured* her that he would finish it by the end of the week.

promise Mom *promised* me that if I got to bed on time all week, on Friday night I could rent a movie and stay up late to watch it.

pledge Ms. Owens called the public television station and *pledged* to give $200 to support their programs.

guess   estimate speculate presume

VERB: to have an idea about something without being sure that it is right.

guess I didn't know the answer, so I *guessed* 'c' because that seemed the most likely. Jeff hasn't been at soccer practice this week; I *guess* he's on vacation.

estimate There was a big turnout for the St. Patrick's Day parade, and the police *estimated* the crowd at about 100,000 people.

speculate It isn't known for sure how people first came to America; scientists have *speculated* that they crossed over from Asia following herds of animals.

presume When he entered the office for his 9:00 interview, the woman at the front desk said, "Good morning, sir. I *presume* you are Mr. Smith?"

▶ **Guesstimate** is a new word, made by combining *guess* and *estimate.* People use it to make a statement that is more definite than a guess, but not as careful as an estimate: "We have 200 miles to go. I *guesstimate* that we'll be there in four hours." We recommend that you not use this "compromise word" in writing, but choose either *guess* or *estimate* according to how exact you want to be.

guest   visitor company caller

NOUN: someone who is at another person's home for a meal or a short stay.

guest Mom said that since Aunt Peggy was our *guest* for dinner, I should have offered her the meat platter first, before I served myself.

visitor Her sister lives next door to her and is a frequent *visitor* at her house.

company The kitchen table is big enough for our family to eat at, but when we have *company* for a meal we use the dining room table.

caller Many people have a "welcome mat" outside the door where *callers* can wipe their feet before entering the house.

habit   routine custom practice ritual

NOUN: a usual way of acting or behaving.

habit Randy has a *habit* of biting his nails, and he's trying to stop doing it. When I get the morning newspaper, I always read the weather report first—it's just a *habit* of mine.

routine She's going to take some vacation time later this month; she wants to get away from the *routine* of office work.

custom In Spain it is the *custom* during the hot months to take a midafternoon nap or rest called a "siesta."

practice The boss makes it a *practice* to introduce himself to new employees when they join the company.

ritual Religious ceremonies often involve *rituals* that are meant to be followed exactly.

Mr. Delmo has a **habit** of yawning when he is bored.

He follows an exact **routine** when he cooks on the outdoor grill.

hang   suspend dangle sling

VERB: to fix or fasten something from above, leaving the lower part free.

hang On sunny days we *hang* the laundry outside to dry. When he's studying for a test, Ben *hangs* a sign on his bedroom door saying "Please Do Not Disturb."

suspend The huge steel beam was lifted by a crane and *suspended* above the building as the workers prepared to move it into place.

dangle The magician hypnotized a member of the audience by *dangling* a watch in front of her face until she fell into a deep sleep.

sling A hammock is a simple bed made by *slinging* a heavy cloth between two trees or posts.

happen   occur befall arise transpire

VERB: to take place; to come into being.

happen   Arturo reads the sports pages every morning to find out what *happened* the day before in major-league baseball. I'm not sure exactly when Custer's Last Stand was, but I know it *happened* some time in the 1870's.

occur   The passing of Halley's Comet near the earth last *occurred* in 1986.

befall   In the Middle Ages, pilgrims traveling to a religious shrine went in groups, because they never knew what might *befall* them on their journey.

arise   The Coca-Cola Company changed its plan to eliminate the original flavor of this soda after great public protest *arose* over the decision.

transpire   The judge instructed the witness to tell the court exactly what had *transpired* on the morning of the robbery.

happy   glad cheerful joyous

ADJECTIVE: having or showing a pleasant feeling.

happy   James thought he had done badly on the test, so he was *happy* to get a B$^+$. I don't mind watching your dog for you while you're away; in fact I'd be *happy* to do it.

glad   Everyone was *glad* to see Sara when she came home from college for a visit.

cheerful   The store clerk was very friendly and always greeted her customers with a *cheerful* smile.

joyous   It was a *joyous* occasion as all the Smiths' children and grandchildren gathered to help them celebrate their 50th wedding anniversary.

Antonyms: **unhappy, sad.**

hard   difficult demanding tough rigorous

ADJECTIVE: not easy to do or understand.

hard   Moving the books to the attic was *hard* work; I never realized a box of books was so heavy. Math is *hard* for me, so I ask my older sister for help.

difficult   Chess is a *difficult* game to learn, but most people who do learn the game enjoy playing it.

demanding   Mr. Jones is a *demanding* boss who expects his staff to work long hours and to be available for his calls at all times.

tough   It is *tough* to hit home runs in the St. Louis Cardinals' Busch Stadium because the fences are so far away.

rigorous   People who want to be Navy fighter pilots have to go through a very *rigorous* training period before they earn their pilot's wings.

Antonyms: **easy, simple.**

hate detest despise abhor loathe

VERB: to dislike very much; have strong feelings against.

hate The American colonists *hated* the fact that they had to pay heavy taxes to the English government. I *hated* that movie and left before it was even half over.

detest The two neighbors had a fight about their property line, and now they *detest* each other and never speak.

despise I thought the green blouse might look nice on her, but she said, "No, not green! I absolutely *despise* that color."

abhor Indian national leader Mohandas Gandhi *abhorred* violence and always urged his followers to seek change only by peaceful means.

loathe It's said that the French queen Marie Antoinette *loathed* the common people of her kingdom and joked about the fact that they were starving.

Antonym: **love.**

have own hold possess

VERB: to be in possession of; keep or control as one's own.

have The Olsens *have* a home computer that they use to keep track of household bills. Do you *have* any ideas for how we can get the dog to stop barking so much?

own Chuck made the final loan payment on his car last month, and now he *owns* it completely by himself.

hold The great boxer Joe Louis *held* the title of heavyweight champion of the world for many years.

possess During the early 1800's, a very wealthy banking family known as the House of Rothschild actually *possessed* more riches than many countries.

head leader director chief boss

NOUN: a person who is at the top; someone who is in charge.

head In the U.S. the *head* of a state government has the title of governor. Henry Ford made inexpensive cars available to millions of Americans during his years as *head* of the Ford Motor Company.

leader In the years before the Civil War, Harriet Tubman was the *leader* of a group that helped Southern slaves escape to freedom in the North.

director J. Edgar Hoover is known for his long service as the *director* of the Federal Bureau of Investigation.

chief Quanah Parker was a famous Comanche *chief* who turned his people away from war to life on a reservation in Texas.

boss The movie *Scarface* deals with the life of Al Capone, the powerful Chicago crime *boss* of the 1920's.

healthy   fit able-bodied robust

ADJECTIVE: having or showing good health.

healthy To remain *healthy,* it helps to have a proper diet and plenty of sleep. She just had a vacation at the beach, and she looks *healthy* and relaxed.

fit Experts recommend walking or swimming as good ways for adults to keep *fit.*

able-bodied In World War I, many posters and advertisements called upon *able-bodied* men to join the army.

robust Years of working hard on the farm made him a strong, *robust* young man.

Antonyms: **unhealthy, sickly.**

▶ A distinction can be made between the two similar words **healthy,** meaning "having or showing good health," and **healthful,** meaning "producing good health." A *healthful* diet with fruits and vegetables can keep a person *healthy.*

hear   listen heed eavesdrop

VERB: to notice or pay attention to something said.

hear Josh had the radio on really loud and didn't *hear* his mother calling him for dinner.

listen The coach told Ernie not to swing at any high pitches, but he didn't *listen* and took a swing at one over his head.

heed She's going to *heed* her doctor's advice and try to stop smoking.

eavesdrop The man sitting next to me was talking on a portable phone, and I *eavesdropped* on his conversation.

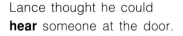
Lance thought he could **hear** someone at the door.

His sister sometimes will **eavesdrop** when he is talking on the telephone.

heavy   bulky hefty burdensome weighty

ADJECTIVE: greater than usual in weight, size, or amount.

heavy The refrigerator moves on wheels because it is too *heavy* to be lifted and carried. Being the captain of a navy ship is a *heavy* responsibility.

bulky The box was large and *bulky* and we had a hard time getting it in the door.

hefty The two football co-captains came onto the field: the tall, lean quarterback and beside him the *hefty,* powerful defensive tackle.

burdensome The *burdensome* duties of leading his country in World War II caused great strain to President Franklin D. Roosevelt.

weighty The question of how the U.S. can develop new sources of energy is a *weighty* problem that has been the subject of much study.

<u>Antonym:</u> **light.**

▶ The word **heavy** can apply either to things that actually have physical weight, such as a *heavy* rock, or to a weight on the mind, such as a *heavy* responsibility. Of the synonyms, *bulky* and *hefty* usually mean physical weight; *burdensome* and *weighty* usually describe a weight on the mind.

height   altitude elevation

NOUN: the distance from the top to the bottom of something.

height The Sears Tower in Chicago is the tallest building in the United States, with a *height* of 1454 feet. Whenever Rob goes for a checkup, the nurse measures his *height* and weight.

altitude In 1932, the physicist Auguste Piccard ascended to an *altitude* of 55,500 feet in a hydrogen balloon.

elevation Florida is very flat, and the highest point in the state has an *elevation* of only 345 feet above sea level.

help   assist aid support collaborate

VERB: to do part of the work; do what is needed or wanted.

help When Dad does yard work I *help* by getting tools for him and carrying away trash. Stacy had trouble with a math problem, and her sister *helped* her to do it.

assist A flight attendant stood at the door of the plane to *assist* the entering passengers in finding their assigned seats.

aid The Red Cross *aids* people who have lost their homes in a flood or storm.

support Senators from both political parties promised to *support* the President's efforts to bring peace to the Middle East.

collaborate Richard Rodgers and Oscar Hammerstein *collaborated* to create many famous musicals, such as *The King and I, South Pacific,* and *Oklahoma!*

hide   disguise conceal camouflage veil

VERB: to put or keep out of sight.

hide When I first came in, I didn't see Andrew because he was *hiding* behind the sofa. Tall, thick bushes *hide* the pond from view until you are right next to it.

disguise Emma Edmonds *disguised* herself as a soldier and became a spy for the Union Army during the Civil War.

conceal The refrigerator in this kitchen is *concealed* inside a large wood cabinet.

camouflage The marines *camouflaged* their vehicles to make it difficult for enemy aircraft to spot them.

veil In some Muslim countries, women are *veiled* so that their faces cannot be seen except for their eyes.

Jason crouched down to **hide** behind the rock.

Many animals have a brownish color that **camouflages** them in the wild.

high   tall lofty towering soaring

ADJECTIVE: reaching far up above the ground.

high It was a clear, sunny day, with just a few *high* clouds floating across the blue sky. The main room of our public library has a very *high* ceiling.

tall The *tall* building you see in the center of the New York skyline is the Empire State Building.

lofty The *lofty* peaks of the Rocky Mountains provide the background for the famous western movie *Shane*.

towering The Los Angeles Lakers had a powerful team in the 1980's, led by the clever guard Magic Johnson and the *towering* center Kareem Abdul-Jabbar.

soaring He gazed up and watched a *soaring* hawk as it circled in the sky above.
Antonym: **low**.

hint   clue tip suggestion notion

NOUN: some information that is meant to help someone or to answer a question.

hint Mom asked me to name the capital of Ohio, and then gave me a *hint* by saying it was named for a famous explorer. *"Hints* from Heloise" is a newspaper column that gives ideas for fixing things around the house.

clue I could tell halfway through the movie that the woman's husband was really the killer, because there were so many *clues* that he had done it.

tip Someone gave my dad a *tip* to buy stock in the Acme Company— the price is supposedly going to go way up.

suggestion Mrs. Lee has a file of *suggestions* for students who need ideas for science projects.

notion We wanted to stop by her house, but we didn't have the slightest *notion* where she lived.

hire   employ engage retain

VERB: to get someone to do work for pay.

hire My brother was just *hired* by Wolf's Department Store to sell sporting goods. Dad has to *hire* someone to cut down that old tree at the back of our yard.

employ All international airlines have to *employ* pilots who speak English, because that is the language used for radio communication.

engage The movie *Driving Miss Daisy* describes what happens when a wealthy businessman *engages* a chauffeur to drive his elderly mother around town.

retain The pop singer has *retained* a lawyer to represent her in a lawsuit against her former manager.

Antonyms: **fire, dismiss.**

hit   strike punch pound slug swat

VERB: to go hard against; give a blow to.

hit You could hear the crack of the bat when the batter *hit* the ball out of the stadium. The car's brake slipped and it rolled backward, *hitting* another car.

strike In soccer the rules state that a player can be put out of a game if he *strikes* another player.

punch Boxers have to wear heavy gloves so that they will not cause so much injury as they *punch* each other.

pound Before cooking the piece of veal she *pounded* it flat with a wooden mallet.

slug The newspaper said that the movie star had lost his temper and *slugged* a photographer who was trying to take pictures of him.

swat A fly landed on the table, and Carl *swatted* it with a rolled-up newspaper.

Mom had to **hold** Bobo so he couldn't get at Aunt Jean's cat.

Now Bobo is **confined** to the back porch when Aunt Jean comes to visit.

hold   retain detain restrain confine

VERB: to keep in a certain place or position.

hold The doctor asked Steven to *hold* still while she looked in his ear. A corral is a fenced-in place for *holding* farm or ranch animals, especially cattle.

retain In football a team must gain ten yards in four plays to *retain* possession of the ball.

detain The man was *detained* by the airport police while they carefully searched his luggage for illegal drugs.

restrain After the surgery, Deborah's knee was put in a cast to *restrain* its movement.

confine The judge ordered the convicted shoplifter to be *confined* in the county jail for 30 days.

Antonyms: **release, free.**

hole   hollow cavity

NOUN: an open place in something solid.

hole When the lake is frozen, fishermen make *holes* in the ice to drop their lines through. Dad cut *holes* in a sheet for Jill, so she could be a ghost on Halloween.

hollow Squirrels and chipmunks often make their homes in the *hollow* of a dead tree trunk.

cavity Christina has not had any new *cavities* in her teeth since she learned to brush them properly.

home   residence quarters lodging

NOUN: the place where someone lives.

home Although she works in New York City, her *home* is in Northport, a small suburb on Long Island.

residence The British royal family normally lives in London, but they have a summer *residence* at Balmoral, Scotland.

quarters In former times expensive houses were often built with extra bedrooms, to provide living *quarters* for the servants of the household.

lodging The new freshman dormitory was not ready in time for the fall term, and students had to find *lodging* in nearby motels.

This pond is the **home** of many kinds of wildlife.

The scientist is using a tent as temporary **lodging** while he studies the pond.

honor   credit recognition esteem

NOUN: praise or respect given or due to a person.

honor Sandra felt that it was a great *honor* to be chosen as captain of the softball team by her teammates. The highest award that an American soldier can win in battle is the Congressional Medal of *Honor.*

credit In accepting the Nobel Prize, the scientist gave *credit* to his two assistants for aiding him in his research.

recognition The Parents' Club gave Mrs. Rivera a brass plaque in *recognition* of her years of outstanding service as the school's drama teacher.

esteem The "Ashcan School" of painting sounds unimpressive, but actually it is a nickname for a group of painters who are held in high *esteem* by art critics.

hope   faith confidence optimism

NOUN: a strong wish for something and a belief that it will happen.

hope Helen has been studying ballet dancing for years and has the *hope* of becoming a professional dancer. In 1849 many people went to California with the *hope* of finding gold there.

faith I'm not sure where I lost my wallet, but I have *faith* that some honest person will find it and return it.

confidence The bank expressed *confidence* that Mr. Davis will repay his loan, because he's paid back all the other money he's borrowed.

optimism He has real *optimism* about how well his business will do this year.

hopeful   confident optimistic

ADJECTIVE: having or showing hope.

hopeful She has just finished writing a book, and she's *hopeful* that she can find a publisher for it.

confident His job interview went very well, so he's *confident* he'll get the job.

optimistic The basketball coach has four out of five starters back from last year, and she is *optimistic* about the team's chances this year.

hopefully

▶ Many people object to the use of **hopefully** to mean "I hope that" or "It's to be hoped that," as in *"Hopefully, it won't rain for our picnic tomorrow."* This is a fairly new sense of the word, but it seems to be here to stay. The reason is that there is no real synonym for this meaning, so people find it to be a useful word.

hot   steaming boiling sweltering sultry

ADJECTIVE: having a high temperature; very warm.

hot The sand was *hot* against my feet as I walked across the beach. Car engines are cooled by water or air so that they do not get too *hot*.

steaming A *steaming* bowl of soup was just the thing to have after we came in from ice skating.

boiling To cook the beans, put them in a pot of *boiling* water for ten minutes.

sweltering It was another 90° day, and the newspaper headline said, *"Sweltering City Gets No Relief from Heat Wave."*

sultry New Orleans, a southern city on the Gulf of Mexico, is known for its *sultry* summer weather.

Antonym: **cold.**

The Wrights live in a
brick house in the city.

They spent their vacation in
a little **cottage** at the beach.

house   cottage mansion dwelling

NOUN: a building for one family or a few people to live in, separate from other buildings.

house They decided to move out of their apartment in the city and buy a *house* in the suburbs.

cottage When Dennis went to Ireland, he visited the little country *cottage* where his grandmother was born.

mansion The city of Beverly Hills, California has many large *mansions* owned by movie stars.

dwelling Many people think that the Eskimos lived in igloos, but actually they just used them as temporary *dwellings* while hunting in the winter.

however   yet nevertheless

CONJUNCTION: in spite of that; but still.

however All the advance tickets for tonight's concert have been sold; *however,* there will be some seats available at the door.

yet There is a big sign at the entrance to our street, "No U Turn," *yet* for some reason people always turn around here anyway.

nevertheless The contract seemed to be fair and clearly written; *nevertheless,* she's going to have a lawyer check it over before she signs.

▶ Some books on writing say that you should only use **however** within a sentence, and not to start a sentence. *However,* we don't think that's a good rule.

hug embrace squeeze clasp

VERB: to put one's arms tightly around someone or something.

hug Tina *hugged* her parents and kissed them goodbye before she left. My little brother loves his teddy bear and always falls asleep *hugging* it tightly.

embrace In some cultures it is the custom for two men who are close friends to *embrace* each other when they meet.

squeeze When we go to visit Grandpa, he *squeezes* me in his arms and then swings me up over his head.

clasp Uncle Bob was nervous when Mom asked him to hold the baby, and he *clasped* him against his chest as if he were afraid he'd drop him.

humane human humanitarian compassionate

ADJECTIVE: acting as a person should; showing kindness.

humane The Geneva Convention sets rules of war, including *humane* treatment for all prisoners. Our local *Humane* Society has begun a campaign to stop people from abandoning unwanted pets.

human People who claim to have seen the abominable snowman say that this creature exhibits *human* emotions.

humanitarian Congress approved $50 million in *humanitarian* aid for victims of the war, including food and medical supplies.

compassionate The American social worker Jane Addams won the Nobel Peace Prize for her *compassionate* efforts to help poor people.

Antonyms: **inhumane, inhuman.**

hurt injure harm damage impair mar

VERB: to cause pain or loss to; affect in some negative way.

hurt Kelly *hurt* her arm when she tripped over a rock while running in the yard. Billy kept telling Mom not to *hurt* him when she took the splinter out of his foot.

injure The Eagles' quarterback was *injured* in the last game and won't be able to play this week.

harm People used to think it was healthy to have a suntan, but now doctors warn that too much sun can *harm* the skin.

damage While he was taking the battery out of the car, some of the acid spilled on the fender and *damaged* the paint.

impair A cataract is a condition of the eye in which the lens becomes cloudy, which *impairs* the vision.

mar When he went back to visit the lake, he saw that the beautiful view he remembered was now *marred* by the sight of abandoned cars and piles of trash.

if   whether

CONJUNCTION: in the case that; should it be that.

if I want to go with you, but I have to ask my mom *if* it's all right.

whether When the Civil War began, it was not clear *whether* the United States would remain one nation or be divided in two.

important   significant meaningful notable

ADJECTIVE: worth caring or being concerned about; having value or meaning.

important You need good ideas in your paper, but correct spelling and grammar are *important* too. Passover is an *important* holiday in the Jewish religion.

significant The televised debates with Richard Nixon played a *significant* role in the election of John Kennedy as President.

meaningful They found the play to be funny, but not particularly *meaningful*.

notable On *notable* occasions such as holidays, the mayor often gives a speech.

include   contain involve cover

VERB: to be made up of; have as a part.

include This book *includes* an index listing all the topics covered in the book. The science of biology *includes* the study of plant life.

contain Packaged foods have a label listing the ingredients the food *contains*.

involve Beside the road were the two cars actually *involved* in the accident, as well as several others whose drivers had stopped to help.

cover The final exam in math is going to *cover* material from the entire course.

The team picture **included** the coaches and team mother.

One coach got **involved** in an argument with the umpires during a playoff game.

income   wages salary earnings profit gain

NOUN: money that comes in to a person or a business.

income That author gets a good *income* from the sale of his mystery books. She needs to find a better-paying job, because she doesn't have enough *income* to pay all her bills.

wages A "W-2" is a tax form showing the *wages* a person has earned in a year from working for a certain company.

salary He was hired as the manager of the store at a *salary* of $30,000 per year.

earnings Pro tennis players not only win prize money from playing, but also have large *earnings* from endorsing rackets, clothing, and other products.

profit The amount of money a business takes in, minus the amount it spends, is its *profit* for the year.

gain If you buy a house and later sell it for more money, you may have to pay tax on the *gain* from the sale.

information   news data evidence material report

NOUN: a group of facts that are known about something.

information Joan went to the library to get *information* for her science report. My dad reads a newsletter that gives *information* about the stock market.

news The Battle of New Orleans was actually fought after the War of 1812 ended; the *news* that the war was over had not reached the troops.

data The great advantage of computers is that they can store huge amounts of *data* and make rapid use of it.

evidence Scientists have found *evidence* that people were living throughout the Americas as much as 10,000 years before Columbus arrived.

material To gather *material* for a book on Ronald Reagan, the writer interviewed people who served under him in the White House.

report I saw a *report* on TV about the effort to clean up the oil spill in the harbor.

inside   interior inner internal

ADJECTIVE: included or enclosed in something.

inside Matt sat by the window, and I took the *inside* seat. From here you can watch the ice skaters go by as you sit in a comfortable *inside* temperature of 70°.

interior The car is painted red on the outside, and the *interior* color is gray.

inner This raincoat has an *inner* lining that can be taken out in warmer weather.

internal She had no serious cuts or bruises from the fall, but the doctor is concerned that she might have some *internal* injuries.

Antonyms: **outside, exterior, outer, external.**

insurance   safeguard security assurance

NOUN: something that provides protection against loss or damage.

insurance In this state drivers must have *insurance* that will pay for the cost of an accident. On their camping trip in the desert, they carried extra water as *insurance* against running out.

safeguard Many cars have a "child lock," a *safeguard* against the door's being opened from the inside while the car is moving.

security Their new house has a *security* system that causes an alarm to go off if someone tries to break in.

assurance Dan bought the stain remover with the clerk's *assurance* that it would take the spot out of his coat.

interest   curiosity attention notice

NOUN: a feeling of wanting to know more about something.

interest Henry has a great *interest* in the Civil War, and he has collected many books about it. The tourists visited all the historic points of *interest* in the downtown section of the city.

curiosity At the age of two or three, children have great *curiosity* and are always looking at things and picking them up.

attention We all paid close *attention* while the magician pulled a rabbit out of his hat, but we couldn't see how he did it.

notice Apparently the thief was a very ordinary-looking man, because no one took any *notice* of him when he entered and left the store.

Antonyms: **disinterest, indifference.**

interesting   fascinating absorbing intriguing engrossing

ADJECTIVE: causing or creating interest.

interesting Nicole thinks French is an *interesting* subject and she's going to take it as her major in college. There's an *interesting* story in the paper today about how gorillas care for their young.

fascinating My sister thinks Princess Diana is a *fascinating* person and reads everything she can find about her.

absorbing The mystery movie was so *absorbing* that I lost track of the time and didn't realize how late it was.

intriguing The *intriguing* question of who built Stonehenge, a huge ancient monument in England, has attracted the attention of many scientists.

engrossing Sam is reading an *engrossing* book about life in the Middle Ages.

Antonyms: **uninteresting, boring.**

invent discover create initiate conceive

VERB: to make or think of for the first time.

invent In 1793 Eli Whitney *invented* the cotton gin, which helped to make the United States the largest cotton producer in the world. The Sumerians in ancient Mesopotamia are believed to have *invented* the first system of writing.

discover While they were studying uranium, Marie and Pierre Curie *discovered* two new elements, radium and polonium.

create Walt Disney *created* the famous cartoon character Mickey Mouse.

initiate The museum *initiated* a program for young members to serve as guides.

conceive The author F. Scott Fitzgerald *conceived* the idea for his book *The Last Tycoon* while working as a screenwriter in Hollywood.

In 1609 Galileo **invented** a telescope that allowed him to view the heavens.

He used this telescope to **discover** the moons of the planet Jupiter.

irritated annoyed aggravated exasperated

ADJECTIVE: to be angry or impatient; be bothered.

irritated Valerie was *irritated* when Denise didn't return her phone call. He gets *irritated* when his morning paper is late because he likes to read it with breakfast.

annoyed The neighbors were *annoyed* by the dog's constant barking.

aggravated Mr. Young was *aggravated* because only a few students turned up for drama club, when so many had said before that they were interested.

exasperated She was so *exasperated* by the long wait at the checkout counter that she finally walked out without her order.

jail   prison   penitentiary

NOUN: a place where prisoners are kept.

jail The people who rioted in the town square were held overnight in the city *jail* and then released for a later trial.

prison At his trial the bank robber was found guilty and sentenced to four years in the state *prison.*

penitentiary For many years dangerous criminals were held in Alcatraz, a federal *penitentiary* on an island in San Francisco Bay.

▶ **Jail** usually refers to a local building where prisoners are held for a short time awaiting trial or release; **prison** refers to a building in a separate location where convicted criminals are sent to serve a longer sentence.

Artie was **jealous** of Hugo because he could lift so much.

Hugo was **envious** of Artie's beautiful new sports car.

jealous   envious resentful covetous

ADJECTIVE: wanting something another person has or can do.

jealous Sam gets really *jealous* when he thinks his girlfriend is showing an interest in another boy.

envious None of Dave's friends made the all-star team, and they were *envious* of him when they saw him walking around in his all-star jacket.

resentful Mrs. Jones felt *resentful* toward her boss because he made so much more money than she did.

covetous The Bible says not to be *covetous* of things that your neighbors have.

job   task duty chore assignment

NOUN: something that is worked at or done.

job Babysitting was Annette's first paid *job*. Craig's teacher congratulated him for the fine *job* he'd done on his science project.

task A lot of records were lost from the computer memory, and Lisa had the *task* of putting all the same information back in again.

duty The *duty* of the Secret Service is to protect the President and his family.

chore Each child in the family has a daily *chore,* from setting the dinner table to taking out the garbage.

assignment Mario knew calculus was going to be a tough course when the teacher gave a long *assignment* on the first day of class.

joke   gag jest wisecrack

NOUN: something that is done to make people laugh.

joke Annie's favorite birthday present was a book of "knock-knock" *jokes.* When he was little, Charlie thought hiding from his mother was a great *joke.*

gag I've seen that comedian on TV three times now, and he always tells the same *gags* about his mother-in-law.

jest She had a serious expression on her face when she told me, so at first I didn't realize she was speaking in *jest.*

wisecrack As the school marching band went by, Jeff tried to amuse his friends by making *wisecracks* about their uniforms.

jump   leap spring vault

VERB: to use the legs to move up into the air.

jump The leftfielder *jumped* to catch the ball just as it was about to go over the fence. The cat *jumped* onto the kitchen counter and stared out the window.

leap When Ernie heard the good news, he *leaped* into the air with joy.

spring Ballet dancers *spring* into the air from bent knees and then land gracefully in the same position.

vault Jack stepped back, took a running start, and *vaulted* over the hedge.

just

▶ As an adverb, **just** has many meanings. In each of the following sentences, you could substitute **just** for the word in italics: This blouse fits *exactly* right. We have *barely* enough food for everyone. That family *recently* moved here. I *only* called to say hello. Our house is *immediately* north of the lake. *Just* is a useful word, but you don't have to use it. If another word sounds right, use that instead.

keep   retain   reserve   maintain

VERB: to have or hold for a time; have and not give up.

keep I thought Chuck was just lending me his tape, but he said I could *keep* it. You can *keep* books out of the library for three weeks without paying a fine.

retain The boxer defeated his opponent and *retained* his title as champion.

reserve The sign in the restaurant said, "We *reserve* the right to refuse service to anyone who is not properly dressed."

maintain The wealthy family has a large apartment in the city and also *maintains* a vacation home in the country.

Antonyms: **discard, relinquish.**

kind   kindly warm-hearted sympathetic compassionate

ADJECTIVE: wanting to help others and make them happy.

kind It was *kind* of Gary to carry Mrs. Helman's groceries to her car. Our school bus driver always has a *kind* word for everyone, even on cold, rainy mornings.

kindly The book *Heidi* is the story of a young orphan girl who goes to live in a mountain cabin with her *kindly* old grandfather.

warm-hearted The Nelsons are a *warm-hearted* family who make all visitors to their home feel welcome.

sympathetic The nurse's *sympathetic* manner put Ricky at ease right away.

compassionate Fran's service in the Peace Corps made her more *compassionate* toward people in poorer countries of the world.

Grandma says that we should always be **kind** to animals.

Grandpa was **sympathetic** when I told him how we lost the game.

king   monarch sovereign lord

NOUN: a person who inherits the rule of a country, or who is thought to have the power of such a ruler.

king In 1534 *King* Henry VIII declared himself head of the Church of England. The movie star Clark Gable was so popular he was called the *King* of Hollywood.

monarch Queen Boadicea was the female *monarch* of a tribe in England that revolted against the Romans in A.D. 61.

sovereign At the Battle of the Boyne in 1690, Protestant troops wore orange in honor of their *sovereign,* William of Orange.

lord During the Middle Ages, powerful *lords* controlled large areas of land, almost like separate countries.

knock   bang tap rap thump

VERB: to strike with a hard blow or blows.

knock Even though John didn't see any lights on in the house, he *knocked* on the door, hoping someone would answer.

bang I can always tell the days when Eric is practicing his pitching, because you hear the ball *banging* against the garage door.

tap She wanted to get the attention of her friend sitting inside, so she *tapped* lightly on the window and waved.

rap In early American schools a teacher might *rap* a child on the knuckles with a ruler for misbehaving.

thump When Grandpa thinks the people in the apartment downstairs are making too much noise, he *thumps* his cane on the floor to make them stop.

know   understand realize recognize comprehend grasp

VERB: to have information in the mind; be familiar with.

know I *know* the movie starts at 7:15, because I just checked the newspaper listing. My dad is a big Elvis fan and *knows* the words to all his songs.

understand If you read them carefully, the instructions are easy to *understand*.

realize When the golfer found his ball it was behind a big tree, and he *realized* there was no way to play a shot to the green from there.

recognize Mom could tell that the movie was filmed in her old neighborhood in New York; she *recognized* a lot of the buildings.

comprehend When Albert Einstein first published his scientific findings, his theories were so advanced that not many people could *comprehend* them.

grasp The teacher told us the answer to the math problem, but I just can't seem to *grasp* the theory behind it.

land   earth   ground   soil   terrain

NOUN: a part of the surface of this planet that is not covered by water.

land   The Smiths bought some *land* in Florida and they are going to build a retirement home there. Frogs can live on *land* as well as in water.

earth   As we drove along, we could see the freshly plowed *earth* stretching for miles alongside the highway.

ground   When he reached port after months at sea, the happy sailor bent down and kissed the *ground* beneath his feet.

soil   Its rich *soil* makes the state of Iowa one of the world's leading farm areas.

terrain   Hannibal, a great general of ancient Carthage, crossed the rugged mountain *terrain* of the Alps to attack the Romans.

last   final   closing   concluding   ultimate

ADJECTIVE: coming after all others; at the end.

last   On the *last* day of school, we handed in all our books and cleaned out our desks. Hawaii and Alaska were the *last* two states to join the United States.

final   She was second in the tennis tournament—she won all her earlier matches but lost the *final* one.

closing   At the end of the meeting, the principal made a few *closing* remarks.

concluding   The TV miniseries starts tonight and will be on all week; the *concluding* episode will be shown Friday.

ultimate   When movies first came out on videotape they were meant to be sold, but the *ultimate* result has been that people mainly rent rather than buy them.

Antonyms: **first, opening, beginning.**

later   afterward   thereafter   presently   subsequently

ADVERB: after the present time or a certain time; after some stated time.

later   In summer it gets dark *later* than it does in winter. All the seats were filled when the meeting began, and those who came in *later* had to stand in back.

afterward   The play is over at 10:00, and there will be a party for the cast *afterward*.

thereafter   The Battle of Midway was a great turning point in World War II, and *thereafter* the Americans advanced while the Japanese retreated.

presently   The announcer came on stage to say that the orchestra had finally arrived and that the concert would begin *presently*.

subsequently   The Industrial Revolution started in Britain, and *subsequently* spread to Western Europe and the United States.

Antonym: **earlier, previous, prior.**

laugh   chuckle giggle chortle

VERB: to make the special sounds that show one finds something funny.

laugh The students *laughed* when their teacher walked into class on Halloween morning dressed as Count Dracula.

chuckle The movie wasn't very funny, but the audience did *chuckle* at a few of the jokes.

giggle Michelle and Laura sat *giggling* at a table in the library, as they passed silly notes back and forth to each other.

chortle In his hiding place, Ricky *chortled* quietly to himself as he watched the other children looking all over trying to find him.

Ms. Kent **led** her class into the City Museum.

The guard **directed** them to the dinosaur exhibit.

lead   guide direct steer

VERB: to show the way; go along before or with.

lead In this restaurant the head waiter meets people when they come in and *leads* them to their table. Joey had been fishing at the lake before, and he *led* us to his favorite spot next to an old dock.

guide The mountain climbers hired a local climber to *guide* them along the trail up the mountain.

direct During rush hour, a policeman is usually stationed at the corner of First and Main to *direct* traffic.

steer To *steer* a bicycle, you turn the handlebars in the direction that you want to go.

least   slightest tiniest

ADJECTIVE: the smallest amount or quantity.

least Helen is a fussy eater who won't eat an apple if there's the *least* bit of peel on it. I don't care which way we go, just take whichever road has the *least* traffic.

slightest He wiped and polished the car over and over until there was not even the *slightest* trace of dirt on it.

tiniest Krill are among the *tiniest* creatures of the sea, often less than an inch long, yet certain whales depend entirely on them for food.

Mr. Samuels **leaves**
for work at about 7:30.

The train to the city
departs at 7:39.

leave   depart exit withdraw retreat

VERB: to go away from a place.

leave The show was so boring that many people in the audience got up to *leave* before it was over. Andrea will *leave* home in the fall to go to college in Ohio.

depart At this airport, flights going overseas *depart* from one of the first four gates of the terminal.

exit The script of a play has directions telling the actors when to come on stage and when to *exit.*

withdraw The secretary led the visitor into the president's office, introduced them to each other, and then *withdrew* quietly from the room.

retreat The general ordered a second attack by his reserve troops, causing the enemy soldiers to *retreat* from the battlefield.

<u>Antonyms:</u> **stay, remain.**

legal legitimate rightful lawful permissible

ADJECTIVE: according to law; allowed by law.

legal It is not *legal* in this city to burn leaves in your yard, because burning causes air pollution. He got a speeding ticket for driving 70 miles an hour, which is 15 miles above the *legal* limit.

legitimate The followers of Prince James Stuart believed he had a *legitimate* claim to the throne of England, because his father had been king.

rightful Each man claims that the valuable painting belongs to him, and a judge will have to decide which one is the *rightful* owner.

lawful The minister turned to the bride and said, "Do you take this man to be your *lawful* wedded husband?"

permissible Smoking is no longer *permissible* on airplane flights within the United States.

Antonyms: **illegal, unlawful.**

less fewer

ADJECTIVE: not as much as some stated or known amount.

less The doctor told him he should try to eat *less* salt than he does now.

fewer *Fewer* people use this park in winter than during the summer.

▶ **Fewer** is a better choice than **less** for individual things that can be counted one by one: It's easier to lose weight by eating *less* food at each meal, than by eating *fewer* meals altogether. However, certain set phrases don't follow this pattern: "Express checkout line: 9 items or less." "Answer in 25 words or less."

let allow permit enable authorize grant

VERB: to cause to happen; be willing to have happen.

let Joel's parents would not *let* him play high school football because they were afraid he'd get hurt. Mom told the babysitter not to *let* the dog in the house.

allow The history museum *allows* children under 12 to get in free.

permit No one is *permitted* to take out books from the reference section of the library.

enable Going to summer school *enabled* her to graduate from college in three years instead of four.

authorize Only the president, vice president, and treasurer of the company are *authorized* to sign company checks.

grant The captain *granted* Private Jones permission to leave the base for three days to visit his sick mother.

Antonyms: **forbid, prohibit, bar.**

letter   note message memo report dispatch

NOUN: a written communication sent from one person to another or others.

letter Mr. and Mrs. Peng got a *letter* from the bank notifying them that their home loan had been approved.

note She left a *note* for her son telling him she had gone to the store for an hour.

message There was a *message* for Ms. Adams at the hotel desk that her secretary had called from the office.

memo The boss sent a *memo* to the sales manager, telling her that he wanted to open a new West Coast sales office.

report The principal prepared a *report* comparing the daily attendance at school this year with last year's attendance.

dispatch The correspondent sent a *dispatch* back to his newspaper from the front lines, describing the battle he had seen.

level   grade rank status stage

NOUN: a certain position in some order or progression.

level The National Hockey League is the highest *level* of hockey in North America. Calculus is a difficult course that is usually taught in college, not at the high school *level.*

grade The best *grade* of beef is called "Prime;" below that is "Choice."

rank In the army a full colonel has a higher *rank* than a lieutenant colonel.

status In the Middle Ages, members of royal or noble families had the highest *status,* while poor farm workers had the lowest.

stage Learning to walk is one of the early *stages* in a child's development.

lie   untruth falsehood fabrication perjury

NOUN: something a person says that is not true.

lie The man told a *lie* when he said he'd never met the famous gangster, because the police have several photos of them together.

untruth The mayor says he will sue the newspaper for printing *untruths* about him in its story on his business dealings.

falsehood The dictator had spoken of his desire for peace, which was an obvious *falsehood* because he invaded a neighboring country just one week later.

fabrication His tale of being an honor student in college is just a *fabrication;* the fact is that he barely graduated.

perjury If a witness in court says something that he knows to be false, he can be charged with the crime of *perjury.*

Antonyms: **truth, fact.**

lift raise hoist elevate boost

VERB: to cause to move up into the air.

lift Dean *lifted* the bags out of the shopping cart and put them into the trunk of the car. Football players often *lift* weights as a way to become stronger.

raise Tracy *raised* her hand to show that she knew the correct answer.

hoist As the sailing ship moved out into the harbor, the crew moved quickly to *hoist* the sails.

elevate The movie's director sits in a special mechanical chair that is *elevated* above the set so that he can look down on the actors.

boost Bobby couldn't reach the first limb of the tree, so his mom *boosted* him up.

likely liable probable possible

ADJECTIVE: more or less certain to happen; to be expected.

likely If this snow keeps up, it's *likely* school will be closed tomorrow. The news reports say that Judge Lee is the *likely* choice for the vacant Supreme Court seat.

liable I don't think you should try to drive into the city at this hour—you're *liable* to run into a lot of traffic.

probable Wes decided to go to the beach, even though the weather forecast calls for *probable* showers this afternoon.

possible It's *possible* that the Eagles can still win the league championship, but they can't afford to lose any more games.

<u>Antonyms:</u> **unlikely, doubtful.**

It's **likely** that Dwayne can make his shot from so close to the hole.

It's **possible** that Len can make his shot too, but it will be hard to do.

line   row column file

NOUN: a group of people or things side by side or one behind the other.

line In front of the theater there was a long *line* of people waiting to buy tickets.

row The corn was planted in the field in neat, straight *rows*.

column Charlie watched the ants as they moved along the sidewalk in a long, unbroken *column*.

file The teacher had the class stand in single *file* at the edge of the playground.

list   register agenda roster roll

NOUN: a series of names, numbers, or other items written one after the other.

list When Mom goes to the supermarket she makes a *list* of all the things she needs to buy. Andrew wrote a *list* of the people he wants to invite to his party.

register Everyone who came to the wedding signed the guest *register*.

agenda Before the sales meeting, the boss prepared an *agenda* telling when each person would speak and what they would talk about.

roster The coach gave us a *roster* with the name, address, and phone number of each player on the team.

roll A teacher keeps a record of all the students in the class in a *roll* book.

little   small miniature tiny minute

ADJECTIVE: not big in size or amount.

little Mom still has the teddy bear she kept in her room when she was a *little* girl.

small Mice are *small* animals, and often live near people without being seen.

miniature Kerry got a *miniature* dining room set to go with her doll house.

tiny It was a damp, foggy night, and *tiny* drops of moisture had collected on the car windshield.

minute The ameba is a *minute* creature that can only be seen with a microscope.

Antonyms: **big, large.**

live   reside stay dwell

VERB: to make one's home.

live The Baggios *live* in Apartment 3-F. Many different kinds of wild animals *live* on the plains of Africa.

reside To go to this school, you must *reside* somewhere within School District 5.

stay During spring vacation he's going to *stay* with his grandmother for a while.

dwell American Indians of the Great Lakes area used to *dwell* in dome-shaped bark huts called wigwams.

lively   active energetic brisk vigorous

ADJECTIVE: full of life or spirit; showing energy.

lively The band marched onto the field, moving at a *lively* pace. Our family is interested in politics, and we had a *lively* discussion about the race for senator.

active She's a very *active* person and takes part in several sports as well as working and raising a family.

energetic Margaret felt *energetic* and decided to take on the spring cleaning.

brisk The doctor recommended that Grandma take a *brisk* walk after breakfast every morning.

vigorous After a *vigorous* workout in the pool, John likes to relax in the spa.

Antonyms: **lazy, sluggish, idle.**

The band played a **lively** tune that made everyone want to get up and dance.

Though he's getting on in years, my grandpa is still **active** and healthy.

local   native regional provincial

ADJECTIVE: having to do with a certain place rather than a general area.

local In this paper world news stories are in Part A, and *local* news is in Part B. Our *local* radio station broadcasts high school football games on Friday nights.

native These eucalyptus trees are now planted all over Southern California, but they are *native* to Australia.

regional In the college basketball championship, the winners of the four *regional* tournaments go on to play for the national title.

provincial The candidate for mayor said that his opponent had a *provincial* view of the world, because he had never been away from his home town.

logical   rational sound reasonable sensible

ADJECTIVE: showing correct thinking; based on fact or reason.

logical Because of her long experience as mayor of the state's largest city, she is a *logical* choice to run for governor.

rational The power must have been off for a while when we were away—that's the only *rational* explanation for all the clocks being so wrong.

sound Before I went off to college, my father gave me some *sound* advice that I've always remembered.

reasonable The boss said her idea sounded *reasonable* and agreed to try it out.

sensible I read over the math problem carefully, and choice 'b' seemed to be the only *sensible* answer.

lone   alone isolated solitary lonely

ADJECTIVE: not with another or others; by oneself or itself.

lone Texas is called the *Lone* Star State because its flag has a single star on it. It was winter and the beach was deserted, except for a *lone* jogger running along.

alone Stacy likes to sit in her room with a book when she wants to be *alone*.

isolated Mom grew up in a big city, and she says she wouldn't want to live out in the country because she would feel too *isolated*.

solitary The author Henry David Thoreau led a *solitary* existence, living by himself at Walden Pond.

lonely That town is a *lonely* spot, just a gas station and a few buildings in the middle of miles and miles of empty desert.

Seal Island has just one **lone** house. It's a **lonely** place, far from the mainland.

long   lengthy extended drawn-out prolonged

ADJECTIVE: covering a great distance or lasting a great time.

long I hadn't seen her in a *long* time and I was surprised at how tall she'd grown. *Gone With the Wind* is a *long* book—it took me most of the vacation to read it.

lengthy On the opening day of the Little League season, a local politician made a *lengthy* speech, while the players waited impatiently for the game to begin.

extended The modern medical practice is for new mothers to take their babies home soon after birth, instead of having an *extended* stay in the hospital.

drawn-out He thought the movie was too *drawn-out* and would have been better if it had been a half hour shorter.

prolonged The play *The Man Who Came to Dinner* tells of a man who turns a simple invitation to dinner into a *prolonged* visit lasting for weeks.

Antonyms: **short, brief.**

lose   forfeit yield waive

VERB: to fail to keep or have; give up.

lose In this game if you wait too long to move, you *lose* your turn and the next player gets to go. After World War I Germany *lost* all its former colonies in Africa.

forfeit In most states, convicted criminals have to *forfeit* their right to vote while they are in prison.

yield The senator from Maine was supposed to speak next, but he agreed to *yield* to his fellow senator from Georgia.

waive In certain cases, a defendant may *waive* the right to a trial by jury and choose to be heard by a judge only.

Antonyms: **find, recover, regain.**

lost   missing misplaced vanished

ADJECTIVE: that cannot be found or located.

lost Mrs. Wells put up signs all around the neighborhood asking if anyone had seen her *lost* cat. Cory lives next to a golf course and often helps people look for *lost* balls that they have hit into the woods.

missing Many people joined the search for the two *missing* campers, until a helicopter finally spotted them wandering in a canyon.

misplaced I don't think my bracelet is really gone; it's just *misplaced* somewhere in the house and will turn up eventually.

vanished In the southwestern U.S. there are many large, impressive cliff houses built by the Anasazi, a *vanished* tribe that lived in this area until about 1300 A.D.

Antonyms: **found, returned.**

loud   noisy blaring deafening resounding

ADJECTIVE: having a great or strong sound.

loud Thunder makes a *loud* sound. Jimmy didn't see the ball coming toward him, so I called to him in a *loud* voice, "Look out!"

noisy He had a hard time sleeping when he visited the city because it was *noisy*.

blaring They had their radio turned up all the way, and the *blaring* sounds annoyed other people sitting nearby on the beach.

deafening The plane raced down the runway and took off with a *deafening* roar.

resounding Actor James Earl Jones is known for his powerful, *resounding* voice.

Antonyms: **quiet, soft.**

Chris likes to have **loud** music on while he studies.

I wonder how he gets A's when he studies in such a **noisy** room.

love   adore admire respect

VERB: to care for or feel strongly about someone or something.

love Alex *loves* his new baby brother and wants to pick him up and hug him all the time. Maria *loves* to play tennis, and you'll always find her on the courts.

adore Andrea just *adores* that singer; she has pictures of him all over her room.

admire Many people *admire* Mother Teresa of India for the way she has spent her life helping others.

respect The boss *respects* his workers' opinions and listens carefully to them.

Antonym: **hate.**

▶ **Love** and **like** share the same meaning, but *love* is a much stronger word: I *like* frozen corn, but I *love* to eat fresh summer corn that's just been picked.

low   short squat stubby

ADJECTIVE: close to the ground or surface.

low The pitch was too *low* and the umpire called it a ball. Mom cut off the *low* branches of the tree so that we would have room to sit under it.

short Girls who are good in gymnastics are often very *short,* and several famous champions have been less than five feet tall.

squat There are no skyscrapers in that part of the city, just row after row of *squat* brick houses clustered close together.

stubby The dachshund is an unusual-looking breed of dog, with its long, tube-like body and its small, *stubby* legs.

Antonyms: **high, tall.**

loyal   faithful true reliable devoted steadfast

ADJECTIVE: committed to or keeping faith with someone or something.

loyal During the Revolutionary War, colonists who remained *loyal* to England were called Tories. She's a *loyal* friend who never criticizes me behind my back.

faithful Every morning Mr. Sosa goes past our house on his daily walk, with his *faithful* dog at his side.

true *True* to his word, Eric showed up at eight o'clock sharp to help us with the work, just as he'd said he would.

reliable Mr. Thomas said he was sure that none of the bank employees could have taken the money, because they were all very *reliable.*

devoted Laura sent a fan letter to her favorite movie star, and she signed it, "From your most *devoted* admirer."

steadfast Even in the worst days of the Civil War, Abraham Lincoln remained *steadfast* in his belief that the Union must be preserved.

luck   fate fortune destiny

NOUN: the way things can happen in life by accident, without being planned.

luck He wasn't sure of the answer so he guessed, and by *luck* he was right. The shot was going wide when it hit a player in the back and bounced in our goal—what bad *luck.*

fate The plane had to make an emergency landing in a parking lot that was usually crowded with cars, but by a happy twist of *fate* it was empty that day.

fortune Brenda went to a Gypsy woman who tells *fortunes,* and the woman told her that she would soon be taking a long trip.

destiny In her book the singer said that even when she was an unknown high school student, she always felt it was her *destiny* to become a famous star.

machine   motor engine machinery

NOUN: any device that uses energy and motion to do work.

machine A dishwasher is a *machine* that can automatically wash and dry dishes. In an expensive coat, the stitches on the buttonholes are often sewn by hand, rather than by *machine.*

motor The sailboat has a *motor* for use when there is not enough wind to sail.

engine Because of the higher cost of gas today, modern cars usually have smaller *engines* than the cars of the 1970's.

machinery People who work in a book-printing plant wear ear plugs to shut out the constant noise of the *machinery.*

magic   spell charm sorcery witchcraft

NOUN: a special power that is supposed to make a person able to control what happens or to do things that would normally be impossible.

magic Common forms of *magic* include making a coin disappear or pulling a rabbit out of a hat. Just after Davey said that he hoped it would snow tonight, snowflakes began to fill the air, as if by *magic.*

spell The story of Rip Van Winkle tells how Rip drinks a strange brew that causes him to fall under a *spell* and sleep for twenty years.

charm Sandra has an old copper penny that her grandmother gave her, and she carries it in her wallet as a good-luck *charm.*

sorcery It was once thought that people could use *sorcery* to make someone ill.

witchcraft In 1692, a famous series of trials was held in Salem, Massachusetts, accusing people of practicing *witchcraft* to harm their neighbors.

main   major leading chief primary foremost

ADJECTIVE: great in size or importance.

main I'll meet you at the library, right in front of the *main* entrance. They had a number of reasons for buying the house; the *main* one was the low price.

major O'Hare in Chicago is one of this country's *major* airports.

leading The popular movie *The Sound of Music* stars Julie Andrews in the *leading* role of Maria.

chief The roller coaster is the *chief* attraction at the Playland amusement park.

primary The news program presented several stories, but the *primary* focus of the show was the President's visit to the Soviet Union.

foremost Ireland has produced many writers in its history, including James Joyce, one of the *foremost* authors of the twentieth century.

Antonyms: **minor, lesser.**

majority   plurality

NOUN: the higher number; the most.

▶ **Majority** and **plurality** are often confused, because both of them can refer to the winning vote in an election. To be exact, a *majority* is more than half of all the votes cast; that is, over 50%. A *plurality* is the highest number of votes cast for any candidate. If there are more than two people running, this could be less than 50%. Suppose Smith gets 45% of the vote, while Jones gets 40% and three other candidates divide the other 15%. Smith has a plurality, but not a majority.

make   manufacture create construct produce fashion

VERB: to bring something into being, especially by assembling parts or materials.

make Dad is *making* beef stew for dinner tonight. The director John Ford *made* many famous movies about the Old West.

manufacture Much of the clothing that is now sold in the United States is *manufactured* abroad.

create For this play, the set designer has *created* a set that makes you feel exactly as if you are on a street in old New York.

construct The famous Pyramids of ancient Egypt were *constructed* more than four thousand years ago.

produce Japan *produces* a wide variety of electronic equipment, such as TV sets, stereos, and VCRs.

fashion A number of large tree branches had fallen during the storm, and the boys put them together to *fashion* a kind of play house.

Ronna and her brother Marty
made a racing car out of boxes.

Their father works in a factory
that **manufactures** sports cars.

male   masculine manly virile

ADJECTIVE: having to do with the sex that can father babies.

male A *male* moose is called a bull and the female is called a cow. The Supreme Court had only *male* judges until Sandra Day O'Connor was appointed in 1981.

masculine "Prince" is a *masculine* title; the feminine counterpart is "princess."

manly The poet Walt Whitman described Abraham Lincoln as being a typical *manly* specimen of the American West.

virile In the late 1980's, Hollywood made many action movies featuring *virile* stars such as Sylvester Stallone and Arnold Schwarzenegger.

Antonyms: **female, feminine.**

The **male** lion has a large mane of hair around its head.

The lion is often used as a football mascot because it has a strong, **masculine** image.

man   male fellow guy

NOUN: a male person who is no longer a boy.

man Dad says that when he was a boy he hated to eat vegetables, but now that he's a *man* he eats them because they're good for him.

male The female mallard duck has a plain brownish color, while the *male* is more brightly colored.

fellow My older sister is dating a nice *fellow* that she met at college.

guy Marty is on a bowling team with some of the *guys* from his office.

▶ The word **man** can also be used to mean all people, rather than just the male sex: "If history teaches us anything, it is that *man . . .* is determined and cannot be deterred." (John F. Kennedy) Some people object to this usage because it seems to leave out females; they prefer that *people* or some other word be used instead.

many several numerous various

ADJECTIVE: being large or great in number.

many *Many* kinds of wild animals live on the plains of Africa. *Many* people in the United States now use computers in their work.

several The author will appear on the *Tonight* Show to talk about her new book, and also on *several* other TV and radio shows.

numerous After the town was hit by a hurricane, *numerous* offers of help poured in from all over the country.

various This warm-up jacket comes in *various* colors, including black, red, gray, and blue.

Antonym: **few**.

mark label tag stamp brand

VERB: to put an identifying sign or symbol on something.

mark As the newspaper editor read over the story, he *marked* each page with his initials to show he'd checked it. White lines *mark* the edges of a baseball field.

label The box was *labeled* "Local tomatoes—home grown," so I guess they're really fresh.

tag The clerks *tagged* all the shirts with the discount prices before the holiday sale began.

stamp As the books were checked out, the librarian *stamped* a due date inside the front cover of each one.

brand In the Old West, cattle on the range were always *branded* with a special kind of mark to show who owned them.

mass heap pile stack bundle

NOUN: a body or group of things of no particular shape; an indefinite amount.

mass There had been a storm out at sea, and *masses* of seaweed had washed up on the beach. The Los Angeles highway system has to handle the huge *mass* of people who drive to work every day in the city.

heap Brian was too tired to hang up his clothes when he went to bed, so he just left everything in a *heap* on the floor.

pile They have a big *pile* of wood by their back fence for burning in the fireplace in the winter.

stack My dad loves to read, and every Tuesday night he goes to the library and comes home with a big *stack* of books.

bundle Bob keeps a *bundle* of old rags in the closet to use for odd cleaning jobs around his apartment.

master   leader ruler authority lord

NOUN: a person who has power or control over others.

master   That dog is very well-trained; all his *master* has to do is clap his hands and he comes right over. In the time when people had slaves, a slave belonged to his *master,* who could actually buy or sell him as if he were property.

leader   At exactly eight o'clock, the *leader* of the orchestra walked on stage and gave the signal for the concert to begin.

ruler   General Francisco Franco was the *ruler* of Spain from the time that his forces won a civil war in 1939 until his death in 1975.

authority   The person who is the head of the FBI is the highest law-enforcement *authority* in the United States.

lord   During the Middle Ages powerful *lords* held large areas of land and ruled over all those who lived there.

match   compare equal touch rival

VERB: to be similar to or as good as.

match   James told me to jump as far as I could and then he would *match* my jump. The computer company said that for every person who gave $100 or more to the public TV station, they would give a *matching* amount.

compare   Grandma still likes to watch movies, but she says there are no modern stars to *compare* to her old favorites like Bette Davis and Carole Lombard.

equal   Because pitchers do not pitch as many games as in the past, it is unlikely anyone will ever *equal* Jack Chesbro's record of winning 41 games in a season.

touch   Although there are some good French-style restaurants in this town, they can't *touch* the ones we ate in last summer in France.

rival   He says that nothing can *rival* the thrill of skiing down a mountain slope.

matter   affair concern issue

NOUN: something that has to be done or dealt with.

matter   Dad's boss called him at home last night and they had a conversation about some business *matters.* The principal is concerned about all the damage at her school, and she says it's a *matter* for the police.

affair   I saw Rachel and Heather arguing outside school, but I stayed away because it's none of my *affair.*

concern   All the main roads have been cleared of snow; the main *concern* now is plowing the side streets.

issue   There will be a special town meeting tonight to discuss the *issue* of building a new city hall.

mature   adult grown-up ripe

ADJECTIVE: fully grown or developed.

mature *Mature* redwood trees can be over 300 feet tall and 20 feet in diameter. Her mom told her to act more *mature* and stop making those silly faces at her little brother.

adult A caterpillar develops into a butterfly in its *adult* stage.

grown-up Tennis writers have called on that player to take a more *grown-up* attitude toward the game and stop fussing so much when he loses.

ripe To make banana bread, you'll need to have plenty of *ripe* bananas.

Antonyms: **immature, undeveloped, childish.**

maybe   perhaps possibly conceivably

ADVERB: that may be; that can happen or could be true.

maybe The sky is getting really dark—I think *maybe* we're in for some rain. If we hang this birdhouse in the back yard, *maybe* some birds will come and live in it.

perhaps It is now known that the Vikings sailed to America long before Columbus, and *perhaps* other European sailors did so as well.

possibly If we keep playing as well as we have lately, we could *possibly* win the rest of our games this season.

conceivably Of course, he might *conceivably* win the lottery, but it isn't realistic for him to make plans now about how to spend the money.

Antonyms: **certainly, definitely.**

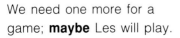

We need one more for a game; **maybe** Les will play.

He hits the ball too far; **perhaps** he would do better at baseball.

meal   feast banquet snack

NOUN: the food served or eaten at one time.

meal I'd like to go back to that restaurant; I had a really good *meal* there last time. We all try to be home by six, so that we can have our evening *meal* together.

feast We always look forward to Thanksgiving dinner at Grandma's—she puts on a real *feast* with all different kinds of food.

banquet The Rotary Club is having a *banquet* this Friday at noon to honor all the students in town who have straight-A averages.

snack Katie fixed some popcorn for a *snack* while we were watching a movie on TV last night.

mean   cruel nasty malicious vicious heartless

ADJECTIVE: wanting to hurt others.

mean Making fun of her like that was a *mean* thing to do. Jerry thought that his father was being *mean* not to let him go camping with his friends.

cruel The story of Cinderella tells of the *cruel* treatment Cinderella receives from her stepmother and stepsisters.

nasty The fans thought the home-team runner was safe, and they shouted out *nasty* remarks to the umpire when he was called out.

malicious I know that what Jennie said hurt your feelings, but I don't think she was being *malicious* when she said it.

vicious The newspaper columnist was called "the Poison Pen" because of his *vicious* attacks on politicians that he didn't like.

heartless The Roman emperor Nero was a *heartless* dictator who murdered many people to stay in power, including his own mother.

Antonyms: **kind, good.**

meaning   sense significance import

NOUN: the way a thing is meant; the thought or idea that is intended.

meaning The Spanish word "adios" has the same *meaning* as English "good-bye." My baby brother doesn't know how to talk yet; so far he just makes sounds that don't have any real *meaning*.

sense Steve left me a note that seems to say, "Melon at five. Please," but no matter how I read it, that just doesn't make any *sense*.

significance When people choose numbers for a bank code, they usually pick ones that have some *significance* to them, such as their birth date.

import In his first speech as President, John F. Kennedy said that the U.S. would land a man on the moon; these words had great *import* for our space program.

meet   face encounter confront

VERB: to come into the presence of; come upon.

meet My brother and I are going into the city today, and Dad is going to *meet* us there for lunch. She hopes that when she visits Hollywood she'll get to *meet* some movie stars.

face Mark wants to drop out of college, but he doesn't see how he can go home and *face* his parents with the bad news.

encounter As the mayor walked through the streets, she kept *encountering* people who shouted hello and wished her good luck.

confront They tried to sneak in a side door without paying, but as they walked in, an usher *confronted* them and said, "Where are your tickets?"

Antonyms: **avoid, miss.**

Whenever we're downtown, we always **meet** friends on the street.

The policeman **confronted** the man and told him to move along.

memory   recollection reminiscence remembrance

NOUN: someone or something that is remembered.

memory My mom has a good *memory;* she can look at her old high school yearbook and name everyone in the pictures.

recollection Studs Terkel's book *Hard Times* is made up of interviews in which people provide their *recollections* of the Great Depression of the 1930's.

reminiscence On Alumni Weekend the members of the Class of 1955 came back to the campus and shared *reminiscences* of their old college days.

remembrance *Remembrance* Day is a holiday in Canada to honor the veterans who served in World War I and World War II.

mental   intellectual intelligent psychological psychic cerebral

ADJECTIVE: having to do with or using the mind.

mental My grandmother does the newspaper crossword puzzle every morning; she says it's good *mental* exercise. I've never seen the Midwestern prairie, but from the "Little House" books I have a *mental* picture of it.

intellectual The professor enjoys *intellectual* hobbies, such as reading and playing chess.

intelligent I asked Uncle Larry if he thinks there is *intelligent* life on any other planet, and he laughed and said, "Are you sure about *this* one?"

psychological There is nothing wrong with her physically, so her headaches must be caused by something *psychological.*

psychic The man claimed to have *psychic* abilities that enabled him to know what other people were thinking.

cerebral He takes a very *cerebral* approach to watching football, analyzing every play carefully but never getting excited or rooting for either team.

merry   jolly jovial blithe

ADJECTIVE: full of fun, high spirits, and good cheer; very happy.

merry A breeze was blowing in from the ocean, and even at a distance we could hear the *merry* voices of the children as they ran in and out of the waves.

jolly Santa Claus is usually shown in pictures as a *jolly* man with a long white beard and a big smile.

jovial At the office party the boss was in a very *jovial* mood, telling jokes and laughing.

blithe The comedy actress Goldie Hawn often plays *blithe* characters who are carefree and fun-loving.

Antonyms: **gloomy, glum.**

mess   disorder clutter disarray

NOUN: a place or situation that is dirty, disorganized, and often unpleasant.

mess My brother is a pretty good cook, but when he finishes a meal the kitchen is really a *mess.* The whole house is being painted, and all the rooms are a *mess.*

disorder The clothing for sale was not arranged by size or style, but just piled up in large bins, and there was a general sense of *disorder* about the place.

clutter It was a typical attic, filled with old clothes, stacks of books, discarded toys, broken furniture—all the usual *clutter.*

disarray When they returned home after the earthquake, they found their house in complete *disarray.*

Billy was sitting in the **middle,** in the **midst** of all the bags and boxes.

middle　midst center midpoint

NOUN: a place that is halfway between two other points.

middle The car ran out of gas and came to a stop in the *middle* of the road. Those fish like deep water; you have to be out in the *middle* of the lake to catch them.

midst I wasn't sure if Ben was there yet, but then I saw him standing in the *midst* of a crowd of people in front of the theater.

center To start a basketball game, the referee throws the ball up between the two teams at the *center* of the floor.

midpoint The geographical *midpoint* of the state of Pennsylvania is located, logically enough, in Centre Country.

▶ **Middle** and **midst** are more often used to describe general locations than exact ones. **Center** and **midpoint** refer to places that are more precisely at or near a central point.

mind　intelligence brain intellect

NOUN: the part of a person that can think; the part that learns, knows, decides, and remembers things.

mind Tim has a really good *mind,* and I know he would get good grades if he studied harder.

intelligence The ability to devise tools for work is one thing that separates human *intelligence* from the mental activity of animals.

brain I can't believe I forgot my books again—I'm just not using my *brain* today.

intellect The mystery stories of Arthur Conan Doyle tell how the detective Sherlock Holmes uses his brilliant *intellect* to solve difficult cases.

minor   unimportant lesser inferior

ADJECTIVE: not as important as another or others.

minor A young pitcher has just joined the New York Yankees from their *minor* league team in Columbus, Ohio. The car was badly banged up in the accident, but the driver had only a few *minor* cuts and bruises.

unimportant When gas was very cheap in the 1950's and 1960's, most people thought it was *unimportant* whether or not a car got good mileage.

lesser F. Scott Fitzgerald became famous for his novel *This Side of Paradise,* but today it is considered one of his *lesser* works.

inferior The man sued the store because he said he'd paid for a very expensive Oriental rug, but actually received one of *inferior* quality.

Antonyms: **major, main.**

miss   skip forgo refrain abstain

VERB: to not do or use something; to fail to do, see, or know something.

miss Jared got 90% on the math quiz; he got the first nine questions right and *missed* the last one. I *missed* the 8:05 train and had to wait for the one at 8:30.

skip She had a lot of shopping to do, so she *skipped* lunch and spent her lunch hour at the store.

forgo For a TV show on Martin Luther King, a famous black actor gave readings of King's speeches, and he agreed to *forgo* his usual fee and appear for free.

refrain Passengers must *refrain* from smoking on an airline flight.

abstain In the voting, 58 senators voted for the bill, 40 voted against it, and two *abstained* and did not vote at all.

mistake   error slip blunder oversight

NOUN: something done, said, or thought in the wrong way.

mistake He got on the uptown bus by *mistake* and ended up going ten blocks out of his way. It was a *mistake* to buy that shirt without checking the size; it turned out to be much too big.

error My paper had only one spelling *error;* I wrote "seperate" instead of "separate."

slip In singing the national anthem, the singer made a *slip* and left out the line "Whose broad stripes and bright stars."

blunder When Napoleon attacked Russia he failed to prepare his army for the cold winter there, and this *blunder* eventually led to his downfall.

oversight We couldn't put Eddie's new riding toy together—by some *oversight* one of the back wheels was left out of the box.

mix   combine blend mingle merge

VERB: to put different things together as one or in one group.

mix He *mixed* a spoonful of sugar into his coffee. If you *mix* the primary colors blue and yellow, you get green.

combine The word "smog" was formed by *combining* "smoke" and "fog."

blend A polar bear's white, almost colorless coat allows it to *blend* in with the Arctic landscape of snow and ice.

mingle After her speech the Senator *mingled* with members of the audience, shaking hands and greeting people.

merge In 1955 this country's two largest labor unions, the AFL and the CIO, *merged* to form the AFL-CIO.

Grandad **mixes** fertilizer with the soil when he plants flowers.

He **combines** different kinds and colors of flowers in his garden.

modern   up-to-date present current contemporary

ADJECTIVE: having to do with the time that is now, or the time just past.

modern The CD (compact disc) player is a *modern* invention. *Modern* homes often have fireplaces, but they are not used for cooking as in pioneer days.

up-to-date That encyclopedia publishes a new edition every year to be sure that all its information is *up-to-date.*

present Paris has been the capital city of France from the year 987 right up to the *present* day.

current Our teacher often cuts out *current* articles on science from newspapers.

contemporary The City Art Museum is now holding a show called "Visions of Today," which displays the work of seven leading *contemporary* artists.

moment   instant flash minute second

NOUN: a very short, but indefinite, period of time.

moment The phone's been ringing all morning—I haven't had one *moment* to relax. As the President's car passed by us, he looked over for a *moment* and gave us a friendly wave.

instant The lightning was so close that for an *instant* the dark night was as bright as day.

flash The deer heard us, and in a *flash* it turned and raced off into the woods.

minute When you turn on the TV, you have to wait a *minute* before it warms up and the picture comes on.

second Joe's mom called him for dinner, and he said, "I'll be there in a *second.*"

▶ **Minute** and **second** are synonyms for **moment** in their general sense. They also have exact meanings when referring to time, but those are not what is meant in expressions such as "Wait a minute" or "I'll be there in a second."

money   cash funds currency

NOUN: objects that are in the form of coins or paper bills and that have a certain accepted value, for use in buying and selling things.

money Danielle is saving her *money* to buy a new tennis racket. When they went to Italy, they had to change their American dollars for Italian *money.*

cash Gas is cheaper at this station if you pay *cash* instead of using a credit card.

funds He transferred *funds* from his savings account to his checking account to pay his bills.

currency The U.S. has a two-dollar bill, but it is a little-used form of *currency.*

mostly   mainly generally largely primarily chiefly

ADVERB: for the most part; in most cases or situations.

mostly My brother doesn't like rock music; he listens *mostly* to country music. Lemonade is *mostly* water, with some lemon juice and sugar added.

mainly In Los Angeles people travel to work *mainly* in cars, rather than by bus.

generally *Generally,* U.S. schools close for summer vacation, though some are on a year-round schedule.

largely Most of Australia's farms and cities are located on its coasts; the central part of the continent is *largely* desert.

primarily Norman Rockwell drew covers for many magazines, but he is known *primarily* for the ones he did for the *Saturday Evening Post.*

chiefly Though they once ranged all over North America, wolves now are found only in remote northern areas, *chiefly* in Alaska and Canada.

motion movement momentum locomotion

NOUN: the act or fact of moving.

motion In football only one player on the offensive team is allowed to be in *motion* when a play starts. The baby always falls asleep when we go for a ride in the car; I guess the *motion* of the car relaxes her.

movement It's funny to watch my dog Nellie when she's having a dream—she makes little *movements* with her feet like she's running.

momentum The outfielder caught the ball in fair territory, but the *momentum* of his run carried him over into foul territory.

locomotion Parapodia, short projections that resemble legs, are the means of *locomotion* for many kinds of worms.

The TV studio has
movable furniture.

When the news crew goes out on a
story, they use a **portable** camera.

movable portable mobile transportable

ADJECTIVE: able to move or be moved.

movable A hurricane warning had been issued, and we brought in everything *movable* from the yard so that it wouldn't blow away.

portable He took his *portable* radio along to the beach to listen to the ballgame.

mobile The U.S. Marines are a highly *mobile* fighting force that can move troops and equipment quickly from one place to another.

transportable Fresh raspberries spoil very quickly, so they are not *transportable* for sale in locations far from where they grow.

Antonyms: **fixed, immovable, stationary.**

167

As the boat **moved** through the water, they **shifted** their weight to one side.

move   shift transfer remove displace

VERB: to change the place where something is.

move Kelly *moved* over on the bench so that I would have room to sit down. You'll have to *move* the car, because there's no parking here after six.

shift The fullback *shifted* the ball from his right arm to his left as he hit the line.

transfer When he got downtown, Evan *transferred* from the southbound bus to one going east.

remove Maggie *removed* the dishes from the table and put them in the sink.

displace All the new houses being built here have *displaced* many of the wild animals who used to live in this area.

much   plentiful abundant considerable substantial

ADJECTIVE: being a large amount; great in amount.

much She had so *much* homework that she was in her room studying almost all weekend. Let's get going; we don't have that *much* time until the bus gets here.

plentiful The price of oil tends to rise when the supply is scarce, and to drop when it is *plentiful.*

abundant The early settlers in New England found that fish and wild game were *abundant* all over the countryside.

considerable The Senator's suggestion to cut Social Security payments has met with *considerable* opposition from senior-citizen groups.

substantial That actor hasn't made a movie in several years, but he still gets a *substantial* income from the TV commercials he does.

much/many

▶ **Much** and **many** have the same meaning of "a large amount," but *many* is used for individual things that can be counted: *Many* of the students in the school are going to help at the Halloween Carnival. *Much* of the work still has to be done.

must   ought   should

VERB: to have to; be required, compelled, or obliged to do something.

must In this state, children *must* go to school at least until they are 16. All traffic *must* exit here because the highway up ahead is closed.

ought If you're going to be gone longer than you expected, you really *ought* to call home and tell them you'll be late.

should The concert is bound to be sold out, so we *should* buy our tickets soon.

mystery   riddle   puzzle   enigma   maze

NOUN: something that is hard to understand or that needs to be solved.

mystery "The Lost Colony" is the name for an early settlement in Virginia from which all the colonists disappeared; what happened to them is still a *mystery.*

riddle Timmy loves to ask people *riddles,* like "What gets wetter when it dries?" (a towel), and "What gets bigger the more you take away from it?" (a hole).

puzzle Every day our newspaper has a *puzzle* in which you fill in the words under a picture to make a sentence.

enigma The famous author J. D. Salinger remains an *enigma* to many people for the way he suddenly stopped writing books in the middle of his life.

maze Dad says that he hates having to fill out his income tax return, because you have to make your way through such a *maze* of rules and forms.

myth   legend   epic   fable

NOUN: a story from earlier times, especially one of great or important events.

myth The ancient Greek *myth* of Pandora tells how a person's curiosity first brought trouble and evil into the world.

legend The *legends* of King Arthur and his knights are thought to be based in part on a real-life British king who lived about the year 500.

epic Homer's *Iliad* is an *epic* poem hundreds of verses long, telling of the great events of the Trojan War.

fable The *fables* of Aesop are about animals that can talk and that have human faults, such as being jealous of one another.

▶ **Myth** also has another meaning, "a false story or belief," which does not refer to something from olden times: The book says that the idea of "the American family farm" is a *myth,* because modern farms are often owned by big corporations.

name   title label designation

NOUN: the word or words by which someone or something is known.

name The state of Illinois gets its *name* from an Indian tribe that lived in the area. Cougar, mountain lion, and puma are different *names* for the same animal.

title The eldest son of the king or queen of England has the *title* Prince of Wales.

label Many people feel that Mr. Jones lost the election because his opponent was able to pin the *label* of "Big Spender" on him.

designation Before an even larger war caused it to be called "World War One," the war of 1914-1918 had the *designation* "The Great War."

natural   instinctive inherited innate inborn native

ADJECTIVE: present from birth; not needing to be taught.

natural Babe Ruth had great *natural* talent in baseball; no other player has ever been a star as both a pitcher and a hitter. She has a beautiful *natural* singing voice, but it will take years of lessons for her to become an opera singer.

instinctive If you place your finger in a baby's hand, by an *instinctive* reaction it will close its hand to grip the finger.

inherited Some scientists think that children learn language by imitating adults around them, while others believe it is an *inherited* ability.

innate Bats can fly in the dark because they have an *innate* "radar" technique—they send out sounds and then detect objects by the echo.

inborn Chess champion Gary Kasparov showed a remarkable *inborn* talent for the game and could play complicated matches at the age of six.

native Though he had little education, Andrew Carnegie had *native* intelligence and worked his way up from a poor messenger boy to a very wealthy man.

Antonyms: **learned, artificial.**

nature   essence core soul

NOUN: the basic qualities or characteristics that make something what it is.

nature Gorillas can become fierce when aroused by humans, but by *nature* they are rather gentle. Mom never has to tell Bobby to clean his room; it's his *nature* to be neat and orderly.

essence Ernest Hemingway is famous for the "Hemingway style" of writing, the *essence* of which is the use of short, familiar words to express powerful ideas.

core Northern Ireland has long been troubled by violence; the *core* of the problem is that two opposing groups believe they have the right to the land.

soul Author Ben Jonson called William Shakespeare the *soul* of his age, because of the way his plays expressed the spirit of the English character.

near   nearly close closely nearby

ADVERB: at a short distance away.

near A mother bear stays *near* until her cubs can manage on their own. I could tell that the storm was getting *near* by the rumble of thunder.

nearly While Mom drove back from the beach, my sister and I slept in the back seat until we were *nearly* home.

close She always keeps a pot holder *close* to the stove while she is cooking.

closely The star rushed out of the theater to her limousine, *closely* followed by a group of fans asking for her autograph.

nearby Their new apartment is in a nice neighborhood, with a park *nearby*.

Antonyms: **far, distant.**

neat   tidy trim orderly

ADJECTIVE: being clean and in good order; arranged as it should be.

neat Yolande keeps her desk *neat* so that she can find her papers easily. They raked up all the fallen leaves into three *neat* piles.

tidy After we eat over at Grandma's, she wraps up all the leftovers in *tidy* little packages and saves them for her lunch.

trim Mr. Clark keeps a small boat in the harbor, and he works on it every day to keep it *trim* and ready for sailing.

orderly The encyclopedia volumes were arranged on the shelf in an *orderly* row.

Antonyms: **messy, disorderly.**

Dave keeps his side of the closet **neat.**

Rex's side is very **orderly,** with everything arranged by color.

necessary   required essential vital

ADJECTIVE: that must be done or had; needed.

necessary I have plenty of writing paper, so take as much as you feel will be *necessary* for your report. We'll only be gone two days, so it's not *necessary* to stop the mail delivery.

required All high school students have to take certain *required* courses in order to graduate.

essential In order for plants to grow, it is *essential* that they have both light and moisture.

vital Critics often say that the *vital* element in a good story is some conflict or obstacle that the main character has to overcome.

<u>Antonyms:</u> **unnecessary, optional.**

Mr. Lugg **needs** to fix his lawn sprinkler, but he **lacks** the right tools to do the job.

need   require lack want

VERB: to be without; have or feel a necessity for.

need The kitchen *needs* a new coat of paint. You'll *need* a heavy coat and snow boots if you plan to travel to the Midwest at this time of year.

require Raising a puppy into a healthy, well-behaved pet *requires* plenty of time, patience, and loving care.

lack He *lacked* a high school diploma, so it was hard for him to find a good job.

want One of the most famous lines in the Bible is from the 23rd Psalm: "The Lord is my shepherd, I shall not *want.*"

▶ The use of **want** as a synonym for **need** is is an older meaning of the word that is not common today, but it is still found in books, as this example shows.

new   fresh original recent novel

ADJECTIVE: made or done just now or a short time ago; not old.

new In September of each year car dealers display the *new* car models that have just come out. There was a long line of people waiting to see the *new* hit movie.

fresh To get the house ready for sale, they gave the outside a *fresh* coat of paint.

original Every year the students had to write a paper on their summer vacation, and this year Tara had the *original* idea of doing hers in the form of a poem.

recent At ten this evening there will be a special program on the most *recent* developments in the Middle East crisis.

novel Peter's science project is a study of how dogs react to rock music—that's certainly a *novel* topic.

Antonym: **old.**

next   nearest following succeeding

ADJECTIVE: just after the one mentioned; closest in time or space.

next This bread is baked at night so that it can be sold fresh the *next* morning. He had trouble sleeping in the motel because the TV was on loud in the *next* room.

nearest The plane developed engine trouble, and the pilot had to make a quick landing at the *nearest* airport.

following Part one will be shown Friday night, and part two the *following* night.

succeeding By late June the water was warm enough to go swimming, and in the *succeeding* weeks they enjoyed many afternoon swims.

nice   pleasant friendly cheerful delightful agreeable good-natured

ADJECTIVE: pleasing or good in some way.

nice It was *nice* of you to let me borrow your book. A small bouquet of flowers added a *nice* touch to the luncheon table.

pleasant With the sun shining and a cool, steady breeze, it was a very *pleasant* day for the sailboat races.

friendly Our neighbor always has a *friendly* greeting for us when we see her.

cheerful The *cheerful* sound of children laughing and playing floated up from the open window.

delightful It was my first real camping trip, and it was a *delightful* experience.

agreeable Ari asked her boyfriend to put a smile on his face and be *agreeable* when he came to dinner with her parents.

good-natured That dog looks ferocious, but you'll find he's quite *good-natured.*

▶ Try not to overuse **nice** in your writing as a general word of praise. As you can see here, it has many good synonyms that could be used to replace it.

noise   din uproar clamor racket

NOUN: a sound that is loud, unpleasant, or unwanted.

noise People who live near that airport complain about the *noise* from planes taking off and landing. You are not supposed to make *noise* in a library.

din Every machine in the factory was running at full speed, and we stepped into the plant manager's office to escape the *din.*

uproar When the referee changed his call and gave the ball to the other team, there was an *uproar* from the home team fans.

clamor First one impatient driver hit his horn, then another, and soon the air was filled with the *clamor* of honking horns.

racket The baby had a wooden spoon and was making a big *racket* by banging it against a pan.

normal   regular typical natural ordinary

ADJECTIVE: as it usually is; like most others.

normal *Normal* body temperature for humans is 98.6°. I wonder why the dog keeps running over to the door and back; it's not *normal* for her to act like that.

regular In English, a *regular* verb adds "-ed" at the end to show the past, as in: "walk—Yesterday I walk<u>ed</u> home from school."

typical On a *typical* day, Tina will spend about two hours on her homework.

natural I was trying to throw a trick pitch, but the coach told me to stick with my *natural* throwing motion so that I wouldn't hurt my arm.

ordinary Instead of being specially educated at home, Prince Charles of England was sent to a boarding school where he was treated like an *ordinary* student.

<u>Antonyms:</u> **abnormal, irregular.**

notice   observe note discern perceive

VERB: to sense with the eyes; look at; see.

notice He *noticed* that the kitchen faucet was leaking and called the plumber to fix it. I think that Mindy wears that odd hairstyle just so people will *notice* her.

observe The Wild Animal Park is set up so that visitors can *observe* the animals moving about in a natural setting.

note The detective *noted* that the lock on the back door had been broken off.

discern When you first walk into a dark room, it takes a minute for your eyes to adjust so that you can *discern* objects in the room.

perceive The seal sat so still that at first I thought it was just part of the rocks, and it wasn't until I swam near that I *perceived* what it actually was.

<u>Antonyms:</u> **overlook, ignore, disregard.**

Kerry had quite a **number**
of overdue books to return.

She paid a large **amount**
of money in fines for them.

number   amount quantity sum whole

NOUN: a collection of similar things thought of together.

number Quite a *number* of students have been out sick with colds this past week. She's very interested in black history and has a *number* of books on the subject.

amount Jeff's grandmother was not used to having a teenage boy in her house and was amazed at the *amount* of food he could eat.

quantity Dad always likes to keep a *quantity* of wood on hand for the winter, in case we need it to heat the house when the power goes off.

sum Though I like some of Pablo Picasso's paintings much better than I do others, I have to say that the *sum* of his life's work is outstanding.

whole She is going to take out a loan to buy the car, because if she paid cash that would wipe out the *whole* of her savings.

numeral   number figure digit

NOUN: a sign or symbol that represents a certain amount or quantity.

numeral The word "forty" is the same as the *numeral* 40. According to the system of Roman *numerals,* the year 1950 would be shown as "MCML."

number Hockey star Wayne Gretzky is famous for wearing the *number* 99 on his uniform.

figure With a calculator you can add a long column of *figures* quickly.

digit In major league baseball, a player's batting average is shown with three *digits,* such as .354 or .279.

obey   mind heed comply

VERB: to follow a rule, law, order, or instruction.

obey Ernesto is trying to teach his dog to *obey* certain commands. On that long, empty straightaway many drivers do not *obey* the 55-mile-per-hour speed limit.

mind Josh is very stubborn and doesn't always *mind* what his parents say.

heed Afterward Ellen was glad she had *heeded* her friend's advice to keep her wedding a small, simple event.

comply The author asked for more time to finish her book, and the publisher agreed to *comply* with her request and extend the deadline by six months.

Antonyms: **disobey, ignore.**

object   protest complain disagree

VERB: to give a reason against.

object Many parents have *objected* to the plan to start school at 8:45 instead of 8:00. In court a lawyer may *object* to something that the other lawyer has asked, if he thinks it is improper.

protest When the umpire called the runner out at home, our coach *protested* that the catcher had actually dropped the ball.

complain He *complained* to the people in the upstairs apartment because they made so much noise late at night.

disagree Randy thinks that he's old enough to get an after-school job now, but his mother *disagrees* and wants him to wait another year.

Antonym: **agree.**

When the City Council voted to ban dogs from the beach, one woman **objected.**

She and a group of dog owners **protested** against the new law.

ocean   sea deep main

NOUN: a very large body of salt water.

ocean The state of Hawaii is made up of a group of islands in the Pacific *Ocean.* Though sharks are thought of as living in the *ocean,* some kinds can also go into fresh water.

sea During the late 1800's, millions of European immigrants crossed the *sea* to come to America.

deep In the time when the powerful British navy sailed all over the world, a famous poet wrote that "Britannia's home is on the *deep.*"

main The waters off the coast of South America were known as the Spanish *Main* in the days when Spanish treasure ships passed through there.

offer   present tender proffer

VERB: to put forward something for another to take or accept.

offer Mom *offered* Aunt Karen another helping of pie, but she said that she'd had enough. Julia wants to take a course in ancient history, but it isn't being *offered* until the spring semester.

present José won the City Club scholarship, and Ms. Ryan *presented* him with a check for $1,000 for his college studies.

tender At the age of 65 the bank president *tendered* his resignation, saying it was time for a younger person to take over.

proffer As the Queen moved down the line of guests, she stopped in front of each person and *proffered* her hand for a handshake.

often   frequently regularly repeatedly oft

ADVERB: happening again and again.

often My Uncle Stan lives near us, and he *often* stops over to watch a ballgame with my Dad. There are woods just behind their house, and in the evening they *often* see rabbits at the edge of the yard.

frequently The temperature *frequently* rises to over 100 degrees in the Arizona desert, especially during the summer months.

regularly She gets her car serviced *regularly,* every time that she drives another 3,000 miles.

repeatedly Although the governor said *repeatedly* before the election that he would not raise taxes, soon after winning office he proposed a new sales tax.

oft Lincoln's Gettysburg Address begins with the *oft*-repeated line, "Fourscore and seven years ago . . ."

Antonym: **seldom.**

OK   acceptable   satisfactory   all right

ADJECTIVE: that is as it should be; good or fine.

OK   Mom says it's *OK* with her if you stay over, as long as your mom says so too.

acceptable   As cars are being made in a factory, workers check them over to be sure that each one is *acceptable.*

satisfactory   Being absent from school won't count against you, as long as you have a *satisfactory* reason.

all right   The PE teacher says it's *all right* with her if we use the gym during lunch.

▶ **OK** can also be spelled **O.K., Okay,** or **okay.** It can also be used as a noun (Get your Dad's OK), verb (Ms. Adams OK'd the deal), or interjection (OK! Let's go!).

old   elderly   ancient   antique   aged   archaic   obsolete

ADJECTIVE: having lived, existed, or been in use for a long time.

old   My dad had long hair in his picture in his *old* high school yearbook. New York's Wall Street has *old* buildings that go back to George Washington's time.

elderly   *Elderly* people in the U.S. are protected against large medical bills by an insurance program called Medicare.

ancient   In *ancient* Egypt the rulers, called pharaohs, were thought of as gods.

antique   We own an *antique* desk that used to belong to my mom's grandfather.

aged   Mary Norton's book *Are All the Giants Dead?* tells of former heroes of fairy tales who are now *aged* and living in quiet retirement.

archaic   New translations of the Bible substitute modern words for *archaic* ones, such as "You have" for "Thou hast."

obsolete   A blunderbuss is an *obsolete* weapon with a short barrel that was used in European wars in the 1700's.

Antonyms: **young, new.**

once   previously   earlier   formerly

ADVERB: at a certain time in the past, but no longer.

once   It was *once* thought that the earth was flat and that it was possible to fall off the edge. India was *once* a British colony, but now it is an independent country.

previously   The ad for the used car said, "This car is in perfect condition; it was *previously* owned by a mechanic who gave it loving care."

earlier   Ronald Reagan did not enter politics until fairly late in his life; *earlier,* he had been a well-known movie actor.

formerly   By bringing water from the Colorado River, farmers in the Imperial Valley created rich farmland where *formerly* there had been an empty desert.

only   just barely merely hardly scarcely

ADVERB: no more than or very little more than.

only The movie theater has a special early show where a ticket costs *only* 99 cents. *Only* one President, Franklin D. Roosevelt, served more than two terms.

just That part of Texas is an empty place, with *just* a few small towns scattered here and there.

barely Our car trip had *barely* started when Petey said, "Are we there yet?"

merely Darlene was afraid she'd broken her wrist, but after the doctor examined it he said it was *merely* sprained.

hardly The snow was falling so heavily this morning that I could *hardly* see the house across the street.

scarcely The great pitcher Bob Feller reached the major leagues at age 17, when he was *scarcely* out of high school.

Jeff was in a hurry and left his locker door wide **open.**

When he got to his class, the door was slightly **ajar.**

open   uncovered ajar unfastened

ADJECTIVE: allowing things to pass through; not shut.

open A wind came in through the *open* window, blowing the papers off the desk. The refrigerator door shouldn't be left *open* like that.

uncovered Don't put the lid on; keep the pot *uncovered* while the stew cooks.

ajar I saw that the door was slightly *ajar*, so I peeked in and called, "Anybody home?"

unfastened Somebody left the latch *unfastened* on the gate and the dog got out.

<u>Antonyms:</u> **closed, shut.**

opposite   opposing contrary contradictory conflicting

ADJECTIVE: completely different.

opposite "Hot" and "cold" have *opposite* meanings. He loves to argue, and he'll express the *opposite* opinion of whatever you say just to start a discussion.

opposing This newspaper has a feature on the editorial page called "Face-Off," in which two columnists present *opposing* views on the same issue.

contrary *Contrary* to what many people think, Columbus did not sail west to prove the earth was round; this had already been known for hundreds of years.

contradictory Senator Jones now says we need a tax increase, which is directly *contradictory* to his campaign promise to cut taxes.

conflicting It will be hard for the jury to decide what happened, because the two main witnesses gave *conflicting* testimony.

Antonyms: **like, similar.**

order   command direct decree

VERB: to tell someone to do something; give a command.

order The police officer *ordered* the driver to pull over. They complained to the hotel's owner that their room was dirty, and she *ordered* her staff to clean it up.

command John J. Pershing *commanded* the American army during World War I.

direct Mrs. Estevez received a letter *directing* her to report for jury duty.

decree King Henry II of England *decreed* that Anglo-Saxon common law should replace ancient Roman law as the legal system of England.

Sgt. Roxx **ordered** the men to stand up straight.

Sgt. Roxx **directed** traffic entering the army base.

origin   source root basis foundation

NOUN: the point from which something comes.

origin The *origin* of our Thanksgiving holiday was a harvest celebration held by the Pilgrims in Massachusetts. For his term paper on the *origins* of rock music, Dennis is reading a lot about the early music of Southern blacks.

source During the 19th century, several European explorers traveled through central Africa, searching for the *source* of the Nile River.

root Words such as "heater," "heated," "heating," and "reheat" are all formed from the *root* word "heat."

basis Author Patricia MacLachlan has said that the *basis* of her famous story *Sarah, Plain and Tall* was an actual event from her own family history.

foundation The Constitution is the *foundation* of the U.S. system of laws and government.

original   earliest initial primeval

ADJECTIVE: having to do with the beginning or source of something.

original The *original* capital of the U.S. was New York City, not Washington D.C. "Budget" now means a plan to spend money, but its *original* meaning was a small leather bag to hold coins.

earliest The *earliest* American settlers probably came from Asia, crossing an ice bridge from Siberia to Alaska about 30,000 years ago.

initial The committee's *initial* reaction to Barbara's suggestion was negative, but gradually she won them over.

primeval When Daniel Boone first went through the Cumberland Gap to the West, all he saw before him was *primeval* forest stretching for hundreds of miles.

other   another alternate alternative remainder

NOUN: being the one that is left.

other The twins look so much alike that even their friends have a hard time telling one from the *other*. I'm going to take this package away with me now, and come back later for the *other*.

another If that book isn't in the library, try *another* by the same author.

alternate Our class is supposed to elect two representatives and one *alternate* to the student council.

alternative Since you didn't order a ticket ahead of time, the only *alternative* is to buy one at the gate today.

remainder The school will use most of the money to buy new textbooks, while the *remainder* will be used for computer programs.

outer outside outward exterior external

ADJECTIVE: away from the center or the inside; farther out.

outer A baseball has a cork center with layers of yarn and rubber around it, then an *outer* cover of leather. We had to wait in the *outer* office until we could go in to see the principal.

outside The central air-conditioning system keeps the office at a constant 72 degrees, even when the *outside* temperature is up in the 90's.

outward He may have felt bad about losing, but his *outward* appearance was all smiles as he offered congratulations to the winner.

exterior When we lived near the ocean, we put a cloth over the car at night to protect the *exterior* finish against the salt air.

external People put rubbing alcohol on their skin; it is for *external* use only and is not meant for drinking.

<u>Antonym:</u> **inner.**

outline profile silhouette contour

NOUN: a line or figure that shows the outer edge and shape of something.

outline Peering into the fog, he spotted the *outline* of the bridge up ahead. On a map the *outline* of Lake Superior looks a bit like the head of a wolf.

profile Instead of showing her looking straight ahead, the artist drew her face from the side, in *profile.*

silhouette It was not morning yet, but from the *silhouette* of the dark mountains against a lighter sky I could tell that the sun was about to come up.

contour As our plane approached New York, we saw the *contour* of the Long Island shoreline below us.

outrageous monstrous atrocious heinous vile

ADJECTIVE: very cruel or wrong.

outrageous The United Nations condemned the *outrageous* bombing of a British hotel by Irish Republican Army terrorists.

monstrous Adolf Hitler has been described as the most *monstrous* dictator in modern history.

atrocious There has been worldwide protest against the *atrocious* slaughter of elephants by illegal ivory hunters.

heinous Because it can put a whole nation at risk, spying against one's own country is regarded as a *heinous* act.

vile The Puritan minister Jonathan Edwards was known for his powerful sermons; he once described people who commit sins as *"vile* insects."

outside   exterior surface covering face

NOUN: the outer side or part.

outside This candy bar has milk chocolate on the *outside* and caramel in the middle. We stayed dry because the *outside* of the tent had been waterproofed.

exterior Their house is filled with expensive paintings and custom-made furniture, but you'd never know that from looking at its plain, simple *exterior.*

surface I spotted the footprints of a deer on the *surface* of the newly fallen snow.

covering The hardest substance in the human body is the *covering* of enamel that protects the teeth.

face The *face* of this watch looks simple, but inside there are very complicated mechanisms.

<u>Antonyms:</u> **inside, interior.**

Some birds built their nest
outside my bedroom window.

The bird flew along just above
the **surface** of the water.

own   hold possess retain

VERB: to have as belonging to one.

own They *own* a sailboat that they take out on the lake every weekend. When he lived in the city, he didn't *own* a car because it was easier to take the bus.

hold If you get a bank loan to buy a house, the bank will *hold* a mortgage on the property until the loan is paid off.

possess The royal family of England *possesses* great wealth in the form of land, buildings, jewelry, and art treasures.

retain The artist is going to allow his paintings to be reproduced in a book, but he will *retain* the rights to the original paintings himself.

pack crowd stuff cram jam

VERB: to fill something tightly.

pack Bruce *packed* three bags with the clothes he'd need for college. On opening day the stadium was *packed* with fans eager to see the start of the season.

crowd As the returning astronauts came in to meet the press, the room was *crowded* with reporters.

stuff Eddie *stuffed* himself on hot dogs and potato chips at the family picnic.

cram Hurrying to get to her appointment on time, Maureen *crammed* her papers into her briefcase and ran out the door.

jam Passengers *jammed* the aisle of the overcrowded subway car.

Rosa got up early so that she'd have time to **pack** her suitcase.

Maria overslept and had to **cram** everything into a sports bag.

pain ache sore pang twinge

NOUN: a bad feeling that is sensed in or on the body.

pain The dentist asked Jim where the *pain* was, so she could locate the infected tooth. Andrew sometimes gets a *pain* in his stomach when he is feeling nervous.

ache I don't like to sit near her at lunch because she is always complaining about all the little *aches* and minor illnesses she has.

sore Lindsay still has a *sore* on her knee from the time when she fell off her bike.

pang If I skip breakfast I start to get hunger *pangs* about ten o'clock or so, and I have to have a snack then.

twinge Grandpa says that he can always tell when it's about to rain, because he starts to feel a *twinge* in his bad knee.

pardon   excuse forgive condone absolve

VERB: to allow something to go on without blame or punishment.

pardon The secretary said, *"Pardon* me for interrupting your meeting, Mrs. Carr, but there's an important telephone call for you." President Gerald Ford *pardoned* Richard Nixon for any crimes that he might have committed as President.

excuse Please *excuse* me for stepping on your foot—I didn't see you there.

forgive I wasn't talking to Heather because of the mean thing she said about me, but I decided to *forgive* her and now we're friends again.

condone Jerry is responsible for his bad behavior, but his parents are at fault too because they *condone* it and never correct or criticize him.

absolve After studying all the facts of the case, the grand jury has *absolved* the mayor of any wrongdoing, and he will not be charged with a crime.

part   piece section portion segment component

NOUN: something that belongs to a thing, but is not all of the thing.

part The movie gets off to a slow start, but the last *part* is really exciting. Mom's car won't be fixed until tomorrow; they had to order a new *part* from the dealer.

piece I can't finish this jigsaw puzzle, because one of the *pieces* got lost.

section When the morning paper comes, Jana always turns to the entertainment *section* first to find out what's happening in show business.

portion American workers have to pay a major *portion* of their income in taxes to the government.

segment An insect's body is made up of three *segments,* which are the head, the thorax, and the abdomen.

component Angela's new stereo system has five *components:* a receiver, a tape deck, a CD player, and two speakers.

participate   share cooperate partake

VERB: to join with others in doing something; take part.

participate In Eastern Europe in 1989, huge crowds of people *participated* in demonstrations calling for free government. He wanted to be in the band, but you can't *participate* in after-school activities if you have failing grades.

share The whole town *shared* in the celebration when the local basketball team won the state tournament.

cooperate The families on our street agreed to *cooperate* in a "neighborhood watch" program to prevent crime in the area.

partake We were all invited to the school library to *partake* of the refreshments provided by the Parents' Club.

particular   exact precise distinct specific express

ADJECTIVE: apart from others; being a certain one.

particular You expect a car to have the steering wheel on the left, but in this *particular* one it's on the right because it was made in England. They'd like to move, but they don't have any *particular* house in mind yet.

exact If you call this number, a voice will come on and give the *exact* time.

precise John F. Kennedy was born right around the time the U.S. entered World War I—on May 29, 1917, to be *precise.*

distinct Frogs and toads may look alike, but they're actually two *distinct* species.

specific The article says today's students don't know as much about geography as past students, but it doesn't give any *specific* comparisons to prove it.

express We were very disappointed that the play's star missed this performance; we bought our tickets for the *express* purpose of seeing her.

partner   colleague associate confederate

NOUN: someone who does something with another person.

partner Mrs. Richards is a *partner* in the law firm of Thompson, Richards, and Weiss. Gina is looking for a tennis *partner* so she can play in the city doubles tournament.

colleague Dr. Evans is a fine surgeon who is well respected by his *colleagues* in the medical profession.

associate The boss could not attend the business conference in Japan, so he sent two of his *associates* to represent the company.

confederate The gang leader and his *confederates* were arrested as they tried to escape the country, and all the stolen money was recovered.

party   celebration gathering affair festivity

NOUN: a gathering of people to have a good time or to mark a special occasion.

party Charlie had a *party* for his birthday and invited six of his friends from school. After the school play, there was a *party* for all the cast members.

celebration The United States had a big *celebration* in 1976, which was the 200th anniversary of the year the nation was founded.

gathering When Maya graduated from high school, her parents had a small family *gathering* at their house to congratulate her.

affair Though she didn't expect to enjoy herself at the neighborhood picnic, it turned out to be a very pleasant *affair.*

festivity I like the food and the prizes at Little League opening day, but we always have to listen to a lot of speeches before the *festivities* begin.

pass   surpass exceed overtake

VERB: to move beyond; go past.

pass The car pulled into the left lane to *pass* a slower car ahead. I *pass* a bakery on the way to school, and the smell of fresh bread always makes me hungry.

surpass Her family thought Rachel would do well in college, but she *surpassed* their expectations by getting all A's for four years.

exceed The French Club needed to raise $7,000 for their trip, and their efforts were so successful that they *exceeded* this total by $1,000.

overtake This jet fighter is fast enough to *overtake* any other plane in the sky.

The Tiger runner has **passed** two others and is trying to **overtake** the leader.

past   history yesterday yesteryear antiquity

NOUN: the time or events that came before now.

past Washing clothes took much longer in the *past,* because it had to be done by hand. He was really surprised when the car broke down; he'd never had any trouble with it in the *past.*

history As America's oldest college, Harvard has a *history* of producing famous graduates, including five U.S. Presidents.

yesterday The movie business is hard to predict, and *yesterday's* big star may be forgotten tomorrow.

yesteryear Though school may seem like hard work to today's children, the children of *yesteryear* had to work right alongside adults on farms or in factories.

antiquity Egypt has many famous structures that have survived from *antiquity,* such as the Pyramids and the Sphinx.

Antonym: **future.**

pay   remit settle compensate reimburse satisfy

VERB: to give money in return for something.

pay Mr. Evans has to *pay* his rent by the first of every month. The bus ride costs $2.25, but senior citizens only have to *pay* $2.00.

remit If you order clothes from the mail-order company, you can *remit* by credit card, personal check, or money order.

settle We waited by the restaurant cash register while Dad *settled* the check.

compensate According to the terms of the insurance policy, if our car is stolen we will be *compensated* for the loss.

reimburse Ms. Conti spent some of her own money on her business trip, and her company *reimbursed* her when she got back.

satisfy The court ordered the man to *satisfy* the claims brought against him.

Mr. Bent is going to **pay** a man to cut down the old tree in his yard.

Now he has to **compensate** his neighbor for damaging his roof.

peace   armistice truce cease-fire

NOUN: a time when things are quiet and calm, free from war or conflict.

peace The Civil War lasted for four long years before *peace* finally came to the nation. President Dwight D. Eisenhower led the U.S. during eight years of *peace* in the 1950's.

armistice *Armistice* Day was celebrated for many years on November 11, the date in 1918 when World War I came to a close.

truce The soldiers approached the enemy lines under a flag of *truce,* which was a sign that they did not intend to attack.

cease-fire The two countries agreed on a temporary *cease-fire,* and fighting will be halted while they try to work out a plan to end the war.

peek glance glimpse peep

VERB: to look quickly or secretly.

peek Matt already knows what he's getting for Christmas; he *peeked* in the closet where the presents are hidden. I thought the baby was asleep, but then I saw him *peeking* out from under the blanket.

glance Miss Hale told me that when I give the speech I should just *glance* down at my notes from time to time, not read from them.

glimpse As the school bus passed, Derek *glimpsed* his friend Anthony waving to him from the back seat.

peep Will was shy about meeting his preschool teacher, and he hung back and *peeped* out from behind his mother's legs.

people persons humanity mankind

NOUN: a group of humans; men and women in general.

people Some *people* say that if you talk to your plants, they will grow better. Before electricity was invented, *people* used candles and gas lamps for light.

persons The police have gotten calls from a number of unidentified *persons* who claim to have seen the escaped gangster here in town.

humanity The question of how to save the environment affects all of *humanity.*

mankind When Neil Armstrong first set foot on the moon, he said, "That's one small step for a man, one giant leap for *mankind.*"

▶ The word **humankind** is now often used as a substitute for **mankind,** on the grounds that *mankind* seems to limit the reference to males only.

perfect ideal flawless faultless impeccable

ADJECTIVE: that cannot be made better; exactly as it should be.

perfect Mike had a *perfect* attendance record in school last year; he wasn't absent once. A *perfect* diamond is worth much more than one that has flaws in it.

ideal It was an *ideal* day for the beach—warm and sunny, with clear blue skies.

flawless Her dive was *flawless,* and each of the judges gave her a "10," which is the highest possible score.

faultless The critic said that the actress playing Lady Macbeth gave a *faultless* performance, the finest he had ever seen in this role.

impeccable Using *impeccable* logic, the prosecuting attorney laid out a step-by-step case that convinced the jury the accused man was guilty.

Antonyms: **imperfect, flawed.**

▶ Remember that **perfect** is an absolute word, much stronger than words such as *great* or *outstanding.* A score of 97% on a test is *excellent;* 100% is *perfect.*

period   age era interval span duration

NOUN: a certain length of time; a given time.

period In our high school, the day is divided into seven *periods* of fifty minutes. The *period* in American history after the Civil War is known as Reconstruction.

age During the Bronze *Age* about 5,000 years ago, people began using this metal to make tools, weapons, and other objects.

era The time when Queen Elizabeth I ruled England is often referred to as the Elizabethan *Era*.

interval On weekdays, trains on this subway line run at ten-minute *intervals*.

span Elephants have a long life *span* and commonly live more than 60 years.

duration The President sent a large naval force to the area and said that they would remain there for the *duration* of the crisis.

permanent   lasting endless perpetual eternal

ADJECTIVE: continuing or enduring a long time.

permanent After spending vacations in Florida for years, he decided to make the state his *permanent* home. The UN met in several different sites around New York before moving to its *permanent* headquarters on the East River.

lasting Many of Franklin D. Roosevelt's New Deal policies had a *lasting* effect on U.S. government, such as Social Security and unemployment insurance.

endless This bridge has an *endless* flow of traffic moving in and out of the city.

perpetual People have often tried to produce a *perpetual*-motion machine, one that would run forever without wearing out or using up all its energy.

eternal Though Shakespeare's plays are hundreds of years old, they do not seem out of date, because they deal with *eternal* problems of human nature.

Antonym: **temporary**.

person   individual human creature being

NOUN: a man, woman, or child.

person There's a prize for the *person* who guesses how many marbles are in the jar. The phone has a button you push to put the *person* who's calling on "hold."

individual The basketball coach wanted his players to think of themselves as a team, not as a group of *individuals*.

human Though several kinds of animals can run 40 miles per hour or better, the fastest speed reached by a *human* is only half that.

creature *E.T.* is a movie about an odd but friendly *creature* from another planet.

being The American Revolution was inspired by the idea that man is created as a free *being* whose rights cannot be taken away by a ruler.

persuade convince urge coax induce

VERB: to make a person believe or do something; win over.

persuade Once the boss has decided something, it's difficult to *persuade* him to change his mind. That car salesman is good at *persuading* people to buy his cars.

convince Michelle was upset at first about having to wear braces, but her parents finally *convinced* her that it was a good idea.

urge The local Republicans feel that Mr. Jones would have a good chance to be elected mayor, and they are *urging* him to run.

coax Brett didn't want to dance, but his girlfriend *coaxed* him out on the floor.

induce The severe lack of rain in Oklahoma in the 1930's *induced* many farmers to leave their land and go to California in search of work.

Anita **persuaded** her Dad to bring Rufus along on their trip.

When they were ready to go, they had to **coax** Rufus into the car.

physical concrete tangible material

ADJECTIVE: having to do with solid things that can be seen.

physical The police searched the area for *physical* evidence, such as tire marks or footprints. Geography involves the study of the *physical* features of the earth.

concrete You keep saying you think it could happen, but are there any *concrete* examples of situations where it actually did happen?

tangible He'll never believe that Indians used to live around here unless he finds some *tangible* object to prove it, such as an arrowhead.

material The ancient Greeks believed that the gods could come down from heaven and enter the *material* world in which humans live.

Antonyms: **spiritual, intangible.**

picture   image   likeness   representation

NOUN: something that shows what a person or thing looks like; a drawing, painting, photograph, or the like.

picture   Mrs. Witt has *pictures* of her two children on her desk at work. For Mom and Dad's wedding anniversary, Robby made a card and drew a funny *picture* of them getting married.

image   In the book on French art, the publisher tried to make sure the *images* in the book looked the same as the actual paintings themselves.

likeness   Brenda doesn't like the photo of her that's in the yearbook; she says it really isn't a good *likeness* of her.

representation   Because newspapers are now able to print in full color, they can provide a more accurate *representation* of what things look like.

pity   sympathy   condolence   compassion

NOUN: a feeling of sorrow about another's unhappiness or suffering.

pity   Roberta felt *pity* for the little lost puppy, so she took it home with her. When the homeless family was interviewed on TV, they said that they did not want *pity* from people, just a chance to find work.

sympathy   The football player stayed on the ground after he was hit, but the other players showed no *sympathy,* saying "Get up, you're not hurt."

condolence   After President Kennedy was killed, thousands of people wrote to express their *condolences* to his widow.

compassion   Albert Schweitzer founded a hospital in Africa and became known for his great *compassion* toward those suffering from disease.

place   location   spot   site   locale

NOUN: a certain part of space; any point in space thought of by itself.

place   That is a nice chair, but I'm not sure that we have any *place* in the house to put it. She found a really good *place* for lunch, a little Italian restaurant down by the harbor.

location   Children's books used to be kept on the first floor of the library, but they've been moved to a new *location* on the second floor.

spot   When Aaron goes to the beach he likes to pick out an empty *spot* to put his blanket, away from other people.

site   The city is conducting a study to determine the best building *site* for the new City Hall.

locale   Because it has many old, interesting-looking neighborhoods, the city of Toronto is often used as the *locale* for feature movies.

plain   simple   unadorned

ADJECTIVE: not fancy or elegant; with little or no detail added.

plain Grandpa doesn't like foreign foods with a lot of seasoning; he prefers a *plain* meal of meat and potatoes. At his job in the bank he always wears a white shirt, a dark tie, and a *plain* blue or gray suit.

simple The early American pioneers lived in *simple* cabins made of logs cut from the nearby forests.

unadorned The Vietnam Veterans' Memorial in Washington is a low, *unadorned* wall of black granite with the names of the Vietnam dead.

<u>Antonym:</u> **fancy, elaborate.**

plan   program   policy   strategy   scheme

NOUN: a way or idea worked out ahead of time for what to do or how to do it.

plan When a new house is being built, the builder follows a *plan* that shows how the rooms should look. It has been a very dry summer, and the city has to come up with a *plan* for saving water.

program The school has begun a *program* to teach English to foreign students.

policy During the 19th century, the United States followed a *policy* of not becoming involved in wars in Europe.

strategy Harry Truman knew he was behind in the race for President in 1948, so he developed a *strategy* of going all over the nation to speak to the voters.

scheme In the book *Charlotte's Web,* the character of Templeton the rat loves to eat and is always thinking up *schemes* to get more food for himself.

The boys had a **plan** to get tickets for the game by getting in line early.

Rusty had a **scheme** to get into the game free.

plant   seed sow till cultivate

VERB: to work to cause something to grow in the ground.

plant When spring comes, we'll *plant* flowers all around the edge of the back yard. Mr. Kubota *planted* a vegetable garden with tomatoes, beans, and peppers.

sow The American pioneer "Johnny Appleseed" (John Chapman) wandered for 40 years over the countryside *sowing* seeds for apple trees.

seed Mom *seeded* the bare patch of ground by the fence to grow some grass there.

till Farmers *till* the soil by breaking it up with a metal plow so that plants will grow more easily.

cultivate Scientists at the state college of agriculture are *cultivating* a new breed of corn that can resist long periods of dry weather.

play   romp frolic cavort gambol

VERB: to do something for fun; pass the time in an enjoyable way.

play After we finish lunch we can go out and *play* in the schoolyard for a while. Eddie wanted me to come over to *play,* but I had to help my dad in the yard.

romp The snowplow had piled snow up along the street, and the boys *romped* through the deep drifts, shouting and laughing.

frolic It was the first time Jessie had ever been to the ocean, and she *frolicked* happily in the waves.

cavort The kittens *cavorted* on the kitchen floor, chasing each other in circles and then rolling around in a ball.

gambol The story of "The Ant and the Grasshopper" tells how the ant works to prepare for winter, while the grasshopper just *gambols* about in the fields.
Antonym: **work.**

please   satisfy delight gratify gladden

VERB: to make someone feel good; give pleasure to.

please Robert has improved his grades in school this year, which *pleases* his parents. I like to shop in that store, because they really go out of their way to *please* their customers.

satisfy We played the first-place team today, and though we'd hoped to win we were definitely *satisfied* that the game ended in a 1-1 tie.

delight Grandma was *delighted* to hear I'd be coming to visit her this summer.

gratify The scientist always felt her theory would work, and she was *gratified* when the test results proved her to be right.

gladden After the long months at sea, the sight of their home port *gladdened* the sailors' hearts.

point   aim goal objective intention

NOUN: the main idea or purpose of something.

point Fire engines are a bright color—the *point* is to make them easy to see. The *point* of Joan Didion's essay "Holy Water" is that water is a precious thing.

aim The *aim* of a pep rally is to get the team and the fans excited about the game.

goal My aunt plans to go on a diet; her *goal* is to lose twenty pounds.

objective *A Bridge Too Far* is the story of a famous World War II attack whose *objective* was to capture a bridge across the Rhine River.

intention I had every *intention* of getting up early this morning, but I slept right through the alarm.

Larry always wears a hard hat on the job; that's company **policy.**

Most of the men wear jeans and boots; that's the usual **practice.**

policy   procedure practice routine

NOUN: a plan that guides the way something is done.

policy The store's *policy* is that if you return an item that was bought there, you must show the sales slip. The Good Neighbor *Policy* was an effort by the U.S. to have good relations with the nations of Latin America.

procedure Before the flight, the pilots went through the standard *procedure* of checking all the plane's controls and instruments.

practice Though the usual *practice* is to vote at a voting booth, some people mail in their ballots instead.

routine He has an exact *routine* when he gets dressed in the morning—he always puts his clothes on in the same order, even down to which sock goes on first.

polite courteous well-mannered proper civil

ADJECTIVE: having or showing good manners.

polite Angela is very *polite* and always says "Please" and "Thank you." "Miss Manners" (Judith Martin) writes a newspaper column on *polite* behavior.

courteous Airline ticket agents are trained to be *courteous* to people they serve.

well-mannered Kenny's teacher said she enjoys having him in the class, because he's a friendly, *well-mannered* boy.

proper In past times it was not considered *proper* for a woman to travel alone.

civil I didn't expect him to greet us like long-lost friends, but he could at least have given us a *civil* hello.

Antonym: **rude.**

The waitresses at Rip's Diner are very **polite** to their customers.

The waiters at Château de Maison are **civil,** but not very friendly.

poor needy penniless destitute

ADJECTIVE: not having enough money to pay for things that are needed.

poor A large part of the world's population is too *poor* to afford proper food.

needy Each year during the holiday season *The New York Times* publishes a series of articles to raise money for *needy* people in the city.

penniless The old folk tale of "Dick Whittington" is about a *penniless* orphan boy whose cat helps him to gain a fortune.

destitute Some large cities now provide shelters for *destitute* people so that they will not be on the streets in bad weather.

Antonyms: **rich, wealthy.**

▶ The word **broke** also can be a synonym for **poor,** but this word is more suited to everyday conversation than to serious writing.

popular   likable admired celebrated

ADJECTIVE: having many friends; well-liked.

popular Megan is *popular* with the other children in her class because she is so friendly and outgoing. Many novels for teenage readers are about "loners" who are not part of the *popular* group at their schools.

likable Craig is certainly a *likable* person, but he doesn't seem serious enough to run for class president.

admired Public-opinion polls usually rate Eleanor Roosevelt as the nation's most *admired* First Lady, because of her many efforts on behalf of human rights.

celebrated Audie Murphy was a *celebrated* soldier of World War II, receiving 24 medals from the U.S. government.

Antonyms: **unpopular, disliked.**

population   inhabitants residents populace citizenry

NOUN: the people who live in a place, or the number of these people.

population Argentina is almost as big a country as India in land area, but the *population* of India is 25 times as large as Argentina's.

inhabitants The American Indians are now called "Native Americans," because they were the first *inhabitants* of the Americas.

residents Many *residents* of the city have protested against the plan to put a new highway through the downtown area.

populace In the Middle Ages, only people who had special occupations learned to read and write; the general *populace* was not educated at all.

citizenry In 1789 the *citizenry* of Paris rebelled against King Louis XVI, setting in motion the French Revolution.

position   stand attitude viewpoint stance

NOUN: a way of thinking; an opinion on a certain matter.

position Because there is so much strong feeling on both sides, the Senator doesn't want to a take a *position* on that issue.

stand The President has changed his *stand* on the question of taxes and says that he is now willing to support a tax increase.

attitude At first the team didn't like the new coach's methods, but their *attitude* changed after they won a few games.

viewpoint He has a popular radio show where listeners call in to express various *viewpoints* on the major issues of the day.

stance The mayor has taken a tough *stance* on street crime; she favors much longer prison terms for those who are convicted.

postpone   delay defer suspend shelve

VERB: to put off until some later time.

postpone   The tennis match was *postponed* until tomorrow because of the rain. It's supposed to be bad luck to *postpone* a wedding after you've set a date for it.

delay   Our flight was *delayed* for half an hour as we waited for the planes ahead of us on the runway to take off.

defer   When students borrow money to pay for college, they are often allowed to *defer* payment on the loan until a later date.

suspend   No trains are running now on the 7th Avenue subway line; service has been *suspended* while workers repair a break in the tracks.

shelve   The Senate committee *shelved* the tax bill until the next session.

▶ **Cancel** and **postpone** are often thought of as synonyms, but when something is *postponed*, it is put off to a later time. When it is *canceled*, it is called off for good.

Mr. Zellch invented the Waterizer to **pour** himself water automatically.

Something went wrong with it and water is **gushing** out.

pour   flow stream gush drain

NOUN: to move in a smooth and steady way, as a liquid from a container.

pour   Arnie asked me to *pour* a glass of orange juice for him. The rain was *pouring* down, and she ducked into a doorway to keep from getting soaked.

flow   They often catch fish for dinner in the brook that *flows* past their cabin.

stream   Tears *streamed* down her cheeks as she watched her son go off to his first year at college.

gush   Water *gushed* out of the broken pipe, creating a flood in the basement.

drain   The Mississippi River *drains* into the Gulf of Mexico near New Orleans.

power   control authority influence jurisdiction

NOUN: an ability to decide or affect what others do.

power In former times, kings and queens had a lot of *power*. According to the Constitution, only Congress has the *power* to declare war on another country.

control The dictator Joseph Stalin had total *control* over the Soviet Union.

authority As head of production for the movie company, she has the *authority* to decide which movies they will make.

influence When a decision was made to cut the defense budget, Senator Smith used his *influence* to make sure that no projects were cut in his own state.

jurisdiction Although it lies within the state of Arizona, the Grand Canyon is a national park and is under Federal *jurisdiction*.

powerful   mighty forceful potent vigorous

ADJECTIVE: having great power or effect; strong.

powerful With its *powerful* jet engines, the Concorde airliner flies faster than the speed of sound. In the 19th century, Great Britain was a very *powerful* nation, controlling an empire that stretched all over the world.

mighty According to legend, Arthur became king of England after pulling a sword from a stone with a *mighty* effort.

forceful The play *Evita* deals with Argentina's Eva Peron, whose *forceful* personality won her millions of followers.

potent Penicillin is a *potent* drug that is widely used to fight infections.

vigorous President Theodore Roosevelt was known as a *vigorous* leader who brought great energy to everything he did.

Antonyms: **powerless, impotent, weak.**

practical   useful sound sensible reasonable

ADJECTIVE: suited for actual use; making good sense.

practical Joe wanted to get his mother a *practical* gift for the kitchen, such as a clock or a toaster. The Scottish engineer James Watt developed the first *practical* steam engine; earlier ones were too large and too expensive.

useful This knife looks quite impressive, but it isn't very *useful* because it has to be sharpened all the time.

sound The boss thinks the idea is a *sound* one and is going to go ahead with it.

sensible Letting the children pick out their own books for book reports seemed to be the most *sensible* way to do it.

reasonable Though they were asking a price of $200,000 for the house, they felt that $185,000 was a *reasonable* offer and agreed to sell.

Celia **practices** the piano at home every afternoon.

She played the piano at school while the singers **rehearsed.**

practice   drill train rehearse

VERB: to do something again and again, in order to become better at it.

practice Our soccer team *practices* twice a week after school and plays its games on Saturdays. In this math book, after you learn a skill you do some problems to *practice* what you've learned.

drill I won't panic if there's a fire in school, because we've *drilled* over and over about what we're supposed to do.

train Brandon *trained* his dog to sit still by giving her a bit of food every time she did it correctly.

rehearse Before a play is performed, the actors *rehearse* their parts to be sure that they know all their lines.

praise   approval compliment acclaim

NOUN: words or actions that show a high opinion of a person or thing.

praise Charlie received *praise* from his teacher for his book report. The mayor gave the Red Cross *praise* for the way they provided help after the earthquake.

approval Mel is doing well at his new job, and the boss showed her *approval* of his work by giving him a raise in pay.

compliment Her children are very well-behaved—she gets a lot of *compliments* from people about how polite they are.

acclaim American pianist Van Cliburn received worldwide *acclaim* when he won an international piano competition in Moscow.

predict   foretell   forecast   prophesy

VERB: to state that something will happen in a certain way.

predict Before the baseball season starts, sportswriters *predict* the order in which they think the teams will finish. Using a computer to analyze past elections, the TV station *predicted* the winner of the election before the polls closed.

foretell Fortune tellers claim they can *foretell* what will happen by studying messages from tea leaves, crystal balls, and playing cards.

forecast This weekend's weather report *forecasts* sunny days and clear, cool nights.

prophesy In ancient Rome, people believed that it was possible to *prophesy* the future from such signs as the flight of birds.

present   current   existing   contemporary

ADJECTIVE: going on now; at this time.

present He feels that his *present* job doesn't pay enough money, so he's looking for a new one. There used to be three newspapers in this town, but at the *present* time there's only one.

current The word "deer" once meant any kind of wild animal, but in *current* use it means only one certain kind.

existing The most famous document of English government, the Magna Carta of 1215, is so rare today that there are only four *existing* copies.

contemporary Many *contemporary* writers have been influenced by the short stories Ernest Hemingway wrote in the 1920's.

Antonyms: **former, past.**

pressure   stress   strain   anxiety   tension

NOUN: a negative feeling that arises from some influence or situation that a person has to deal with.

pressure She likes to go camping on weekends to get away from the *pressures* of her job. My uncle is an air traffic controller—having to direct all those planes in the air really puts him under constant *pressure.*

stress For many modern women, trying to raise a family and succeed at a job at the same time can produce a lot of *stress.*

strain The *strain* of working such long hours has finally affected his health, so the doctor has told him to take a long rest.

anxiety The big math test is coming up, and she's feeling a lot of *anxiety* about it.

tension The *tension* in the crowd was rising, and the police were afraid that a riot might break out.

pretend mimic impersonate simulate feign

VERB: to act as if something is true or real when it is not; put on a false show.

pretend Holly *pretended* she didn't hear me when I asked her to help with the dishes. The boys like to make a "fort" with the sofa cushions and *pretend* they are out in the wilderness.

mimic Justin *mimicked* Mom's voice when he answered the phone and told me to get home right away.

impersonate The man who wore a fake police uniform was arrested and charged with *impersonating* an officer.

simulate New pilots practice on the ground in a training device that *simulates* the conditions of actual flight in the air.

feign Some kinds of animals will *feign* death or injury to distract a predator that is threatening them.

pretty beautiful lovely fair attractive

ADJECTIVE: pleasing to the eyes; nice to look at.

pretty I like Stacy's new hair style—it really makes her look *pretty.* In the midst of all the tall buildings of the city, we were surprised to find a *pretty* little park with trees and a pond.

beautiful Greta Garbo's perfect features made her one of the most *beautiful* movie stars of all time.

lovely From that hill you get a *lovely* view of the valley and the ocean beyond.

fair Folk tales often tell how a handsome prince rescues a *fair* young maiden from some danger or evil.

attractive The dinner table made an *attractive* scene, with the fine china and silver set on a snowy white tablecloth.

Antonym: **ugly.**

▶ **Pretty** and **beautiful** have the same meaning, but *beautiful* is a stronger word. English often has such pairs of words; others are *like/love* and *good/excellent.*

prevent prohibit bar block

VERB: to keep something from happening, especially something unwanted.

prevent She kept her dog on a leash to *prevent* him from running off. Doctors say that heart disease can be *prevented* in many cases by proper diet and exercise.

prohibit In this city, people are *prohibited* from smoking in public buildings.

bar After he was convicted of gambling, he was *barred* from playing pro football.

block The Senator spoke on and on for hours, in an effort to *block* the proposal from coming to a vote.

Ms. Williams was promoted
and now has a **private** office.

On her desk, she has some family
pictures and other **personal** items.

private   personal confidential intimate

ADJECTIVE: not meant to be shared with or known by others.

private A diary is a book where you can write down your *private* thoughts. That star is known for playing action heroes, but in his *private* life he's a quiet person.

personal When I sent my aunt a letter at her office, I marked it *"Personal"* so that it wouldn't get mixed in with all her business mail.

confidential The boss told his assistant that he was thinking of moving the company to Texas, but he said this was *confidential* information.

intimate I saw my friends talking in a corner at the party, but I didn't go over to them, because it looked like they were having an *intimate* conversation.

Antonym: **public**.

prize   award reward premium bonus

NOUN: something that is won, as in a game or contest.

prize Rafael's painting won first *prize* in the school art contest. Contestants on that TV game show compete for *prizes* worth thousands of dollars.

award Mrs. Bernstein got the city's annual "Citizen of the Year" *award* for her many hours of volunteer work in the community.

reward When Jill returned the lost cat, its owner gave her a ten-dollar *reward*.

premium The bank was giving a free toaster as a *premium* to anyone who opened a new account.

bonus The test has an extra question at the end that is worth a five-point *bonus*.

probably   likely probably presumably supposedly

ADVERB: according to what could happen; what may or might be.

probably I'd say from the look of the sky that we'll *probably* have snow today. Please answer the phone; it's *probably* Dad calling from the office.

likely The mayor will *likely* win the election because his opponent is unknown.

possibly Some animal has been eating away at our vegetable garden—it may be a rabbit, or *possibly* even a deer.

presumably Someone reported them for not following the city's water-saving rules; *presumably* it was a neighbor who noticed their sprinklers going.

supposedly The new school will *supposedly* open this September, but looking at it now I don't see how it can be ready by then.

problem   difficulty predicament obstacle dilemma

NOUN: something that is hard to deal with; something that can cause trouble.

problem He's having a *problem* with the brakes in his car and has to get them fixed. The main *problem* with the puppy is that he's always chewing on things.

difficulty The movers had some *difficulty* getting the piano through the door.

predicament Ellen got herself into a big *predicament*; two different boys asked her to the dance and she said yes to both of them.

obstacle Sidney Poitier had to overcome a lot of *obstacles* to succeed as an actor, because when he began his career there were very few good roles for blacks.

dilemma Congressman Jones is faced with a *dilemma*—the President expects him to vote for this bill, but the people in his district are against it.

Jennifer had a **problem** deciding how much rice she should put on.

She made the wrong decision, and now she has a real **predicament.**

process   method   procedure   means

NOUN: a series of actions done in a certain way to make or do something.

process We're in the *process* of painting the kitchen, so everything's a mess in there. Many teachers of English now use the Writing *Process,* which requires a student to go through certain steps to write a paper.

method In the famous essay "A Nice Cup of Tea," author George Orwell gives his *method* for making a perfect cup of tea.

procedure Dad still doesn't understand the *procedure* for programming the VCR and has to get Randy to help him.

means During the strike, commuters who usually rode the train to work had to find other *means* of getting to the city.

promise   pledge   word   vow   oath

NOUN: a statement by a person that he or she surely will do something, or that something surely will happen.

promise Kevin made a *promise* not to tell anyone about our secret hiding place. Mom said, "If you let Becky sit in the front seat now, you can sit there on the way back—that's a *promise."*

pledge When the public TV station has a fund-raising show, people call in to make *pledges* that they will give a certain amount of money.

word All cadets at the U.S. Military Academy have to give their *word* that they will not lie, cheat, or steal, or allow others to do so.

vow Many couples now change the traditional wedding *vows,* promising to "love, honor, and respect" each other rather than to "love, honor, and obey."

oath The witness placed his hand on the Bible and took an *oath* to tell the whole truth and nothing but the truth.

proper   appropriate   suitable   fitting

ADJECTIVE: suited to a certain use or purpose.

proper If you're going to go mountain climbing, be sure you have all the *proper* gear. Marilyn had a difficult time learning the *proper* way to swing a golf club.

appropriate Jason wasn't sure what to wear to the wedding, and his dad said that his navy blazer and gray slacks would be *appropriate.*

suitable The teacher thinks that "Deserts" is not a *suitable* topic for my report, and told me to narrow it down to one particular desert.

fitting Since my grandmother likes the theater so much, we thought it would be *fitting* to give her tickets to a show as a birthday gift.

Antonym: **improper.**

property   belongings possessions goods assets

NOUN: something that is owned by a person.

property He's only supposed to drive the car for business, because it's actually the *property* of his company. Our next-door neighbor's tree was growing over onto our *property,* and he said we could trim some of the branches.

belongings Pioneers going to the West in the 1800's carried all their *belongings* in covered wagons drawn by oxen.

possessions The writer is going to spend a year living in a mountain cabin, with few *possessions* other than what he needs to live.

goods It took Martha five trips to move her household *goods* to her new house.

assets The *assets* of the business include the products it has for sale and the land and buildings it owns.

proud   conceited vain arrogant

ADJECTIVE: thinking highly of oneself or of something one has done.

proud Maya was *proud* of the fact that she got all A's on her report card. Larry really doesn't know how to use the computer, but he's too *proud* to ask for help.

conceited Adam doesn't say hello in school because he's very shy, but people often think he's *conceited* and trying to avoid them.

vain Georgia is very *vain* and spends hours in front of the mirror trying out different hairdos and makeup.

arrogant He has an *arrogant* manner and always thinks he's right about things.

Antonyms: **humble, modest.**

Suzy was **proud** of the medal she won at camp.

Her brother said she was **conceited** to wear it around her neck at home.

prove   verify demonstrate establish substantiate corroborate

VERB: to show that something is true, valid, or as it is said to be.

prove Katie is determined to *prove* to the coach that she should be in the starting lineup. French scientist Louis Pasteur *proved* that bacteria cause disease.

verify When Joe went to cash the check, the bank teller asked to see his driver's license to *verify* that he was the person named on the check.

demonstrate To *demonstrate* that air has weight, Miss Ross showed us how a basketball filled with air weighs more than one that is not inflated.

establish A person accused of a crime does not have to show that he is innocent; it is up to the state to *establish* his guilt.

substantiate Legends say that St. Brendan, an Irish monk, sailed to America centuries before Columbus, but there is no evidence to *substantiate* this.

corroborate The man claims he was at home at the time of the robbery; however, no one else was there who could *corroborate* that statement.

provide   supply furnish equip

VERB: to give what is needed or wanted.

provide The soccer league *provides* uniforms for the players, but they have to buy their own shoes. Mom wants to plant a tree by the house to *provide* some shade from the afternoon sun.

supply The Colorado River *supplies* water to several states in the western U.S.

furnish I asked my father for help with my math homework, and he said, "I'll show you what to do, but I'm not going to *furnish* you with the answers."

equip All new cars sold in this country must be *equipped* with seat belts.

public   general popular common communal

ADJECTIVE: serving or meant for many people or everyone; not private.

public This beach is *public* property, and anyone may swim here. The principal told his wife last month that he planned to resign, but the *public* announcement was not made until today.

general In his best-selling book *In Search of Time,* the British physicist Stephen Hawking explains complicated scientific theories for a *general* audience.

popular Hawaii is a very *popular* vacation spot for American travelers.

common In the college dormitory, students have their own private bedrooms, plus the use of a *common* kitchen and TV room.

communal In olden times, people had to get water from a *communal* source such as a river or a town well, rather than having it in their homes.

Antonyms: **private, exclusive.**

pull   tow haul drag draw tug

VERB: to hold something and move it toward or along with oneself.

pull Sam has a little red wagon that he uses to *pull* his toys around with him. When you tie the rope, be sure to *pull* the knot tight.

tow The car broke down, and a truck had to *tow* it off the highway for repairs.

haul Someone finally *hauled* away the old mattress that was left in the alley behind our house.

drag A big tree branch fell in the road during the storm, and we *dragged* it to one side so that cars could get by.

draw At their cabin in the mountains, they have to *draw* water from a well to do their washing and cooking.

tug He felt something *tugging* at his line and realized that he'd caught a fish.

Antonym: **push.**

Billy **pulled** his little brother around the yard on the sled.

Dad used the sled to **haul** some wood in from the car.

pure   clean fresh unpolluted

ADJECTIVE: free from dirt, germs, or harmful substances.

pure This is *pure* Canadian maple syrup, with no artificial flavoring or chemicals added. The chemistry teacher uses distilled water for his experiments so that it will be absolutely *pure*.

clean After the rain shower, even the downtown area looked bright and *clean*.

fresh Henry likes to get away to the beach and breathe the *fresh* ocean air.

unpolluted He likes being way out in the desert, where the sky is still *unpolluted* by smoke from cars and factories.

Antonym: **impure, contaminated.**

purpose goal intent design

NOUN: the reason why something is made or done.

purpose The *purpose* of this sitting-up exercise is to make your stomach muscles stronger. I don't know what this painting is supposed to be; it looks like the artist just dripped paint on the canvas without any *purpose.*

goal The *goal* of the library's reading program is to have each child read at least five books during the summer.

intent It is perfectly legal to change your name, if you do so without any *intent* to fool or cheat people.

design Dennis Connor won the America's Cup sailing race with a two-hull boat whose *design* made it possible for the boat to go very fast.

push press shove nudge thrust

VERB: to move forward against something.

push Lupe likes to *push* the shopping cart for her mother when they go to the market. He *pushed* the doorbell and waited for someone to answer.

press If you want to record something on the VCR, just *press* this button here.

shove The teacher saw Brian *shove* the other boy out of the way to get ahead in line, so she made him go to the end.

nudge Rebecca *nudged* Helen with her elbow to get her attention.

thrust A cold wind blew up from the river, and he turned up his coat collar and *thrust* his hands deep into his pockets.

Antonym: **pull.**

put place set lay position deposit

VERB: to cause to be in a certain place.

put She saw a pretty stone on the ground and she picked it up and *put* it in her pocket. That hamburger meat is for the weekend; please *put* it in the freezer.

place Our paper boy *places* the paper carefully on our front doorstep, rather than just tossing it in the driveway.

set The phone was ringing as she walked in, and she *set* her packages down on the table to answer it.

lay When you bring in the laundry, please just *lay* the clothes out on the bed.

position The detective *positioned* himself so that he could see both the front and back doors of the house, in case anyone came out either way.

deposit As the Mississippi River flows south, it carries dirt with it and *deposits* this dirt along its banks at the lower end of the river.

quality   characteristic attribute trait property

NOUN: something that makes a person or thing what it is.

quality An unusual *quality* of balsa wood is that it is so light in weight. I read a book about Winston Churchill; the one *quality* that stood out for his whole life was how determined he was.

characteristic The most noticeable *characteristic* of a giraffe is its long neck.

attribute I was surprised to see Kyle waiting there so quietly; patience is not an *attribute* that I would usually associate with him.

trait The color of a person's eyes is a *trait* that is passed down from a parent.

property Diamonds have a *property* called cleavage, which makes it possible to split them so that they have flat, even surfaces.

quickly   rapidly swiftly hastily

ADVERB: moving or acting with speed.

quickly She heard the mail truck coming, so she *quickly* sealed her letter and went out to mail it. I'm surprised that Jeff got an 'A' on the test; he finished so *quickly* that I thought he'd left out half the questions.

rapidly A microwave oven cooks food much more *rapidly* than a regular oven.

swiftly When the jackrabbit heard me open the door, it ran *swiftly* out of the yard and up into the brush.

hastily Brett did the last part of his paper too *hastily,* and there were a lot of spelling mistakes in it.

Antonym: **slowly.**

Heather had to dress **quickly** to leave for school in time.

At school, she realized that she'd dressed too **hastily.**

quiet   silent still noiseless soundless

ADJECTIVE: with little or no noise.

quiet Everyone stayed *quiet* until Angela came in, and then they all shouted "Happy Birthday!" At first the woods seemed *quiet,* but soon we heard the soft rustling of small animals.

silent A person who is arrested by the police may choose not to answer their questions; he has the right to remain *silent.*

still On the hot, *still* August nights in Iowa, you can almost hear the corn grow.

noiseless Compared to our noisy old refrigerator, this new one is almost *noiseless.*

soundless Because the crowd noise is so loud, football coaches use *soundless* methods to communicate with players on the field, such as hand signals.

Antonyms: **noisy, loud.**

quite   completely entirely totally wholly fully

ADVERB: all the way; to the full extent.

quite The painters aren't *quite* finished yet, but they'll be done by tonight. When Billy doesn't have a friend to play ball with, he's *quite* happy to play by himself.

completely Alex forgot to save his paper in the computer memory, and now it has to be *completely* retyped.

entirely Four of the five Great Lakes border on both the U.S. and Canada, but Lake Michigan lies *entirely* within the United States.

totally Carthage was a great city of the ancient world, but it was *totally* destroyed in war, and none of its buildings are standing today.

wholly He was *wholly* responsible for the accident—the other car was stopped at a red light, and he hit it from behind.

fully When they are *fully* grown, gorillas can weigh well over 400 pounds.

Antonyms: **partly, partially, somewhat.**

quote   cite

VERB: to repeat the words of another person.

quote In his farewell speech to Congress, General Douglas MacArthur *quoted* the words of an old British army song, "Old soldiers never die, they just fade away."

cite Martin Luther King's "I Have a Dream" speech *cited* famous documents such as the Bible, the Declaration of Independence, and the Gettysburg Address.

▶ When you **quote** someone, you repeat the exact words. When you **paraphrase,** you use the same thought but not the exact wording. "To *quote* Dr. King, 'I have a dream' for America." "To *paraphrase* Dr. King, I dream of a better America."

rain   rainfall precipitation showers downpour

NOUN: drops of water falling to earth from the sky.

rain You'd better take your umbrella; it looks like we're going to get some *rain.* The baseball game had to be called off because of *rain.*

rainfall An area that gets less than ten inches of *rainfall* per year is considered to be a desert.

precipitation The Weather Bureau records all forms of *precipitation,* including snow, hail, and sleet.

showers The forecast calls for scattered *showers* this morning, though it should clear up later in the day.

downpour Frank was caught in a sudden *downpour* and got soaking wet.

There was a light **rain** when the game started.

Later it became a **downpour.**

rate   speed velocity pace tempo

NOUN: a measurement of movement or other activity.

rate That job calls for a person who can type at a *rate* of 50 to 60 words a minute. This article says that the population of our city is growing at a very fast *rate.*

speed We see lightning before we hear thunder, because the *speed* of light is greater than that of sound.

velocity Major-league baseball scouts use a device called a radar gun to measure the *velocity* of a pitcher's fastball.

pace Because the lead runner set too fast a *pace* during the first lap, he got tired and fell behind the others later in the race.

tempo The band marched out onto the field to the lively *tempo* of John Philip Sousa's "Stars and Stripes Forever."

rather   sooner   preferably

ADVERB: by choice or preference; more readily.

rather Dad asked whether I wanted rice or potatoes with the chicken, and I said I'd *rather* have rice. She wants to go to a movie, but he said he'd *rather* just stay home and rent a videotape.

sooner The city's new express bus isn't getting much business; I guess people would *sooner* be stuck in traffic in their own cars than ride the bus.

preferably When you go to the library, see if you can pick out a book for me— *preferably* a good mystery story.

reach   arrive gain attain achieve

VERB: to come to a certain place or position.

reach Monica was the first runner to *reach* the finish line. It took the jury only two hours to *reach* a verdict, and they found the defendant guilty.

arrive Our plane will leave Chicago at 7:00 and *arrive* in St. Louis an hour later. "Zero" is the answer to the math problem, but how did you *arrive* at that answer?

gain After climbing for hours, they finally *gained* the summit of the mountain. The Australian runner *gained* the lead in the last lap and held on to win.

attain Sandra Day O'Connor was the first woman ever to *attain* the position of Supreme Court Justice.

achieve William Faulkner *achieved* great fame as a writer, including the 1949 Nobel Prize for Literature.

ready   prepared set available qualified ripe

ADJECTIVE: in the condition needed to go into use or action.

ready Annie is so excited about her trip to New York that she was all packed and *ready* to go a week ago. Mom always keeps the spare room *ready* in case any unexpected guests come to stay.

prepared Grant had been studying for weeks, so he knew he was well *prepared* for the final exam.

set I think everything is all *set* for the party, but let's check once more to be sure.

available The mechanic told us that the part he needs to fix the car won't be *available* until tomorrow.

qualified Bruce passed the bar exam and is now *qualified* to practice law in the state of California.

ripe He thinks the time is *ripe* for a new family restaurant in town, and wants to open one in the Hillsdale shopping center.

Antonyms: **unready, unprepared.**

real   genuine actual authentic true valid

ADJECTIVE: being in fact as it appears to be; not artificial.

real   This is just a toy gun, but from a distance it looks *real.* "Fool's gold" is an ordinary mineral that can be mistaken for *real* gold because of its yellowish color.

genuine   The museum's expert examined the painting to be sure that it is a *genuine* work by Rembrandt.

actual   This microscope allows you to view objects at 100 times their *actual* size.

authentic   The Colonial Museum has constructed a building that looks just like an *authentic* log cabin from pioneer days.

true   In the movie the actress had blonde hair, but her *true* hair color is brown.

valid   To make sure the man's signature on the check was *valid,* the teller compared it to his signature that was on file in the bank records.

Antonyms: **artificial, imitation, false.**

really   actually truly indeed

ADVERB: in fact; as is the case.

really   Did Eddie *really* score five goals in the game today? Dad likes to joke that he had to walk through the snow to get to school, but he *really* went by bus.

actually   Though it might seem that elephants are slow and clumsy, *actually* they can run quite fast.

truly   The critic said that Ireland has produced many good novelists and one *truly* great one, James Joyce.

indeed   In his speech the Senator said, "We should all pay attention to problems of the environment; *indeed,* we must pay attention."

reason   cause explanation motive grounds

NOUN: a fact that explains why something happens as it does.

reason   The *reason* we were late is that we got stuck in a big traffic jam. One of the main *reasons* for the Revolutionary War was that the American colonists did not want to pay heavy taxes to England.

cause   After the warehouse mysteriously burned down, the fire department tried to determine the *cause* of the blaze.

explanation   I used to wonder why ice, which is frozen water, floats on water—the *explanation* is that air gets trapped inside the ice as it forms.

motive   It didn't seem that such a wealthy man would have a *motive* to steal, but it turned out he needed extra money to pay for his gambling losses.

grounds   In 1954 the Supreme Court ruled it was illegal to have separate school systems for blacks and whites, on the *grounds* that this violated the Constitution.

Mr. Lewis **received** some visitors from his company's office in Japan.

When his sisters came to visit, Mr. Lewis **welcomed** them warmly.

receive   welcome accept admit accommodate

VERB: to permit to enter; meet with or greet.

receive The President *received* the French ambassador in the Oval Office. That movie was not well *received* by the critics; several even gave it "0 stars."

welcome On the first day of school, the teacher stood at the classroom door to *welcome* all her students to her class.

accept Lanny was *accepted* by the University of Connecticut for next fall.

admit He's been having dizzy spells, and he was *admitted* to the hospital for tests to find out the cause.

accommodate When we travel with our dogs, we always check ahead to find a hotel that can *accommodate* pets.

recent   current fresh latest

ADJECTIVE: happening, done, or made just before the present.

recent The teacher said that for my report on computers I should get the most *recent* information possible, because it's a field that's always changing. Many new citizens have come to the U.S. from Southeast Asia in *recent* years.

current The Queen of England is coming to America next month—there's a story about it in the *current* issue of *Newsweek* magazine.

fresh Derek got paint on his shirt when he sat on the park bench; he didn't see the sign that said *"Fresh* Paint."

latest I like Maurice Sendak's books, but I haven't read his *latest* one yet.

Antonyms: **old, dated, remote.**

record   report account document

NOUN: a written statement of facts, events, or other such information.

record When you get a bill from the phone company, it has a *record* of all the calls you've made. My Uncle Ted is a bird watcher, and he has a notebook with a *record* of the different kinds of birds he's seen.

report Cheryl is doing a *report* for school on the early history of her town, so she went to the library to look at some old newspapers from that time.

account Charles Lindbergh's book *The Spirit of St. Louis* is an *account* of his famous airplane flight from New York to Paris.

document She has a locked box in her dresser where she keeps important family *documents* such as her children's birth certificates.

Joe asked the man to move so that he could sit down, but he **refused.**

Joe asked the woman if she wanted a seat, but she **declined** the offer.

refuse   decline reject spurn veto

VERB: to turn down; say no to.

refuse The umpire called him out, but he *refused* to leave the base, saying that he was safe. Many people want to buy that house, but she has always *refused* to sell.

decline When the Senator was asked about the reports that he hoped to run for President, he *declined* to answer, saying, "No comment."

reject She had hoped that the magazine would publish her story, but they *rejected* it because it was too long.

spurn Anthony *spurned* our offers of help, saying that he'd rather do it himself.

veto If the President does not approve of a bill passed by Congress, he can *veto* it so that it does not become a law.

Antonym: **allow, accept.**

reliable   dependable responsible trustworthy trusty

ADJECTIVE: that can be trusted.

reliable Our paper boy is very *reliable* and drops the paper off at 7:30 every morning without fail. This encyclopedia is a *reliable* source of information.

dependable The car is old and has a lot of mileage, but it's still *dependable* and doesn't break down or need major repairs.

responsible Jennie's parents know she is *responsible* enough to babysit for her little brother while they go out for the evening.

trustworthy Bank tellers have to be *trustworthy,* because their work calls for them to handle large sums of money.

trusty The frontiersman Davy Crockett told many stories of his great hunting feats with his *trusty* rifle, "Old Betsy."

Antonyms: **unreliable, undependable, irresponsible.**

religious   holy sacred divine spiritual

ADJECTIVE: having to do with religion.

religious Renaissance paintings often have *religious* themes, such as scenes from the life of Christ. Many Hindu *religious* ceremonies are performed in the home, including marriages.

holy Mecca, the birthplace of the prophet Muhammad, is the most *holy* city of the Muslim religion.

sacred The *sacred* writings of the Jewish religion are contained in the five books of Moses, also known as the Torah.

divine In the Middle Ages it was believed that kings had a *divine* right to rule that came directly from God.

spiritual Father Charles Coughlin, a Catholic priest, had a popular radio show in the 1930's in which he spoke on political issues rather than *spiritual* matters.

remark   comment note mention

NOUN: something that is said; a short comment or opinion.

remark The comedian made some funny *remarks* about today's news. Jerry said he wished school went on all summer—I wonder what he meant by that *remark*.

comment All the candidates for mayor were asked for their *comments* on how they would handle the city's budget problems.

note The sports reporter wrote a story on yesterday's game, and added some brief *notes* at the end about next week's game.

mention After winning the Oscar, the actor thanked many people in his speech, but for some reason he made no *mention* of his co-star in the movie.

remember   recall remind recollect reminisce

VERB: to bring or call back to the mind; think of again.

remember I *remember* the day my baby brother came home from the hospital— he looked so tiny lying there in his crib. Tom didn't *remember* his friend's phone number and had to check the phone book.

recall Heidi couldn't *recall* ever having met the Swensons before, although they seemed to know her.

remind An old song was playing on the radio, and Mom said it *reminded* her of when she was in high school.

reminisce The group of veterans got together once a year to *reminisce* about their days in World War II.

recollect My Uncle Tony has the nickname "Ace," but no one in the family can *recollect* exactly how he got it.

Antonym: forget.

report   describe relate state narrate

VERB: to give the details of something in writing or speech.

report When Mr. Klein got back from Japan, he sent a memo to his boss to *report* on the trip. Our local radio station is *reporting* that there is a big fire burning in the hills north of town.

describe The book *describes* how Maria Tallchief became a famous ballet dancer.

relate After Kara got home from the party, she called her friend to *relate* in great detail what went on there.

state The lawyer asked the witness to *state* in her own words what she had seen on the night of the robbery.

narrate I watched a National Geographic TV show on wolves that was *narrated* by the actor Robert Redford.

request   favor service petition

NOUN: something asked for or called for.

request On this radio show people can phone in and give a *request* for a song they want to hear. He doesn't like regular airline food, so when he flies he makes a *request* for a special seafood meal.

favor Could you do me a *favor* and lend me ten dollars until next week?

service Waiters in a restaurant provide *service* to customers by taking their order and bringing their food.

petition She is going around the neighborhood to get people to sign a *petition* that would require the city to put a traffic light on our corner.

required   compulsory   mandatory   imperative   requisite

ADJECTIVE: made necessary; called for or needed.

required U.S. history is a *required* course in this high school; you have to pass it to graduate. Wearing a helmet at bat is *required* in Little League baseball.

compulsory In some countries, serving in the army is *compulsory* for both men and women.

mandatory Though many safety experts say that all cars should have protective air bags, not all do, because it is not *mandatory.*

imperative Since you missed the first three meetings, it's absolutely *imperative* that you attend this one.

requisite He didn't get the job because he doesn't have the *requisite* experience.

research   investigation   study   probe   scrutiny

NOUN: the careful study or testing of something to learn new facts.

research Juan went to the library to do *research* for his term paper. The author Antonia Fraser did extensive *research* for her famous book *Mary Queen of Scots.*

investigation The detective made a careful *investigation* of the house and yard in a search for clues.

study For years Janet has been interested in the *study* of ancient Egypt.

probe The newspaper published a special series of articles as part of its *probe* into corruption in the building industry.

scrutiny The political records of the candidates came under close *scrutiny* by the League of Women Voters.

Kim is doing **research** for her science report on frogs.

We went to a pond near school to make a **study** of the wildlife there.

resist   oppose defy combat withstand

VERB: to fight or go against.

resist France was defeated by Germany early in World War II, but some French people continued to *resist* even after the surrender.

oppose Many Americans *opposed* U.S. involvement in the Vietnam War and carried out protests against it.

defy The American naval hero John Paul Jones is famous for the way he *defied* British forces who asked him to surrender.

combat In 1955 Jonas Salk developed a vaccine that could be used to *combat* polio, which had long been a deadly disease.

withstand Castles of the Middle Ages were built with high stone walls to help them *withstand* enemy attacks.

Antonyms: **submit, yield.**

respect   honor esteem admiration regard

NOUN: a good opinion of the worth or value of something.

respect I disagree with him, but I *respect* the fact that he wasn't afraid to speak out. Tim asked his Grandma for advice; he has a lot of *respect* for her opinion.

honor The Nobel Peace Prize was awarded to Ralph Bunche in 1950, making him the first black American to receive this *honor.*

esteem George Washington was held in high *esteem* by the people of his time.

admiration In the 1930's Amelia Earhart won the *admiration* of many for her courage as a pilot.

regard He's a selfish person who shows little *regard* for the feelings of others.

Antonyms: **disrespect, scorn.**

rest   break recess pause respite

NOUN: a time of sleep, relaxing, or not being active.

rest When they were halfway up the hill, they stopped for a *rest*. He's worn out from working such long hours at the office, and he needs a few days *rest.*

break Many American businesses have a "coffee *break"* in the middle of the morning when people stop work for a short time.

recess At 10:15 the class has *recess* for 20 minutes, and the children can go out to play on the playground.

pause The actor forgot what his next line was, and there was a long *pause* as the other actors waited for him to speak.

respite They drove straight through without a stop, except for one brief *respite* when they pulled off the road to enjoy the view of the ocean.

result effect consequence outcome upshot

NOUN: something that happens because of something else.

result As a *result* of the Spanish-American War, the island of Cuba became free of Spain. He waited anxiously to learn the *results* of his medical exam.

effect One *effect* of our city's rapid growth has been an increase in air pollution.

consequence He got three speeding tickets within a year, and as a *consequence* his driver's license was suspended.

outcome The election was so close that all the votes have to be counted again, and it will be at least a week before the final *outcome* is known.

upshot A large group of parents met with the principal to protest the plan for year-round schools—the *upshot* of the meeting is that the plan will not be used.

The **results** of the test showed that the water was polluted.

As a **consequence,** the beach had to be closed.

return recur revert recover

VERB: to go or send back to some place or condition.

return Birds can fly far south in winter and then *return* the next spring to the place where they had been. I have to *return* this book to the library, because it's due today.

recur The song was played at the beginning of the movie, and then the melody kept *recurring* in the background all through the film.

revert I noticed some clothes on the floor of Jed's room; I hope he hasn't *reverted* to his old habit of leaving everything scattered around.

recover She was quite sick for a while, but now she's *recovered* her health and she's back at work.

rich   wealthy   affluent   prosperous

ADJECTIVE: having a lot of money, property, or other valuable things.

rich   John D. Rockefeller became *rich* by owning a huge oil business. Tennis was once a *rich* person's sport, but now all kinds of people play the game.

wealthy   Many *wealthy* families from Milwaukee and Chicago have summer homes on the Wisconsin lakes.

affluent   Fairfield County, Connecticut is an *affluent* suburban area near New York City featuring large homes and expensive shops.

prosperous   Though its economy was nearly destroyed by World War II, West Germany recovered and became Europe's most *prosperous* nation.

<u>Antonym:</u> **poor.**

All students have the **right** to borrow books from the library.

Only seniors have the **privilege** of eating lunch out in the yard.

right   prerogative   privilege   power

NOUN: something that is fair and proper for a person to do or have.

right   The *right* of free speech means that a person cannot be arrested for saying something against the government. American citizens have the *right* to move or travel from one state to another as they wish.

prerogative   People usually cast their vote by means of a voting machine, but they also have the *prerogative* of sending in a written ballot by mail.

privilege   Having a driver's license is a *privilege* that can be taken away if you do not drive carefully.

power   The Supreme Court has the *power* to reverse a decision that has been made by a lower court.

rock   wave sway swing toss

VERB: to move back and forth or from side to side.

rock If the baby has a hard time getting to sleep, Mom *rocks* her gently in her arms. When we went out rowing, Marty kept *rocking* the boat back and forth to try to scare me.

wave Tara *waved* her hand over her head so that we would see her in the crowd.

sway A light wind blew up off the lake, causing the trees along the shoreline to *sway* back and forth.

swing To bunt a ball in baseball, you don't *swing* the bat, you just hold it out straight in front of you.

toss During the storm, huge waves *tossed* the ship about on the water.

room   space range expanse extent

NOUN: any area having a certain purpose or identity.

room They want to add an extra *room* to the house to use as a home office. Our garage is so full of tools and other things that there's no *room* for the car.

space Though Millie uses most of her garden to grow vegetables, she has a little *space* on the side for flowers.

range The coyote once lived only in the West, but now its *range* extends over almost all of North America.

expanse Much of the state of Texas is part of the Great Plains, a broad *expanse* of flat, dry land.

extent I had thought of New York City as being just Manhattan Island, so when I saw the whole city from the air I was amazed at its vast *extent.*

rough   rugged coarse uneven bumpy

ADJECTIVE: having an irregular surface; not smooth or even.

rough To reach the cabin, you get off the paved highway and drive five miles over *rough* dirt roads. I don't like to wear that sweater, because the wool is too *rough* against my skin.

rugged The state of Maine is known for its *rugged* coastline, with hundreds of rocky bays and inlets.

coarse Sandpaper has a *coarse* surface that is rubbed against wood to make the wood smooth.

uneven They want to replace their kitchen floor because the linoleum has gotten warped and *uneven* from water spilling on it.

bumpy It was a *bumpy* plane flight down to Miami because of the thunderstorm.
Antonyms: **smooth, even.**

round circular spherical globular

ADJECTIVE: shaped like a ball or a globe, or like a circle or curve.

round The letter **i** is made with a straight line and a small *round* dot. The ball used in football is not *round*, which causes it to bounce in an odd way.

circular An ice skater forms a figure 8 by joining together two *circular* patterns on the ice.

spherical The shape of the earth is not exactly *spherical;* it is slightly flattened at the North and South Poles.

globular When children blow soap bubbles with a stick, the bubbles come out through the hole in a *globular* shape.

rude impolite impertinent insolent sassy

ADJECTIVE: showing or having bad manners.

rude She was *rude* to the caller and slammed the phone down without saying good-bye. It was *rude* of him to push ahead to the front of the line.

impolite It is *impolite* to interrupt when someone else is speaking.

impertinent When the professor asked for comments, one *impertinent* freshman said, "Let me correct you on something, Prof."

insolent He has an *insolent* attitude in school and never wants to do what the teachers say.

sassy The actress Thelma Ritter received many Oscar nominations for playing sharp, *sassy* characters who were always ready with a quick remark.

Antonym: **polite, courteous.**

rule law regulation code statute

NOUN: a statement telling what is allowed or not allowed.

rule In this school there is a *rule* against running in the halls. We have a *rule* in our house—no watching TV on school nights until your homework is done.

law Virtually every country in the world has *laws* against crimes such as murder and robbery.

regulation The state of California enforces strict smog *regulations* to control air pollution by cars.

code Many businesses follow a dress *code* that states what kind of clothing is acceptable to wear to work and what is not.

statute Some crimes have a *statute* of limitations, which means that there is a limit on how long afterward someone can be charged with the crime.

▶ The terms **rule** and **law** are very close; a *law* is usually made by a government and is more official and more exact than a *rule.*

rumor   gossip hearsay talk

NOUN: a story or report that is believed and passed on without any proof.

rumor The girls raced down to the Park Hotel when they heard a *rumor* that their favorite rock group was staying there. Because the Bears are having such a poor season, there are *rumors* that the coach will be fired.

gossip For many years Louella Parsons wrote a newspaper column in which she reported *gossip* about the private lives of movie stars.

hearsay If a witness in court says he saw something happen, that is evidence, but if he says someone told him it happened, that is just *hearsay.*

talk Asked for a comment on the story that the city was in financial difficulty, the mayor said, "This city is not broke—that's just a lot of *talk!"*

run   dash race sprint charge

VERB: to go by moving the legs more quickly than when walking.

run In the marathon event you have to *run* more than 26 miles. If there is a fire here you are supposed to walk, not *run,* to the nearest exit.

dash The pitch got by the catcher, and Jones *dashed* home from third with the winning run.

race He was late for his bus, so he *raced* out the door and down to the corner.

sprint The football coach timed how fast each player could *sprint* 40 yards.

charge In the Civil War, many battles involved the troops of one side *charging* on foot toward the enemy troops.

▶ It's not certain which verb in English has the most different meanings, but **run** is the one with the most definitions in modern dictionaries. Among these many meanings are: to *run* a business; to *run* for mayor; to *run* into trouble; a train that *runs* to Boston; a play *running* on Broadway; a program that *runs* on a computer.

The boys had to **run** around the track.   Mike **sprinted** at the end and finished first.

sad unhappy lonely gloomy mournful depressed

ADJECTIVE: feeling sorrow.

sad Alex was *sad* when his good friend moved away to another city. I liked the movie *Bambi,* but it was *sad* when the mother deer died in the fire.

unhappy Megan was *unhappy* about losing the lucky charm bracelet her grandmother gave her.

lonely Carl was *lonely* when he first went away to college; he missed his family.

gloomy It was a *gloomy* November day, with dark clouds hiding the sun and a cold rain falling.

mournful The great country singer Hank Williams was famous for such *mournful* tunes as "I'm So Lonesome I Could Cry" and "Cold, Cold Heart."

depressed She was *depressed* about losing her job, so I'm glad she found another one so quickly.

Antonym: **happy.**

safe secure unhurt protected impregnable

ADJECTIVE: free from harm or danger.

safe To be *safe,* we always wear life jackets whenever we go out in the boat. People are afraid to go into that park at night; they don't think it's *safe.*

secure Dana loved the *secure* feeling of being snug in bed while a storm raged outside.

unhurt The car was badly damaged when it hit the tree, but the driver was completely *unhurt.*

protected A turtle is *protected* from attack by its heavy shell.

impregnable The British fortress of Singapore was thought to be *impregnable* to attack by sea, but the Japanese took it in 1941 by attacking from the land side.

Antonyms: **dangerous, unsafe.**

sale exchange auction bargain

NOUN: a selling or trading of something.

sale The week before Thanksgiving, the supermarket has a special *sale* on turkeys. Most states charge a tax on the *sale* of such items as clothing, furniture, and automobiles.

exchange The tenants received a month's free rent in *exchange* for painting their apartment themselves.

auction An *auction* of Oriental rugs was held at a local hotel, and some rugs sold for as much as $100,000.

bargain There is a discount store near us that has great *bargains* on clothing.

same identical equal equivalent alike

ADJECTIVE: being exactly like another.

same The Evening News show is on at the *same* time every night. The words "theater" and "theatre" have different spellings but the *same* meaning.

identical Jon and Jim are *identical* twins, so it's hard to tell which one is which.

equal The recipe for the cream sauce calls for *equal* amounts of flour and butter, two tablespoons each.

equivalent Water freezes at 0° Celsius; this is *equivalent* to 32° Fahrenheit.

alike Of all the millions of snowflakes that fall, no two are shaped exactly *alike*.

The Johnson family all wore the **same** colors to the football game.

The cheerleaders were all wearing **identical** outfits.

say tell express state voice utter

VERB: to make something known in words; speak in a certain way.

say I'll *say* "Go" as the signal to start the race. Dave told me he was going out, but he didn't *say* where he was going.

tell When Bobby goes to bed, he likes to have his mom *tell* him a bedtime story.

express The mayor asked for questions from the audience, and several people *expressed* their disagreement with his plan.

state When I called, I got a recording asking me to *state* my name and message.

voice No one will know what you think about that if you don't speak up and *voice* your opinion.

utter When she told me about it, I was so surprised I couldn't *utter* a single word.

saying   expression phrase proverb motto

NOUN: a well-known group of words.

saying If Mom wants me to speed up, she uses the old *saying,* "He who hesitates is lost;" to slow me down she has another, "Look before you leap."

expression "Have a nice day" is an *expression* that is used so often that it has almost become meaningless.

phrase The single word "break" also appears in many common *phrases,* such as "break up," "break down," "break in," and "break out."

proverb The *proverb* "a stitch in time saves nine" means that if you deal with a small problem right away, it won't become a bigger one later.

motto "Be prepared" is the well-known *motto* of the Boy Scouts of America.

scare   frighten alarm startle upset

VERB: to cause fear; make afraid.

scare The campers told ghost stories at night to *scare* one another. The children were *scared* by the thunder and lightning, so they all huddled together in bed.

frighten The dog's barking *frightened* the little girl, and she began to cry.

alarm Late last night she was *alarmed* by a clanging noise outside her window; it turned out a raccoon had knocked over her garbage can.

startle I *startled* Mom when I touched her; she hadn't heard me come in.

upset Usually I don't mind flying, but I do get *upset* if the plane starts bouncing around in a storm.

Antonyms: **reassure, comfort.**

Royce was **scared** by the ghost story he was reading.

He was **startled** when the wind suddenly blew the door shut.

schedule   timetable program agenda

NOUN: a list of items that will occur or be done in a certain order.

schedule For the soccer season we get a *schedule* telling when and where our team plays and who we play. According to the airline *schedule,* there is one nonstop flight from here to New York, at 7:45 A.M.

timetable The railroad publishes a *timetable* listing all the trains running to and from the city and the time they leave.

program Here's the *program* for the Thanksgiving show—we'd better get there early, because it says that Jimmy's class does their song first.

agenda The sales manager had prepared an *agenda* for the sales meeting, telling which product would be discussed at each time during the day.

scream   shriek howl screech wail

VERB to make a loud, often high-pitched noise.

scream Cindy went to see a scary movie, and she *screamed* when the monster appeared. Everyone *screamed* as the roller coaster took a sudden drop.

shriek When the magician pulled a rabbit out of his hat, the little children *shrieked* with joy and excitement.

howl The dog was locked outside by mistake, and he was *howling* at the back door to get in.

screech Roger had to jam on the the brakes to avoid hitting a cat, and his tires *screeched* as the car came to a sudden stop.

wail When a fire truck goes by here with its siren on, you can hear the coyotes *wailing* in answer to it.

search   explore inspect scout comb

VERB: to look carefully to find something; go over an area closely.

search The police are *searching* for a man who robbed the bank downtown. Heidi likes to collect old children's books, and she *searches* in bookstores all over town for the ones she wants.

explore President Thomas Jefferson sent the pioneers Lewis and Clark to *explore* the West and report back on what they found.

inspect Before clothes are sold, they are *inspected* by someone to make sure that they have been made properly.

scout Major-league baseball teams *scout* games played by high schools and colleges, looking for promising young players.

comb Many people *combed* the woods looking for the little boy who was lost, until he was finally found by a forest ranger.

secret   confidential hidden undercover covert

ADJECTIVE: known only to one person or a few; kept from most people.

secret The boys have a clubhouse and they won't let in anyone who doesn't know the *secret* password. "The *Secret* Life of Walter Mitty" is a famous story about a quiet, ordinary man who imagines himself having great adventures.

confidential The report is marked *Confidential,* and no one in the company is supposed to read it except the president.

hidden It seemed the man was just looking at the scenery, but he had a *hidden* camera and was photographing planes as they left the military base.

undercover *The Spy Wore Red* was a best-selling book about a woman's life as an *undercover* agent in World War II.

covert The U.S. Central Intelligence Agency engages in *covert* operations to try to learn the plans of enemy governments.

Antonyms: **open, public.**

security   safety protection safekeeping

NOUN: the fact of being secure against danger or loss.

security The office building has a *security* guard who watches to make sure that no one steals anything from the building. The airport has very tight *security* so that no one can get on a plane with a weapon.

safety I know you think that bicycle helmet looks funny on you, but you have to wear it anyway, as a matter of *safety.*

protection When he goes to the beach, he puts on a heavy sunscreen cream as *protection* against sunburn.

safekeeping Mrs. Garson left her jewels with the hotel manager for *safekeeping* while she was in the city.

see   look watch stare regard examine

VERB: to sense with the eyes.

see It was really foggy, and we could only *see* a short way down the road. Dad asked me to look in the mailbox and *see* if the mail had come yet.

look Dick did not *look* where he was going, and he tripped over a rock.

watch Gail left work early to *watch* her daughter play a tennis match at school.

stare The little boy had never seen a jet airliner up close, and he *stared* in amazement at how big it was.

regard She *regarded* the big dog nervously as it moved closer to her.

examine He told us the coin seemed to be genuine, but said he would have to *examine* it closely with a magnifying glass to make sure.

seem   appear resemble

VERB: to look like; give the impression of.

seem Mike *seems* to be upset about something—why don't you ask him what's wrong? She's well over seventy, but she *seems* much younger because she has so much spirit and energy.

appear As it rose over the hills, the full moon *appeared* to be a huge orange circle in the sky.

resemble The harmless bull snake *resembles* the poisonous rattlesnake, and many people are not able to tell the difference.

Mrs. Garcia **sells** her paintings at the Midtown Mall on weekends.

The Lux Gallery is going to **auction** off a famous painting this afternoon.

sell   market auction peddle

VERB: to turn an item over to someone else in return for money.

sell Doug got together some clothes and books to *sell* at his neighbor's garage sale. The import shop on Main Street *sells* beautiful Irish fisherman's sweaters.

market Japanese auto manufacturers have had great success in *marketing* their cars in the United States.

auction Many famous paintings have been *auctioned* at Sotheby's, the well-known London art dealer.

peddle The owner of that supermarket chain got his start many years ago by *peddling* vegetables from a cart.

Antonym: **buy.**

sense   wisdom judgment intelligence reason

NOUN: the ability to use the mind to make decisions.

sense You'll do well on the science test if you study the chapter and just use common *sense* in answering the questions. Emily has a poor *sense* of direction, and she often gets lost.

wisdom King Solomon of ancient times was known for his great *wisdom* in making decisions.

judgment There is no doubt that Shelly is very smart, but she has done some things that don't show good *judgment*.

intelligence Rosa learns new things quickly, which is a sign of high *intelligence*.

reason "Risk" is a game that calls for players to use *reason* rather than just memorizing information.

separate   distinct individual disconnected

ADJECTIVE: apart from others.

separate In some elementary schools, the kindergarten classrooms are kept *separate* from the other classes. Craig's parents are looking for a larger house so each of the children can have a *separate* bedroom.

distinct Most crocodiles are *distinct* from alligators because their snout comes to a point in front, while the alligator's is more rounded.

individual An effective speaker will focus on *individual* faces in the audience rather than try to speak to the entire group.

disconnected Rachel stared out the window while *disconnected* thoughts and impressions floated through her mind.

separate   divide part split sever

VERB: to break into sections or pieces; set or place apart.

separate The first step in making a souffle is to *separate* the egg yolks from the white part of the eggs. Prospectors in the Old West used a pan filled with gravel and water to *separate* gold from worthless stones.

divide The equator is an imaginary line that *divides* the earth into the Northern Hemisphere and the Southern Hemisphere.

part Maria thought her hair would look better if she *parted* it on the side instead of in the middle.

split When he was a young man, Abraham Lincoln earned money by *splitting* logs for fence rails and firewood.

sever Lightning hit the tree, and the largest branch was *severed* from the trunk.
Antonym: **combine.**

series   set succession order sequence

NOUN: a number of things of the same kind that come one after another.

series This TV program is about the *series* of events that led up to the Civil War. The Hardy Boys mystery stories are a popular *series* of books for young readers.

set He bought a matched *set* of pots and pans of various sizes.

succession Several Presidents have served two terms in office, but only Grover Cleveland served two terms that were not in *succession.*

order The actors were listed in the program in the *order* of their appearance on stage, instead of the stars being listed first.

sequence Chris had the right numbers for Grandpa's zip code, but he put them in the wrong *sequence*—he wrote "14017" instead of "10471."

serious   solemn grave somber

ADJECTIVE: involving deep thought or important matters; not light or funny.

serious Dan's mom had a *serious* talk with him about his college plans. Red Buttons, a comedian, won an Oscar for a *serious* role in the war film *Sayonara.*

solemn She's a very *solemn* child who seldom laughs or smiles.

grave The doctor had a *grave* expression on his face as he explained to the patient why she needed an operation right away.

somber In *Guernica,* his painting of a tragic event of the Spanish Civil War, the artist Pablo Picasso used only *somber* grays and black, not bright colors.

Antonyms: **careless, frivolous.**

Jan's a **serious** photographer who takes care with her pictures.

No matter what we did, the guard always kept a **solemn** expression.

service worship rite ritual

NOUN: a religious ceremony.

service Their whole family attends church *services* together each Sunday morning. On the anniversary of the battle, there was a memorial *service* held on the battlefield to honor those who died there.

worship The place of *worship* in the Muslim faith is known as a mosque.

rite At many weddings, the marriage *rites* are followed by a party to honor the bride and groom.

ritual In the Jewish religion, a Bar Mitzvah is a *ritual* that marks a boy's coming of age as a man.

set fix establish secure settle implant

VERB: to put or hold in a certain place or position.

set If no one is home, just *set* the package down on the front porch. Let's *set* a time now for our meeting next week.

fix The school board is looking over all the vacant land in the area, trying to *fix* the spot where the new school should be.

establish The Spanish were the first to *establish* colonies in North America; Mexico City was 100 years old by the time the Pilgrims landed in Massachusetts.

secure I don't think that anchor is heavy enough to keep the boat from drifting away—you'd better *secure* the boat to the dock with a rope.

settle The bird flew back and forth around the yard for a few minutes and then finally *settled* on a large tree branch.

implant The flagpole is *implanted* in the ground with concrete so that it can't be blown over by the wind.

several some various numerous

ADJECTIVE: an indefinite number that is more than two.

several *Several* people at school told her they like her new hairstyle. Though sharks are mainly found in warm seas, *several* kinds do live in cooler waters.

some Most of us ride the bus, but *some* children who live nearby walk to school.

various The drama club wants to raise money for a trip to England, and they are discussing *various* ways to do it.

numerous The newspaper received *numerous* letters of protest from senior citizens about its editorial on Social Security payments.

▶ None of the words above is precise in meaning, but **several** applies to the smallest amount, and it can mean as few as three or four. The other words all describe larger amounts, much larger in the case of **numerous.**

shake   tremble shiver shudder quiver

VERB: to move up and down or from side to side in short, quick movements.

shake *Shake* the carton well before you pour the orange juice. The building is next to the railroad tracks, and the whole place *shakes* when a train goes by.

tremble When Willie put the last block on top, the tower *trembled* for a moment and then crashed to the floor.

shiver The dog sat on the porch, *shivering* with cold and howling to get inside.

shudder We were lucky when our car skidded off the road—I *shudder* to think what might have happened if we had hit a tree instead of a snowbank.

quiver The deer heard us and stood absolutely still, with its only movement the *quivering* of its nostrils as it tried to catch our scent on the wind.

Cathy **shared** her popcorn with her little brother Andrew.

He **divided** his candy bar in half so that he could give her a piece.

share   split divide allot

VERB: to separate a whole into smaller parts to be given out.

share Joe cut the apple into pieces to *share* with his friends. Justin ate his candy bar quickly, so he wouldn't have to *share* it with anyone.

split I don't really want this whole sandwich—I'll *split* it with you if you're hungry.

divide Kim and her brothers *divided* up the work of cleaning the kitchen so that it would get done faster.

allot Mrs. Lerner has a month's vacation to spend in four different countries in Europe, and she is *allotting* one week's time to each.

sharp   keen acute quick cutting

ADJECTIVE: fast and exact in thinking or sensing.

sharp Steven's great-grandmother is 96 years old, but her mind is still *sharp*. With its *sharp* eyes, an eagle can see its prey from high in the sky.

keen David's *keen* intelligence makes him able to grasp new ideas right away.

acute Rabbits have an *acute* sense of hearing and run at the slightest indication of danger.

quick Miguel had the flu and missed a week of school, but with his *quick* mind and good study habits he was able to catch up.

cutting In his movies the comedian Groucho Marx had a *cutting* wit and was always poking fun at self-important people.

Antonym: **dull.**

shift   transport transfer convey

VERB: to move or change from one to another.

shift As the car turned the corner, I heard the boxes in the trunk *shift* from one side to the other. Greg didn't like playing catcher, but he's been doing well since he was *shifted* to the outfield.

transport Oil shipments are *transported* around the world in huge ships called "supertankers."

transfer Mr. Blake has to take a quick course in French; his company is going to *transfer* him to its Paris office next month.

convey When he visited the British Prime Minister, the Vice President *conveyed* the President's best wishes to her.

Antonyms: **stop, stay.**

shine   glow gleam glimmer sparkle twinkle

VERB: to give off a light; be bright.

shine Martha polished the silver candlesticks so they would *shine* brightly for the party. He got his shoes *shined* at the stand in the train station.

glow The embers of the dying fire were *glowing* in the dim room, casting odd shadows on the wall.

gleam As I looked in the dark closet, I saw the cat's eyes *gleaming* in one corner.

glimmer Far across the bay a few lights from the other shore *glimmered* in the darkness.

sparkle The ice-covered bushes *sparkled* in the afternoon sunshine.

twinkle The ceiling of the Space Museum is lighted so that it looks like stars *twinkling* in the night sky.

short   brief quick terse

ADJECTIVE: not long in distance or time.

short It's just a *short* walk from our house to the park, and I go there all the time. Aunt Ann stopped by our house for a *short* visit on her way home from work.

brief The principal began the talent show by making a *brief* welcoming speech, and then he introduced the first act.

quick She made a *quick* stop at the store to pick up some milk for dinner.

terse President Calvin Coolidge had a *terse* manner of speaking; when a woman bet she could make him say at least three words, he answered "You lose."

Antonyms: **long, lengthy.**

show   display reveal exhibit expose

VERB: to allow to be seen; bring into view.

show Kevin took his Dad's old stamp collection to school to *show* it to his class. The American Movie Channel *shows* old Hollywood films.

display The store windows are now set up to *display* the new spring fashions.

reveal The theater curtains opened to *reveal* a stage set that was designed to look like an island in the South Pacific.

exhibit There is a show at the convention center *exhibiting* many new computer products.

expose The ground around the tree had been torn up, and the tree's bare roots were *exposed*.

Antonyms: **hide, conceal.**

Damon **showed** his friends the way to his secret hideout.

He pulled back some branches to **expose** the entrance to a cave.

showy flashy gaudy flamboyant garish

ADJECTIVE: making a show or display; attracting attention.

showy He likes collecting tropical fish because of their bright, *showy* colors. She thinks that wearing a fur coat is *showy,* and she's satisfied with a plain wool coat.

flashy Did you see that *flashy* red sports car that Brent was driving?

gaudy Las Vegas hotels are noted for their *gaudy* furniture and decorations.

flamboyant The writer Tom Wolfe favors a *flamboyant* style of dress; he wears all-white suits and white shoes even in winter.

garish For the party, Jenny wore a *garish* purple polish on her fingernails.

The rose bushes were full of bright, **showy** blossoms.

Jake had on a necktie with a **gaudy** flower pattern.

shrink shrivel decrease condense deflate dwindle

VERB: to make or become smaller in size.

shrink Don't wash that sweater in hot water; it will *shrink* if you do. The Mets are still first, but their big lead over the Cubs has *shrunk* to just one game.

shrivel The dead leaves in the driveway began to *shrivel* up and blow away.

decrease For years the city's population was *decreasing,* but now it's growing.

condense Steve's guidance counselor advised him to *condense* his college essay so that it would fit on one sheet of paper.

deflate The back left tire must have a leak; it seems to be slowly *deflating.*

dwindle Though the play drew large crowds in its opening weeks, attendance has now *dwindled* considerably.

Antonyms: **stretch, increase.**

shy   bashful timid meek diffident

ADJECTIVE: not comfortable in public or in a group of people.

shy Lin is *shy,* and she is nervous when she has to give a report in class. A job in sales is not the best choice for a *shy* person who finds it hard to talk to strangers.

bashful When Duane was introduced to the guests, he felt *bashful* and stared down at the floor.

timid You want to ask Jill to the dance, so don't be *timid* about it—just go do it.

meek The coach told Joni that it was her job as goalie to direct the defense, and that she shouldn't be so *meek* about telling the other players what to do.

diffident The boss wants people to speak out and tell him what they really think, not be *diffident* and hold back their opinions.

Antonyms: **bold, brash.**

sick   ill unhealthy ailing

ADJECTIVE: not in good health; not feeling well.

sick Our teacher is *sick* today, and a substitute will take over the class. I don't want to ride on that roller coaster because I'm afraid I'll be *sick* afterward.

ill Mrs. Banks wrote a note saying that her daughter was *ill* with the flu and would have to stay home from school.

unhealthy He went on a diet to lose weight, but I think he lost too much—it makes him look very *unhealthy.*

ailing A famous story about the baseball hero Babe Ruth tells how he promised to hit a home run to cheer up an *ailing* boy in the hospital.

Antonyms: **well, healthy.**

sickness   illness disease ailment malady

NOUN: a disordered, weakened, or unsound condition.

sickness Was she absent from school because of *sickness,* or did she just have to go somewhere? In a wedding ceremony the bride and groom pledge to love one another in *sickness* and in health.

illness Doctors say that stress is a major factor in many *illnesses*, and they urge people to learn to deal with it.

disease Medical science has been able to control the spread of *diseases* such as smallpox or cholera that used to claim many lives each year.

ailment Many people take aspirin for relief from minor *ailments* such as colds, headaches, and sore muscles.

malady Chad claims to suffer from a mysterious *malady* that prevents him from eating any green vegetables.

side   edge wing border flank margin

NOUN: a point or place away from the center of something.

side Let's plant the roses on the south *side* of the house; that way they'll get plenty of sun. When you set the table, put the forks on the left *side* of the plate.

edge Kate was nervous about going out into the pool, so she hung on to the *edge*.

wing The main part of the White House was built in 1792, but the east *wing* wasn't added until 1942.

border The Halloween napkins were orange, with a black and white *border*.

flank In the army of Alexander the Great, he himself would lead the troops in the center, while other generals commanded the right and left *flanks*.

margin The typewriter is set for a *margin* of one inch on each side of the page.

sign   mark symbol evidence indicator

NOUN: a thing that stands for or shows something else.

sign Dark clouds are a *sign* that rain is coming. Billy did his math homework all by himself tonight—that's a *sign* that he understands the work better now.

mark This red *mark* on the tree means that the trail goes to the right here.

symbol A white dove is often used as a *symbol* of peace, because of the Bible story that tells how this bird brought hope to Noah on the Ark.

evidence His fingerprints in the room were *evidence* that he had been there.

indicator Joe only stops to get gas when the fuel *indicator* is right on empty.

Inspector Lune says these marks are a **sign** that the car thief has been here.

He took a picture of the marks to use as **evidence** in court.

silly foolish absurd ridiculous ludicrous

ADJECTIVE: not serious or intelligent; not showing good sense.

silly David admitted that putting salt in the sugar bowl was a *silly* trick to play on the dinner guests. Anne's joke was *silly*, but she got such a laugh out of telling it that we all laughed along with her.

foolish She felt *foolish* when she realized she'd locked her keys inside her car.

absurd Some people thought it was an *absurd* idea for Christopher Columbus to sail west, and they said he had no hope of finding land.

ridiculous Much of the humor of the "I Love Lucy" show was based on the *ridiculous* situations in which Lucy became involved.

ludicrous In the early days of the automobile there were some *ludicrous* attempts to develop new vehicles, such as a car with a sail behind it like a boat.

Antonyms: **sensible, reasonable.**

similar like comparable akin analogous

ADJECTIVE: not exactly the same but very much alike; of the same kind.

similar Dad's taste in clothes never changes; any new suit he buys is *similar* to the ones he already has. The only true pyramids are the ones in Egypt, but many *similar* buildings were built in America by the Indians.

like The leopard shark gets its name because it has spots *like* those of a leopard.

comparable This new American car is *comparable* to Japanese models such as the Honda Accord.

akin The Senator stated that his opponent's plan to cut American military forces was not only a mistake, but could even be considered *akin* to surrender.

analogous In many ways, the human heart is *analogous* to a pump.

Antonyms: **dissimilar, different.**

since ago subsequently

ADVERB: from then until now.

since Ralph moved to the other side of town last summer, and I haven't seen him *since.* She's trying really hard to quit smoking; she hasn't had a single cigarette *since* Friday.

ago Mr. Sands left for lunch about an hour *ago*, so he should be back shortly.

subsequently The first VCRs to come on the market were very expensive, but *subsequently* the prices dropped.

▶ **Since** is also a synonym for **because.** The two words are very close, and you can choose either one. The only slight difference is that *because* is used more often in short, informal contexts: I like Jim *because* he's so funny.

sincere   honest candid open frank

ADJECTIVE: telling or showing the truth or true feelings.

sincere The runner-up was *sincere* when he congratulated the winner of the spelling bee. Theresa has made a *sincere* effort to improve her grades.

honest I think he's being *honest* when he says the lamp broke by accident.

candid In the interview, the mayor was very *candid,* and he admitted he'd been wrong not to step in to settle the school strike.

open The boss promised that the meeting would be an *open* discussion in which each employee would have the chance to ask him questions.

frank You asked me, so I'll be *frank*—I don't think that dress looks good on you.

<u>Antonyms:</u> **insincere, deceitful.**

single   lone sole unique solitary

ADJECTIVE: being the only one.

single An accident blocked all but one lane, and only a *single* line of cars could get by. The unicorn is pictured with a *single* horn in the middle of its forehead.

lone The night was still, except for one *lone* owl hooting softly in the darkness.

sole He bought his partner's share of the business, and he is now the *sole* owner of the company.

unique The bat is *unique* among mammals; it is the only one that can fly.

solitary When the U.S. Congress voted to enter World War II, there was just one *solitary* vote against it, by Jeanette Rankin of Wyoming.

At lunch time, there was only a **single** empty seat at the counter.

At closing time, there was just a **lone** customer sitting there.

size dimension area extent magnitude expanse

NOUN: the amount of space that something takes up.

size The first thing I noticed about the lion was the huge *size* of its head. He's doing well in high school football, but I don't think he has enough *size* to play college football.

dimension According to this floor plan, the *dimensions* of the living room in the new home are twelve feet by twenty feet.

area Alaska is the largest state in *area,* though it has the smallest number of people.

extent When the governor saw the *extent* of the flooding, he declared the entire county a disaster area.

magnitude The state of Washington had volcanic eruptions before Mount St. Helens, but never one of such great *magnitude.*

expanse Argentina raises huge herds of cattle on the Pampas, a vast *expanse* of flat grassland extending across the center of the country.

skin hide rind pelt peel

NOUN: a surface or outer layer that covers or protects.

skin She wears a wide-brimmed hat when she goes out in the sun, so that she won't get too many freckles on her *skin.*

hide The Indians of the Great Plains used buffalo *hides* for clothing and tents, and buffalo meat was an important part of their diet.

rind Some kinds of expensive cheeses, such as Brie or Stilton, have a hard *rind* that surrounds the cheese.

pelt France built a valuable fur trade in North America in the 1700's, when beaver *pelts* brought a high price for use as hats.

peel In this cake recipe, lemon *peels* are used to make the lemon frosting.

sky atmosphere heavens space

NOUN: the area that surrounds the earth, extending out into the universe.

sky It was a beautiful June morning, and there wasn't a single cloud in the *sky.* He claims that when he was camping out in the desert, he saw a UFO speeding across the night *sky.*

atmosphere The earth's *atmosphere* contains many aerosols, which are tiny solid particles suspended in the air.

heavens The planet Venus can be seen as either the first star of evening or the last star before morning, depending on its position in the *heavens.*

space The moon moves through *space* as it rotates around the earth.

The picture was **slanting** to one side and Dad had to straighten it out.

Chuck **leaned** back in his chair and watched Dad do the work.

slant   lean slope tilt tip

VERB: to move or lie at an angle.

slant School desks are usually made so that the top *slants* down toward the student. The italic form of type *slants* to the right, *like this.*

lean The *Leaning* Tower of Pisa is a famous building in Italy that is at an angle to the ground, rather than straight up and down.

slope Ski trails for experts *slope* more steeply than the trails for beginners.

tilt When you play a pinball machine, you are not supposed to *tilt* the machine to one side to get the ball to roll a certain way.

tip In former times men always wore hats when out on the street, and a man was expected to *tip* his hat when meeting a woman, as a sign of respect.

sleep   rest nap slumber snooze

NOUN: a time when humans or animals relax and stop being active.

sleep Greg is tired because he didn't get enough *sleep* last night. Nocturnal animals, such as bats, get their *sleep* during the day and hunt for food at night.

rest Most day-care centers have a regular time for *rest,* when the children must lie down even if they don't fall asleep.

nap The baby has to take a *nap* for about an hour every afternoon.

slumber Cars were going up and down outside his house all night, but nothing could disturb his *slumber* and he didn't wake up until morning.

snooze I thought Grandpa was sitting there to watch the ballgame, but then I saw he was just taking a short *snooze* in his chair.

slow   gradual sluggish dawdling

ADJECTIVE: taking a long time or longer than usual.

slow Kerry is a *slow* eater and is always the last in the family to finish a meal. There is *slow* traffic all along the Coast Highway today because of the fog.

gradual Experts agree that a *gradual* weight loss over a period of time is healthier than a crash diet to take off weight right away.

sluggish The lower Missouri River flows at a *sluggish* rate, and in some places it's hard to tell that the current is even moving.

dawdling Jason didn't want to come in from playing, and when his mother called him he moved along with a lazy, *dawdling* walk.

Antonyms: **fast, quick, rapid.**

small   little tiny miniature diminutive

ADJECTIVE: not large in size or number.

small The store manager has a *small* office in back, with just enough room for a desk and chair. Shannon keeps a *small* savings account with about $50 in it.

little All the snow is melted now, except for a few *little* patches here and there in the shade.

tiny A sieve has *tiny* holes so that water can go through, but solid things cannot.

miniature Some kinds of dogs, such as the collie and the poodle, have *miniature* breeds that look just like the larger version.

diminutive Bernadette Peters is a *diminutive* actress with a large singing voice.

Antonyms: **large, big.**

▶ **Small** and **little** are very close, and in many situations either word can be used. However, *small* tends to be more exact and more formal: The owl feeds on *small* animals, such as mice and rats. We just got a cute *little* dog we named "Peppy."

smart   intelligent bright clever wise

ADJECTIVE: having a good mind; quick to learn and understand.

smart Annie is very *smart* and catches on to new ideas easily. Jeff thinks he's so *smart* because he was the only one who got 100% on the math test.

intelligent Scientists consider the dolphin to be among the most *intelligent* of animals, along with the chimpanzee and the dog.

bright The teacher said Kelly is a *bright* child who should do well in first grade.

clever Francisco is very *clever* at doing things with computers; he can figure out how to work a new program as soon as he gets it.

wise The Cherokee Indian chief Sequoyah was a *wise* leader who invented an alphabet for his people and taught thousands of them to read and write.

smell   scent aroma odor stench

NOUN: something that can be sensed by the nose.

smell The season of fall makes me think of cool, damp evenings with the *smell* of wet leaves on the ground. Eric likes the *smell* of his dad's after-shave lotion and always wants to borrow some when he has a date.

scent A bloodhound has such a keen nose that it can follow a *scent* that is several hours old.

aroma On Saturday morning, she was awakened by the pleasant *aroma* of fresh coffee being brewed.

odor He spilled some fuel at the gas pump and had to wash his hands to get rid of the strong *odor* of gasoline.

stench When we got back from vacation, I found an old carton of sour milk in the back of the refrigerator—what a *stench!*

sneaky   sly underhanded devious

ADJECTIVE: designed to trick or fool; secret or dishonest.

sneaky I think it was *sneaky* of Rex to try to get a date with Matt's girlfriend while Matt was out of town.

sly The fox has often been called a *sly* animal, because it is so good at getting away from hunters who are following it.

underhanded A noted biography of Lyndon Johnson says he used *underhanded* methods to win an election for Senator after his opponent had gotten more votes.

devious The mail-order business is accused of *devious* sales practices, such as billing twice for the same item or delivering a cheaper item than was ordered.

Antonyms: **open, aboveboard.**

social   sociable neighborly companionable

ADJECTIVE: having to do with friends or friendly relations.

social He doesn't like to stay at the college on weekends, because there are so few *social* activities on campus. Charlie is very bright, but he needs to develop better *social* skills so as not to hurt other people's feelings.

sociable Anita is a *sociable* person who loves to go to dances and to give parties for her friends.

neighborly Everyone in the building was so *neighborly* that Luis felt right at home in his new apartment.

companionable The people in that car pool have all been riding together for a long time, and they are a very *companionable* group.

Antonyms: **antisocial, unfriendly.**

soft   smooth sleek silky

ADJECTIVE: not rough or coarse.

soft Tammy likes to pet the cat to feel its *soft* fur. He prefers wearing cotton sweaters to woolen ones, because cotton is *softer* than wool.

smooth When I rubbed my hand against the baby's cheek, I was amazed at how *smooth* his skin was.

sleek The race horses moved toward the starting gate, their *sleek* coats shining in the sun.

silky The 1940's actress Veronica Lake was known for the way she wore her long, *silky* blonde hair hanging down over one eye.

solid   hard firm stiff

ADJECTIVE: having a definite shape and some amount of firmness.

solid We couldn't plant the tree there—we ran into *solid* rock after digging down only a foot or so. For a few days after the operation he didn't eat any *solid* food, just things like soup or pudding.

hard She always brings a pillow with her to the football games, because she hates sitting on the *hard* concrete seats of the stadium.

firm Deborah has a bad back, so she is supposed to sleep on a *firm* mattress.

stiff For his science project, Terry mounted his rock samples on a *stiff* piece of cardboard.

By January, the lake had frozen **solid** so that we could skate on it.

Jennifer skated so long that her hands got **stiff** from the cold.

something

PRONOUN: an unknown or unnamed thing.

▶ There is no real synonym for **something**. You can still vary your writing, though, by choosing more exact words instead. "Here's *something* safe about this garage door—it won't close if *something* is in the way. *Something* stops the motor automatically." This can become, "This garage door is safe because it won't close if an object is in the way. An emergency device stops the motor automatically."

sometimes   occasionally

ADVERB: now and then; at times.

sometimes We usually have cereal for breakfast, but *sometimes* Dad gets up early and makes pancakes. A pro basketball player lives in our apartment building, and *sometimes* we see him in the elevator.

occasionally My grandparents do come out here to visit us *occasionally,* but usually we go back East to visit them instead.

soon   shortly directly presently

ADVERB: in the near future; before long.

soon If we don't get some rain *soon,* there are sure to be some bad brush fires this summer. The American Ballet Theater is coming to town *soon*, and I'll get tickets as soon as they go on sale.

shortly The announcement said that Flight 67 has just landed and will arrive at the gate *shortly.*

directly When she knocked on his office door, he said, "Have a seat outside; I'm making a quick phone call and I'll be with you *directly."*

presently The nurse took the patient's blood pressure, then told him the doctor would be ready to examine him *presently.*

sore   tender sensitive hurting

ADJECTIVE: causing or experiencing pain.

sore His back is *sore* because he strained it trying to lift a heavy box. After her first ballet lesson, Gwen had to soak in a hot tub to relieve her *sore* muscles.

tender Her cut is healed now, but the skin there is still red and *tender.*

sensitive Nora has light blue eyes that are very *sensitive* to the sun, and she has to wear dark glasses when she's out in bright sunlight.

hurting Alan doesn't want any dinner; his stomach is still *hurting* a bit from the hot dog he had for an afternoon snack.

Antonym: **painless.**

space   span separation gap

NOUN: an open distance or empty area between two things.

space We could see the sunset through the *space* between the two tall buildings. When you type your story, leave extra *space* between the title and the story itself.

span The Golden Gate Bridge in San Francisco has a main *span* of 4,200 feet between its two towers.

separation There's room for six tomato plants by the wall there, allowing for a *separation* of about three feet between plants.

gap The Delaware Water *Gap* is a deep, narrow valley formed between two mountains by the waters of the Delaware River.

My dad has a **special** Cubs hat that he always wears to games.

Uncle Bob has a lucky Cubs hat too, but his is **unique.**

special   particular specific unique

ADJECTIVE: different from others.

special My dad wants to lose weight, and his doctor developed a *special* diet for him to follow. The U.S. Congress gave a *special* award to the British leader Sir Winston Churchill, making him an honorary American citizen.

particular I've been shopping in the mall a lot, but I've never gone into that *particular* store because everything there is so expensive.

specific The ability to sleep while hanging upside down, secured by its claws, is a *specific* characteristic of the sloth.

unique Australia is *unique* among the world's nations in that it is the only one that occupies an entire continent by itself.

<u>Antonyms:</u> **general, universal.**

speech   address lecture sermon oration

NOUN: something that is spoken, especially a formal talk given to a group.

speech On Martin Luther King Day, we saw a re-broadcast of his famous "I Have a Dream" *speech*. The person who has the highest average in the class will give a short *speech* at the graduation ceremonies.

address It is a tradition for the President of the U.S. to go before Congress each January to deliver the State of the Union *Address*.

lecture Many students want to take Professor Ellis's American history class because she gives very interesting *lectures*.

sermon One part of a church service is a *sermon* where the minister or priest gives a talk on how the Bible provides a lesson in good behavior.

oration The Democratic Party chose William Jennings Bryan to run for President in 1896 after he gave a long, powerful *oration* at the nominating convention.

spoil   ruin wreck destroy

VERB: to hurt in a serious way, so that value or quality is lost.

spoil The meat was *spoiled* from being left out in the hot sun and had to be thrown away. A sudden rain shower *spoiled* the picnic because everyone got soaking wet.

ruin Just when my picture was almost finished, I accidentally spilled a jar of paint on it and the whole thing was *ruined*.

wreck The waters off Cape Hatteras, North Carolina are called "The Graveyard of the Atlantic" because so many ships have been *wrecked* there in storms.

destroy In the year 79 A.D., a huge volcano erupted near the Roman city of Pompeii and *destroyed* the entire city.

Antonyms: **preserve, improve.**

spot   dot speck blot patch

NOUN: a small part or area that looks different from what is around it.

spot I spilled some tomato sauce and got a red *spot* on my shirt. This plant has little brown *spots* on all the leaves—it must have something wrong with it.

dot With the gray suit he wore a dark red tie with a pattern of small white *dots*.

speck The tabletop was absolutely clean, with not even a *speck* of dust to be seen anywhere.

blot She left the top off her pen and the ink leaked out, making a large blue *blot* on the paper.

patch The sky was a clear, bright blue, with just a few *patches* of white clouds high out over the ocean.

spread   scatter circulate radiate

VERB: to move or extend out over an area.

spread They picked a nice spot on the beach and *spread* their blanket out on the sand. In Kansas the wheat fields *spread* in all directions as far as the eye can see.

scatter To plant these wildflower seeds, you just clear the ground, water it, and then *scatter* the seeds over it.

circulate Blood is pumped out by the heart and *circulates* throughout the body.

radiate They all sat very close to the campfire when it first got going, but as the heat *radiated* outward they gradually moved farther away.

Antonym: **contract.**

Mrs. Todd **spread** a large cloth out for a picnic lunch.

After they ate, she **scattered** bread crumbs for the birds.

squeeze   press squash compress compact

VERB: to push hard to bring the sides or parts of something together.

squeeze *Squeeze* the tube at the bottom and the toothpaste will come out the top. After eating the grapefruit, he *squeezed* the rind to get out the last of the juice.

press When you make the hamburger, just pat the meat together lightly; don't *press* it tight like a snowball.

squash The store clerk packed the raspberries on top of the bag, so that they wouldn't get *squashed* underneath something heavy.

compress Before the sculptor began to work with the clay, she *compressed* it into a small ball to make it easier to handle.

compact This appliance *compacts* a large amount of trash into a small bundle.

stand bear tolerate endure

VERB: to put up with or face something harmful or unpleasant.

stand I could never be a doctor; I can't *stand* the sight of blood. Jeff studied his lines for the play over and over—he couldn't *stand* the thought of forgetting what to say in front of all those people.

bear Tina was going to make the dog sleep outside, but she finally let him in the house; she couldn't *bear* his howling at the door.

tolerate Cheating on a test is not *tolerated* at this college, and any student who does it will be expelled from school.

endure Anyone who serves on a submarine must be able to *endure* long periods of time in a small and enclosed space.

stare gaze gape gawk

VERB: to look long or hard with the eyes wide open.

stare The batter *stared* straight ahead at the pitcher as he waited for the pitch to come. Rob sat *staring* at the menu for a few minutes, and then he whispered to me, "I can't read any of this—the whole thing's in French!"

gaze He was supposed to be paying attention to the teacher, but instead he *gazed* out the window at the clouds drifting by overhead.

gape She's from a very small town, and when she first visited New York City, she stood on the sidewalk *gaping* at the tall buildings.

gawk The policeman told the crowd that had gathered to look at the accident to stop *gawking* and move along.

The girls **stared** at the man sitting across from them.

He just **gazed** out the window as though he didn't notice.

start begin commence initiate

VERB: to cause to be in motion or in being; get moving.

start On cold mornings we sometimes have trouble getting our car to *start.* Even though your report isn't due for a month, you should *start* it soon or you'll have too much to do at the end.

begin I wait for the announcer to say, "And finally it was Mr. Lincoln's turn;" that's my cue to go on stage and *begin* my speech.

commence The contract to build the house states that the work must *commence* no later than thirty days after the date the contract is signed.

initiate Because of many requests from the parents, the school has *initiated* a program to teach computer skills to students.

Antonym: **end, finish, complete.**

statement remark comment assertion pronouncement

NOUN: an idea expressed in speech or writing.

statement In 1928 Calvin Coolidge withdrew from the race for President with the brief *statement,* "I do not choose to run." That actor says he hates publicity—that's an odd *statement* for a person who's always in the news.

remark The principal made a few *remarks* to welcome the parents to Back to School Night.

comment When asked how he liked California, the comedian Fred Allen made the *comment,* "It's a great place to live—if you're an orange."

assertion The company says its new computer will be a top seller, but many experts question this *assertion,* because the machine is so expensive.

pronouncement A cheer went up in the courtroom when the spectators heard the jury's *pronouncement* of not guilty.

stay wait remain linger tarry

VERB: to continue to be in one place; not move on or leave.

stay Michael has a bad cold and is going *stay* in bed today. Andrew asked his mom if his friend Chuck could *stay* for dinner.

wait Don't try to cross the street yet; *wait* until the WALK sign comes on.

remain The company denied that it had any plans to move to the West Coast and said that its office would *remain* in Boston.

linger The smell of burning wood *lingered* in the air after the fire had gone out.

tarry In the story of Cinderella, her fairy godmother tells her not to *tarry* at the ball, or her coach will turn into a pumpkin.

Antonyms: **go, leave.**

steady   regular frequent habitual consistent

ADJECTIVE: going on and on in the same way; constant or continuing.

steady Lance has had several part-time jobs, but now he wants to get a *steady* full-time job. The soccer coach puts Cathy in the middle of the defense because she's a *steady* player who doesn't make mistakes.

regular They are *regular* customers at the restaurant, and the owner always gives them their favorite table by the window.

frequent Most airlines have programs for *frequent* flyers, by which people can get free tickets after they've flown a certain number of miles.

habitual Pictures of the famous news broadcaster Edward R. Murrow almost always show Murrow, a heavy smoker, holding his *habitual* cigarette.

consistent This train gives very *consistent* service; it always gets to the city on time or at most a few minutes late.

<u>Antonyms:</u> **infrequent, irregular.**

step   stage phase degree

NOUN: an action to reach a goal or a completed state.

step The first *step* in putting together the model is to spread all the pieces out on a flat surface. The President stated that he would take any *steps* necessary to help bring peace to the Middle East.

stage If you write a paper according to the Writing Process, the first *stage* is "prewriting," in which you think about what you want to write.

phase A child passes through several *phases* in growing up, such as the period of learning how to talk.

degree A learner's permit to drive is based on the idea that you learn to handle a car by *degrees* over several months before getting your full license.

stick   fasten attach cling adhere

VERB: to keep fixed in a certain spot.

stick Mom always *sticks* notes on the refrigerator door to remind us about things we have to do after school. I stepped on a piece of gum on the sidewalk, and it *stuck* to the bottom of my shoe.

fasten To *fasten* the seat belt, you push this metal buckle into the plastic slot until it clicks.

attach She *attached* the nameplate to her front door with two large screws.

cling Ivy is a plant that can grow up or along a wall by *clinging* to the surface.

adhere One way to remove a stamp from an envelope for a stamp collection is to soak it in warm water until the stamp no longer *adheres* to the envelope.

still   motionless inert stationary

ADJECTIVE: not moving; without motion.

still When the teacher told everyone to line up, Randy would not stand *still* and kept fooling around with the boy behind him.

motionless "Red light—green light" is an old children's game in which you can run on green but must stop and stay *motionless* on red.

inert Some animals will lie on the ground and remain *inert* to fool a predator, because many predators will chase a live animal but ignore one that is dead.

stationary A *stationary* bicycle is an exercise machine that has pedals like a regular bicycle, but stays in one place.

Antonyms: **active, moving.**

Dad told Kim to sit **still** during the play.

When a plane flies low over the theater, the actors remain **motionless** until it passes.

stingy   cheap tight miserly

ADJECTIVE: not willing to give or share something, especially money.

stingy Charles Dickens's "A Christmas Carol" tells how the *stingy* businessman Ebenezer Scrooge paid his workers very little and kept all his money for himself.

cheap I think that buying clothes at "Super-Save" is a good way to save money, but my brother teases me that I'm just too *cheap* to pay full price at the mall.

tight Grandpa likes to joke that the owner of that shop is so *tight* he still has the first nickel he ever made.

miserly The ancient Greek tale of King Midas describes how this *miserly* man asked the gods for the power to turn everything he touched into gold.

Antonym: **generous.**

stock supply inventory stockpile

NOUN: a collection of things stored for future use or sale.

stock The sweater that I wanted to buy is not in *stock* at this store, so they'll have to order it from the main warehouse.

supply The supermarket prepared for Halloween by bringing in a big *supply* of costumes, masks, and candy.

inventory Auto sales have been slow so far this year, and most local dealers have a large *inventory* of unsold cars.

stockpile The dictator claims he is totally committed to peace, but at the same time his army is accumulating huge *stockpiles* of weapons.

stop quit finish halt cease

VERB: to no longer move, go, or act in a certain way; bring to an end.

stop He *stopped* the car at the red light and waited for it to turn green. She wants to lose weight, and she's going to *stop* eating snacks between meals.

quit Larry decided to *quit* playing on the soccer team, because he wanted to play Pop Warner football instead.

finish Lynn and Tom plan to get married, but she's going to *finish* college first.

halt The government ordered the company to *halt* the sale of their new drug, after many complaints that it has dangerous side effects.

cease The owner of the *Daily Voice* newspaper has announced that it will *cease* publishing after today's issue because it is losing so much money.

The painters **stopped** work at noon to have their lunch.

When they **finished** the job, they put their equipment in the truck.

store   market shop stand

NOUN: a place where goods are sold.

store We went to a toy *store* to pick out a birthday present for Jacob. She forgot to buy milk at the supermarket, so she got some at the little *store* on the corner.

market Dad buys fresh fish once a week at a fish *market* down by the harbor.

shop Luke loves any kind of growing plant, and someday he hopes to own a flower *shop.*

stand A farm *stand* near our house sells fruits and vegetables grown by local farmers.

store   save accumulate reserve amass

VERB: to put away and keep for future use.

store Save that box; it's a perfect size to *store* winter clothes over the summer. Donna will have to *store* some of the furniture from her old place; she doesn't have room for all of it in her new apartment.

save Mom *saves* copies of the local newspaper for Janet, because she likes to read them when she's home from college.

accumulate Their house has a woodburning stove for extra heat in the winter, and they spend a lot of time in the fall *accumulating* wood to burn in it.

reserve The library called to say that the book you *reserved* has been returned and is ready for you to take out.

amass The author Carl Sandburg *amassed* a huge amount of information for his six-volume biography of Abraham Lincoln.

Antonyms: **waste, spend.**

story   tale narrative fiction

NOUN: an account that is made up about some event or person.

story "Rip Van Winkle" is a famous *story* by the American author Washington Irving. When I was little, Mom told me bedtime *stories* about Billy Birdwing, a make-believe boy who could fly.

tale The *tale* of Cinderella appears in hundreds of different versions in many countries throughout the world.

narrative In old novels such as *Tom Jones,* it was common for the author to interrupt the *narrative* to make background comments to the reader.

fiction Karen likes to read factual books of history or biography, but her brother prefers to read *fiction.*

▶ Two of these words, **story** and **narrative,** can also apply to accounts that are true, as in a newspaper *story* or a book of history with a fascinating *narrative.*

straight   direct   unswerving

ADJECTIVE: moving in a line from one point to another; not curved or crooked.

straight   Highway 99 is a *straight* road through the valley, with almost no curves or hills. Claire likes to wear her hair short and very *straight,* without any curls.

direct   If you want to take a bus to the art museum, get on the number 10 bus—that one follows the most *direct* route downtown.

unswerving   Once the captain had decided to return to port, he kept the ship on an *unswerving* course until they reached land.

Antonyms: **curved, crooked.**

strange   odd   peculiar   eccentric   weird

ADJECTIVE: not what is to be expected; unusual in a way that is not normal.

strange   *The Strange Case of Dr. Jekyll and Mr. Hyde* is a famous story of a man who becomes two different people, one good and one evil. My computer is not working right, and I keep getting *strange* messages on the screen.

odd   The movie *E.T.* is about an *odd*-looking alien who visits a family on earth.

peculiar   My friend Heather says she thinks Josh likes me—he has a *peculiar* way of showing it, since he's always trying to tease or bother me.

eccentric   James Thurber's story "The Night the Bed Fell" describes his *eccentric* family, including cousin Briggs, who wakes himself up every hour all night long.

weird   The Haunted Mansion at the amusement park always has *weird* noises coming from inside that are supposed to scare you.

Daisy is acting **strange** and hides whenever she hears the doorbell.

I guess she's afraid of the trick or treaters in their **weird** outfits.

stream   flow flood current tide

NOUN: a moving body of water or some similar substance.

stream The pipe broke, and a *stream* of water came pouring out onto the floor.

flow When you water the flowers, adjust the *flow* of the hose so that they just get a light spray.

flood A *flood* of dirty, swirling rainwater rushed through the streets of the town.

current In early times people used to travel on the Mississippi River on rafts that floated downstream with the *current.*

tide You can walk out to the rocks now, but when the *tide* comes up later this afternoon they'll be under water.

▶ All these words are used in other ways, to describe things that are thought of as moving like water. For example, we can refer to a steady *stream* of traffic going over a bridge, the *flow* of paperwork in an office, a *flood* of phone calls about some issue, the changing *current* of public opinion, or the *tide* of human events.

stretch   extend lengthen prolong

VERB: to spread or draw out to greater length.

stretch He *stretched* the rubber band too far, and it snapped in two. The baby was lying on her back, *stretching* her arm up to reach the toy over her head.

extend In order to measure the sofa, the sales clerk had to *extend* the tape measure to its full length.

lengthen As the other runner drew close to her, Tiffany *lengthened* her stride and pulled farther ahead.

prolong When he announces the award winner, he likes to *prolong* the suspense by taking a long time to open the envelope and read the name.

Antonyms: **shorten, shrink.**

strong   powerful hardy robust

ADJECTIVE: having great physical power.

strong A race horse gets its speed from the large, *strong* muscles of its upper legs. Tennis star Steffi Graf is known for her *strong* forehand shots.

powerful The baseball star Roberto Clemente was signed to a pro contract while only a teenager, after a scout noticed his *powerful* throwing arm.

hardy The first expedition to climb Mt. Everest was guided by Tenzing Norgay, a small but very *hardy* man who belonged to the local Sherpa tribe.

robust Theodore Roosevelt was small and sickly as a boy, but after living on a ranch in the West he developed into a *robust* and healthy young man.

Antonym: **weak.**

student pupil scholar learner

NOUN: someone who attends school or studies something.

student That's a large high school, with over 1,000 *students*. All the children in that family are good *students* who get A's and B's on their report cards.

pupil The teacher's edition of the textbook gives the answers to the questions that appear in the *pupil's* book.

scholar Professor Charles Beard of Columbia University was a noted *scholar* in American history.

learner Steven is a very eager *learner* who loves to pick up new information.

stuff substance material element

NOUN: matter of a particular but often unspecified kind.

stuff I washed all my soccer *stuff,* because I have a game today. He forgot to put chlorine in the pool, and now there's some kind of yellow *stuff* on the walls.

substance Diamonds are the hardest *substance* found on earth.

material The animal-rights group is opposed to the wearing of clothing made from *materials* such as fur and leather.

element The ancient Greeks regarded air, fire, earth, and water as the four basic *elements* of life.

subject topic theme

NOUN: something that is thought about, talked about, or written about.

subject We were discussing our vacation plans, but Max changed the *subject* and started talking about a movie he just saw. In a library, fiction books are arranged by author; nonfiction books are arranged by *subject.*

topic My term paper isn't due until May, but I have to pick a *topic* by April 1st.

theme The films of Frank Capra usually deal with the same *theme,* the efforts of one simple, honest man to overcome powerful people who are against him.

subtract deduct reduce

VERB: to take away an amount from another amount.

subtract To find out how much the dress will cost when it goes on sale, just *subtract* 20 percent from the current price.

deduct The income tax that people owe is based on their total income, but they are allowed to *deduct* certain expenses from the total, such as gifts to charity.

reduce The governor said that he has a plan which will *reduce* the state budget by millions of dollars.

<u>Antonym:</u> **add.**

sudden   abrupt hasty impetuous

ADJECTIVE: happening quickly and without warning; not expected.

sudden John was out jogging when he got caught in a *sudden* rainstorm. Linda had a *sudden* change of plans, and now she can't come to the beach with us.

abrupt The play came to an *abrupt* end, and the audience sat in silence for a minute before they realized that it was over.

hasty Don't be so *hasty* about handing in your paper—it isn't due until Friday, and you haven't checked it over yet for mistakes.

impetuous Carolyn has an *impetuous* nature and often rushes into situations without thinking carefully about what might happen.

Antonyms: **slow, gradual.**

Mom got a **sudden** visit from her boss on Saturday.

We made a **hasty** effort to get the house clean.

suggest   recommend advise propose

VERB: to put forward an idea or plan.

suggest If you want to get there by six o'clock, I'd *suggest* that you leave now, because there's going to be a lot of traffic. The boys were looking for something to do, and Dad *suggested* that they ride their bikes to the park.

recommend Diane wanted to learn about the sinking of the *Titanic,* and the librarian *recommended* the book *A Night to Remember,* by Walter Lord.

advise Though it is possible for an accused person to testify in his own behalf, many lawyers *advise* their clients not to do this.

propose The governor has *proposed* building a new branch of the state college.

support prop brace bolster

VERB: to hold the weight of something; keep from falling or collapsing.

support Don't pull out that bottom book—it *supports* the whole stack. When she goes skating, she fastens her skate laces very tight to help *support* her ankles.

prop The window wouldn't stay up, so we used a block of wood to *prop* it open.

brace During the hurricane, the wind was so strong that he had to *brace* himself against a tree to keep from falling.

bolster When they planted the young tree, they *bolstered* it with wires attached to stakes in the ground, so it would grow straight.

Dad **surprised** Mom with a big party on her birthday.

Mom was **amazed** to see an old friend from high school there.

surprise startle amaze astonish astound

VERB: to cause to feel wonder by something unexpected.

surprise Aunt Julie hadn't seen me in a year, so she was *surprised* at how much I'd grown. Mom never tells us ahead of time what our birthday present will be; she likes to *surprise* us.

startle Susan didn't hear me walk in, and I *startled* her when I came up behind her and said "Hi!"

amaze Even though Beth had heard a lot about the Grand Canyon before she went there, when she saw it she was *amazed* at how big it is.

astonish The TV commercial for the magic show says that "The Great Gascoigne will *astonish* you with his sensational selection of tricks."

astound When Grandpa buys a lottery ticket he always says, "OK, here's the big winner," but I'm sure he'd be absolutely *astounded* if he really won.

surrender   yield submit concede

VERB: to give in to the power of another; accept or admit defeat.

surrender The Civil War ended when Confederate forces under General Lee *surrendered* to General Grant. After a nationwide search for the escaped convict, he finally walked into a police station and *surrendered* on his own.

yield After the workers had been on strike for three weeks, the company *yielded* to their demands and agreed to give them an increase in pay.

submit In the Middle Ages the common people had no real power, so they had no choice but to *submit* to the rule of the king.

concede When the voting results showed that the candidate was far behind his opponent, he *conceded* the election to her.

Antonyms: **resist, withstand.**

survive   endure outlive outlast

VERB: to continue to exist; go on living or being.

survive Turtles have a very long life span; several kinds have been known to *survive* for 100 years. Tall buildings in California have to be built with special reinforcement to help them *survive* an earthquake.

endure A polar bear's thick coat of fur and heavy layers of fat allow it to *endure* the bitter cold of an Arctic winter.

outlive Medical studies show that people who do not smoke tend to *outlive* those who do.

outlast Volvo automobiles have the reputation of being able to *outlast* other cars on the road, and some have been driven more than one million miles.

Antonyms: **end, stop.**

system   organization network scheme

NOUN: a group of things that are related and form a whole.

system The New York City subway *system* carries millions of riders to and from work every day. Many pro football teams use the 3-4 defensive *system,* in which there are three linemen and four linebackers.

organization Mr. Best has left Maxima Computers, Inc. to start his own business; he'd rather work on his own than be part of a large *organization.*

network Los Angeles is served by a complicated *network* of freeways that cross the city in all directions.

scheme In decorating the hotel lobby, the designer used a color *scheme* of greens and blues.

Antonym: **chaos.**

table   chart diagram graph

NOUN: a visual arrangement of words, numbers, or signs, used for reference.

table When you pay income tax, you look up the amount of your income in a tax *table* to see how much tax you owe.

chart Outside the school board office, there is a large *chart* showing each school in the district and the name of its principal.

diagram Our science book has a *diagram* of how blood circulates in the body.

graph The newspaper published a *graph* showing how much money the average family spends in a year for various things.

Mr. Valle told Rafael to **take** the old newspapers out to the garage.

The family has the newspaper **delivered** every morning.

take   bring deliver fetch

VERB: to move something from one place to another.

take It looks like it's going to rain; you'd better *take* an umbrella along with you. He *took* the garbage out to the end of the driveway for the truck to pick up.

bring Where Grandma lives people don't have mailboxes out on the street; the mailman *brings* the mail right up to the front door.

deliver My brother has a job *delivering* pizza to people's houses after they phone in their orders.

fetch I trained my dog to go and *fetch* a stick when I throw it for him.

▶ **Take** and **bring** are used in different ways. You *take* something away from the place where you are, to a different place. You *bring* something to the place where you are, from somewhere else farther away: My mom said she can *take* us to the movies this afternoon, if your mom can *bring* us home afterward.

talent   gift aptitude knack

NOUN: a special ability that is natural or inborn.

talent Pablo Picasso's artistic *talent* could be seen in the realistic portraits he painted when he was only 14 years old. Sheila was able to fit right in at her new school; she seems to have a *talent* for making new friends.

gift Allan has a *gift* for imitating other people, and he does great impersonations of movie stars and politicians.

aptitude Natalie's music teacher says that she shows a real *aptitude* for music that should be developed.

knack Cory has a *knack* for learning languages; he picked up a lot of Spanish just by watching the Spanish-language channel on TV.

▶ **Skill** and **talent** are not quite the same. You can acquire a *skill* from practice or training; you are born with a *talent*. The great hockey player Wayne Gretzky has a *talent* for sensing where the other players are on the ice. When he was a boy, his father built a rink in the back yard, so Wayne could improve his hockey *skills*.

talk   speak converse discuss chat

VERB: to use words to express thoughts and ideas.

talk Babies cannot *talk* when they are first born. The teacher changed Jerry's seat because he spent too much time *talking* to the boy next to him.

speak I wish our school would serve better lunches—maybe we should *speak* to the principal about it.

converse Modern car telephones allow you to *converse* with someone on the phone while you are driving down the highway.

discuss The boss called a meeting to *discuss* the company's plan to set up a new office in Europe.

chat Mrs. Leslie stopped at the corner for a few minutes to *chat* with a neighbor about the weather.

taste   flavor tang flavoring

NOUN: a particular sensation felt in the mouth.

taste The hot, spicy *taste* of the chili made her reach quickly for a glass of water. I've never eaten shark meat, but people say it actually has a mild, pleasant *taste*.

flavor The ice-cream store offers a lot of choices, though Dad usually sticks with his favorite *flavor*, vanilla.

tang At the last minute she added a few drops of lemon juice to the salad dressing, to give it just a little extra *tang*.

flavoring Garlic is used for *flavoring* in many dishes of southern Italy and the south of France.

tax   strain exhaust drain overburden

VERB: to make a heavy demand on; tire out.

tax The boy's constant demands finally began to *tax* his mother's patience. Terry's endurance was *taxed* by the long race, but she still managed to finish.

strain The doctor told him that he should only do light exercise at first, so that he doesn't *strain* his muscles.

exhaust Keeping the fire going all night *exhausted* our supply of firewood.

drain The long swim had *drained* Lucas of his strength, and he hung onto the side of the pool gasping for breath.

overburden She's *overburdened* with work and needs a good long vacation.

teach   educate instruct train tutor

VERB: to bring new ideas to a person; show or tell a person how to do something.

teach The schools *teach* children to read and write. Tim's older sister is going to *teach* him how to swim this summer.

educate Tufts Medical School *educates* people who want to become doctors.

instruct When you buy a VCR, there is a booklet with it to *instruct* you on how to turn it on and work it.

train The army *trains* new recruits to use their weapons and to follow orders.

tutor French is hard for Brandon, and a fourth-year student is going to *tutor* him so that he can keep up with his class.

▶ **Learn** is like **teach,** but it is used very differently. You *teach* another person something; that person *learns* from you: I want to *learn* to count in Spanish. My friend Ramon is going to *teach* me. (Do not say "Ramon is going to learn me.")

Mr. Cleary **teaches** a high school math course.

He also **tutors** students who are having trouble with math.

tease   taunt heckle needle bait

VERB: to annoy or bother someone in a playful way; make fun of.

tease   When Mindy saw her brother's new short haircut, she started *teasing* him and calling him "porcupine-head." Jed was afraid the other boys would *tease* him about his braces, but no one said anything.

taunt   The bully *taunted* the younger boy, trying to provoke him into a fight.

heckle   Chicago Cub fans who sit in the bleachers at Wrigley Field are known for the way they *heckle* players on the other team.

needle   Some comedians will try to *needle* the audience as part of their act, but not everyone finds that funny.

bait   Francie *baited* the little dog by holding a piece of food out and pulling it away every time the dog tried to grab it.

tell   inform notify warn

VERB: to let a person know about something; give information to a person.

tell   Dad asked me to *tell* my brother to come inside for dinner. This watch *tells* you the time, and also the date.

inform   The students publish their own newspaper, The Student Voice, to *inform* their classmates about what is going on at school.

notify   The college sent a letter *notifying* my sister that she has been accepted as a member of next year's freshman class.

warn   In our car a red light goes on to *warn* the driver when there is something wrong with the engine.

Antonyms: **hide, conceal.**

term   condition requirement stipulation restriction

NOUN: a part of an agreement stating some fact or regulation.

term   The Reds have just worked out the *terms* of a new contract with their star pitcher. According to the *terms* of surrender in World War I, France took back the region of Alsace from Germany.

condition   The company offered her the job, under one *condition*—she must be ready to start work immediately.

requirement   It is a *requirement* in this state that you take a course in driver's education before you get your license.

stipulation   The man donated two million dollars to the college he had attended, with the *stipulation* that the money be used for a new library.

restriction   The airline now has a $99 fare to California; the only *restriction* is that you have to buy your ticket two weeks in advance.

test exam quiz trial tryout

NOUN: a set of questions or problems to judge how a person or thing performs.

test After each unit in our history book, there is a *test* on the material in the unit. The auto magazine gave the new car model a road *test* to see how well it drove.

exam Rob got a 'C' on his midterm *exam,* but hopes to get an 'A' on the final.

quiz Each Sunday our newspaper has a current-events *quiz* with questions taken from the week's news.

trial Don trains hunting dogs, and he often enters them in field *trials* where dogs are rated by how well they can follow orders.

tryout If you want to be in the school play, come to the *tryout* this afternoon.

To become a soccer coach, Mom had to take a **test** on the rules.

The league has **tryouts** where the coaches pick players for the teams.

thankful grateful appreciative indebted

ADJECTIVE: feeling or showing thanks.

thankful The car got banged up in the accident, but we're just *thankful* no one was hurt. The Thanksgiving holiday is a time to be *thankful* for what you have.

grateful Mr. Toma accidentally left his wallet in a taxicab, and he was *grateful* to the driver for finding and returning it.

appreciative She got a letter from the mayor saying how *appreciative* he was of the help she'd given him in his campaign.

indebted In accepting the acting award, the actress said she'd always be *indebted* to her high-school drama teacher for getting her started in the theater.

<u>Antonym:</u> **ungrateful.**

theory hypothesis conjecture speculation

NOUN: a set of ideas presented in order to explain something.

theory The research of Louis Pasteur and Robert Koch established the *theory* that diseases are caused by harmful bacteria. The Big Bang *theory* states that the universe began as the result of a huge explosion billions of years ago.

hypothesis The scientist is conducting experiments with a chimpanzee to test her *hypothesis* that animals can learn to use language.

conjecture Whoever stole the jewels went right past the dogs, who didn't bark; so it's Detective Doyle's *conjecture* that the thief is someone they know.

speculation Because many planes and ships have disappeared in the Bermuda Triangle, there is *speculation* that a supernatural force may exist there.

therefore consequently accordingly hence

ADVERB: for that reason; so.

therefore The U.S. Supreme Court has nine members; *therefore* it is not possible to have a tie vote. Though whales live in the ocean, they are mammals; *therefore* they must come to the surface from time to time to take in air.

consequently The 5:45 train broke down in the tunnel; *consequently* all the later trains behind it were delayed.

accordingly On the first day of class the teacher said, "You are all intelligent young people, and when you're here I'll expect you to act *accordingly.*"

hence Japan has almost no oil deposits of its own; *hence* it must import virtually all of its oil from other nations.

▶ These words all are used to show how one thing happens because of another, but **therefore** is the strongest. It usually refers to a thing that follows necessarily: The puzzle said that a man was facing due south and then turned the other way and was still facing south—*therefore* I knew he had to be at the North Pole.

thick solid dense compact

ADJECTIVE: with many parts or objects close together.

thick A *thick* cloud of gray smoke from the forest fire hung over the mountain. The Everglades is a huge swamp area in Florida, much of which is covered with a *thick* plant growth called sawgrass.

solid The temperature dropped during the night, and when we got up in the morning the pond behind the house was *solid* ice.

dense In the *dense* fog, he couldn't see the turnoff for the road to the cabin.

compact This travel umbrella folds up into a small, *compact* form so that it will fit easily into a suitcase.

thin   slim slender lean skinny

ADJECTIVE: having a light body weight for one's height; having little fat.

thin Glen was sick for a while, and his face still looks very *thin.* The ostrich is an unusual-looking bird with stick-like legs and a long, *thin* neck.

slim Even though Ruthie has a big appetite, she does a lot of exercising and always manages to stay *slim.*

slender The ballet dancer had a *slender,* graceful figure and looked as though she were floating on air when she danced.

lean People think of cowboys as tall and *lean,* perhaps because they are often played in movies by actors built like this, such as Clint Eastwood.

skinny Wade started weightlifting at the gym because the other boys teased him about being weak and *skinny.*

Antonyms: **fat, heavy.**

thing

NOUN: any object or item that can be seen and felt, or any subject that can be thought about or talked about.

▶ **Thing** is such a general, all-purpose word that it has no true synonyms. *Object* and *item* apply to some of its meanings but not to others. The "thing" to do with this word is not to look for another word to replace it, but to use a more exact statement instead. "The store sells *things* for sports" can be changed to "The store sells sporting equipment." "An unusual *thing* about the store is its name" can become "The store has an unusual name."

think   believe feel suppose assume expect

VERB: to have an idea in the mind; hold a certain thought or opinion.

think Raise your hand if you *think* you know the answer to the teacher's question. I'm not sure, but I *think* that's her house there, the one on the corner.

believe I learned to ice skate by just getting out on the ice and doing it—I really *believe* that's the best way to learn.

feel His sister was in a bad mood, so he didn't *feel* it was a good time to ask her to help with his homework.

suppose I don't know why Stacy left in such a hurry; I *suppose* she had to go somewhere.

assume Marty wears that Los Angeles baseball cap everywhere he goes, so you have to *assume* he's a Dodger fan.

expect My uncle always sends me a funny card for my birthday, and I *expect* I'll be getting one in the mail any day now.

this/that

ADJECTIVE: being the one spoken or written about.

▶ **This** and **that** are both used to point out a certain thing, but they have different meanings. *This* one is close to you as you speak or write: Look at *this* pretty blue rock I just found. *That* one is farther away from you: I found the rock under *that* big pine tree back there.

Look at **this** nest here—
it has two baby birds in it.

Do you think **that** bird
there is the mother?

those/these

ADJECTIVE: being the ones spoken or written about.

▶ **Those** and **these** refer to something being indicated by the speaker or writer. *These* is the plural of *this* and refers to things that are close: Try one of *these* tomatoes; I just picked them in our garden. *Those* is the plural of *that* and refers to things farther away: *Those* big plants in Mr. Rush's garden—are they tomatoes?

though   although

CONJUNCTION: even if.

though *Though* the weather here is usually sunny, it rained every day last week. Megan can already ride a two-wheel bicycle, *though* she's only four.

although *Although* his opponent received more votes in the general election, Rutherford B. Hayes was chosen as President by the Electoral College.

▶ **Though** and **although** are almost the same and either one can be used in most situations. The only difference is that *although* is more suited to serious writing.

thought   idea   concept   notion

NOUN: something that exists in the mind.

thought When Tina smelled something burning, her first *thought* was that she'd left the oven on. Ben was lost in *thought* and didn't hear me come in the door.

idea Brad has a good *idea* for a topic for his history paper.

concept It's said that the scientist Isaac Newton came to understand the *concept* of gravity after watching an apple drop from a tree to the ground.

notion The movie is about a man who has the odd *notion* that he can invent a car that will run on water instead of gasoline.

throughout   during   everywhere

PREPOSITION: in every part of; from beginning to end.

throughout The rain started about six and lasted *throughout* the night. The girls enjoyed the play and paid close attention *throughout* the entire performance.

during Because of the extreme heat in a desert, animals there are usually active at night and sleep *during* daylight hours.

everywhere Rock music started in the United States, but it's now played almost *everywhere* in the world.

throw   toss   pitch   hurl

VERB: to send something through the air from the hand with force.

throw A runner is out in baseball if you *throw* the ball to first base before he gets there. You can *throw* a flat rock so that it will skip on the surface of the water.

toss Before the football game, the players warmed up by *tossing* a ball around on the sidelines.

pitch Sandy Koufax was the first baseball player to *pitch* four no-hit games—one each year from 1962 through 1965.

hurl A javelin is a metal spear used in track and field competition; a competitor takes a long run and then *hurls* the javelin into the air for distance.

thus   hence   therefore

ADVERB: because of this.

thus Mountain lions shy away from people and *thus* they are seldom seen in the wild. The car has a diesel engine; *thus* it can't use regular gasoline.

hence The President's car is supposed to pass by on this road; *hence* there's tight security all along the route.

therefore There is very little rainfall here, and *therefore* all farm crops have to be watered by irrigation.

tight   taut tense snug

ADJECTIVE: having little room or space; close or confined.

tight Dad tried to put on his old baseball uniform from high school, but the pants were much too *tight* around the waist.

taut Keith held the bowstring *taut* as he aimed the arrow at the target.

tense The leopard crouched with *tense* muscles, ready to pounce on its prey.

snug Jan wears a *snug* woolen cap to keep her head and ears warm in winter.
Antonym: **loose.**

till/until

PREPOSITION: up to the time of.

▶ **Till** and **until** have the same meaning, but *until* is more formal and is more suitable for writing. You could say, "Mom called and said she's working late; she won't be home *till* about seven." But it would be better to write, "Although the U.S. Constitution was signed in 1787, the Bill of Rights wasn't added *until* 1791."

tired   exhausted weary fatigued

ADJECTIVE: lacking energy; needing rest or sleep.

tired Eddie looks *tired* today, because he was up very late last night.

exhausted The runners were *exhausted* when they reached the finish line.

fatigued People affected with that disease become *fatigued* very easily.

weary When we got back from our walk, Grandma sank down in her chair and said, "I'm just going to sit here and rest my *weary* bones for a minute."

After the birthday party, Danny was **tired,** but his mother was **exhausted.**

too also besides likewise

ADVERB: in addition.

too Wherever Chuck goes, his little brother Matt wants to go *too*. This is a scary mystery story, but it has some funny parts *too*.
also She's on a volleyball team and a softball team, and *also* likes to play tennis.
besides I'm going to the deli now—is there anything else we need *besides* milk?
likewise The city has had a large increase in population lately, and the suburbs around it have grown *likewise*.

top peak summit pinnacle

NOUN: the highest part or point of something.

top I saw a hawk sitting on *top* of the fence in our back yard. Visitors to New York often go to the *top* of the Empire State Building to look down over the city.
peak The world's tallest *peak*, Mt. Everest, is over 29,000 feet above sea level.
summit Castles in the Middle Ages were often built at the *summit* of a hill to make them harder to attack.
pinnacle Winning the Best Actor award represented the *pinnacle* of his career.
<u>Antonym:</u> **bottom.**

total sum whole

NOUN: the complete amount.

total In a bowling match, you bowl three games and the person with the highest *total* wins. The meal cost $22.00; including tax and tip the *total* was $26.75.
sum If you add up the numbers 43, 24, 20, and 14, the *sum* is 101.
whole They decided that the house is priced too high for them; making the down payment on it would take up the *whole* of their savings.

totally completely entirely fully utterly

ADVERB: all the way; in every way.

totally The damage from the fire was so great that the house had to be *totally* rebuilt. He is *totally* recovered from his illness and is back at work full time.
completely The car was *completely* out of gas and it rolled gradually to a stop.
entirely Bruce decided to cut out the last section of his paper *entirely*, because it just repeated what he'd already said.
fully Dr. Lee has finished her training and is *fully* qualified to practice medicine.
utterly The lawyer for the defendant asked the judge to dismiss the charges, saying that the prosecution had *utterly* failed to prove its case.

tough   strong sturdy durable

ADJECTIVE: not easily damaged by breaking, cutting, or tearing.

tough The coconut had a *tough* shell, and we had to use a hammer to crack it open. The bottoms of Blair's feet are so *tough* from going barefoot all summer that she can walk on rocks or gravel without noticing.

strong The tire swing was hung from a *strong* rope attached to the old elm tree.

sturdy I noticed that the men working on the construction job all wear *sturdy* work boots rather than sneakers or regular shoes.

durable This coat is made of very *durable* material, and it's lasted me through years of heavy wear.

Antonym: **fragile**.

trade   swap exchange replace barter

VERB: to give one thing for another.

trade I want to *trade* my Space Blasters video game with my friend for a game that he has. She's going to *trade* in her old car to the dealer and buy a new one.

swap When the girls got back from trick or treating, they sat down to *swap* some of their candy with each other so they'd each have what they wanted.

exchange The sweater didn't fit, so he took it back to the store and *exchanged* it for one that was the right size.

replace The car battery was too weak, and we *replaced* it with a new one.

barter In the early days of this country, trappers *bartered* the skins of animals for food and other supplies.

Eddie **traded** his Nolan Ryan card for an Eric Davis card.

Eddie had to **exchange** his jacket for a larger size.

trash   garbage waste rubbish refuse

NOUN: things that are of no use and are to be thrown away.

trash The people who used to live here left so much *trash* behind the garage that we'll have to hire someone to take it to the dump.

garbage This kitchen has a *garbage* disposal where you can get rid of food scraps from a meal.

waste A big problem in the U.S. is how to dispose of harmful chemical *wastes*.

rubbish Dad said we would have to spend the weekend getting all the *rubbish* out of the basement.

refuse In the downtown area of the city there's a large container on every corner for disposing of *refuse*.

▶ **Trash** and **garbage** can both refer to any waste material. However, some people make a distinction between the two, using *garbage* to refer only to food materials and *trash* for other unwanted items such as paper and plastic.

travel   journey tour trek

VERB: to go from one place to another.

travel If I had the time to do it, I would love to *travel* across Canada by train. Counting the stopovers along the way, how long does it take to *travel* by plane from here to Australia?

journey Felipe's ancestors *journeyed* through Mexico to California in the 1830's, and his family has lived here ever since.

tour This summer Alicia and Kevin are going to *tour* the ruins of ancient Greece with their grandparents.

trek In the 1930's, crops failed in Oklahoma because of a drought, and many families left their homes there and *trekked* to California in search of work.

treat   handle manage conduct

VERB: to act or deal with in a particular way.

treat I like Mrs. Ramsey as a teacher because she *treats* everyone fairly and doesn't play favorites. It is against the law to *treat* a pet animal in a cruel way.

handle A police officer arrived soon after the accident, and he *handled* the situation very calmly.

manage Carole *managed* the dress shop entirely by herself when the owner was called away suddenly.

conduct This is Miguel's first job, but you would never know it because he *conduct*s himself in a very mature, professional manner.

Antonyms: **ignore, overlook.**

trim   adorn decorate embroider

VERB: to improve the look of something by adding certain touches or details.

trim When we *trim* the tree at Christmas, we always put a gold star at the top. Aunt Elizabeth made me a pretty blouse for my birthday and *trimmed* the collar and cuffs with lace.

adorn The bride's dress was *adorned* with tiny pearls at the neck.

decorate For my dad's high school reunion, the gym was *decorated* to look just like the old diner where his class hung out in the 1950's.

embroider The Mortons have a set of guest towels that are *embroidered* with the initial "M" in gold thread.

Grandma's apron is **trimmed** with white lace. She **decorated** the cake for the party.

trip   journey tour excursion expedition

NOUN: the act of traveling from one place to another.

trip Joel had to make three *trips* from the car to his dorm room to carry up all his clothes and books. Our family is planning a vacation *trip* to Yellowstone National Park this summer.

journey Before jet airliners came into common use, people made the *journey* from Europe to America by ship.

tour The rock singer is going on a concert *tour* that will take her to cities all over North America.

excursion Last Sunday we got away from the city for a pleasant *excursion* on a boat that sailed up the river and back.

expedition In the 1800's British explorers carried out a series of *expedition*s in central Africa to try to locate the source of the Nile River.

trouble   difficulty problem bother

NOUN: something that causes worry or aggravation.

trouble Ben got in *trouble* with his parents for staying out too late with the car. She thinks she needs glasses because she has *trouble* seeing things at a distance.

difficulty It was cold this morning, and we had some *difficulty* starting the car.

problem The seats in modern airliners often have very little leg room, which creates a *problem* for people who are tall.

bother Dad said cooking was too much of a *bother* and took us out for dinner.

true   correct accurate valid

ADJECTIVE: agreeing with the facts; not false or made up.

true The sentence said, "Lincoln's nickname was Honest Abe," so I put *true* as my answer. The film *The Right Stuff* is a *true* story about the U.S. space program.

correct Juanita had all *correct* answers on her math test and scored 100%.

accurate *The New York Times* has a reputation for *accurate* news reporting.

valid You must sign the check at the bottom, or else it is not *valid*.

Antonyms: **false, incorrect.**

trust   believe depend rely

VERB: to have confidence in the honesty or ability of.

trust Cindy always gets a lot of work as a babysitter because people *trust* her with their children. I want to keep this a secret—can I *trust* you not to tell anyone?

believe That actor is often chosen to sell products on TV; the viewers seem to *believe* what he says.

depend Here comes Jeff now—we can always *depend on* him to be on time.

rely You can *rely* on that encyclopedia to give you accurate information.

Antonyms: **doubt, distrust.**

try   attempt struggle strive

VERB: to make an effort.

try When I opened the door, the dog *tried* to get out. The paper isn't due until Monday, but he's going to *try* to finish it today so he'll have the weekend free.

attempt She cleared the high-jump bar at 6-2, and now she'll *attempt* to do 6-4.

struggle When we paddled the canoe upriver, we had to *struggle* against a strong current going downstream.

strive As he accepted the nomination for President, he said that he would *strive* to be worthy of the trust his party had placed in him.

turn   roll spin revolve rotate twirl

VERB: to move in a circle or part of a circle.

turn Aaron heard someone calling him and *turned* around to see who it was. At the end of daylight saving, you *turn* the hands of the clock back one hour.

roll The children played a game where they lie down and *roll* down the hill.

spin The pro basketball player showed us a trick where he holds the ball up and *spins* it around on one finger.

revolve The period of a year is based on the time that it takes the earth to *revolve* around the sun.

rotate The earth *rotates* on its axis once every 24 hours as it goes around the sun.

twirl Sherry marched at the head of the band, *twirling* her baton over her head.

You have to **turn** the handle
to get the coin in the meter.

The hotel door **revolves**
to let people in and out.

type   kind sort class category

NOUN: a group of things that are alike in some way and different from others.

type In spite of its name, the guinea pig is not a pig but a *type* of rodent. This disk wouldn't work in my computer; it's made for a different *type* of machine.

kind What *kind* of dessert would you like to have for dinner tonight?

sort That car is fine for a person who likes something fast and sporty, but it's not the *sort* of car for a family with young children.

class A new player in professional baseball starts out on a team in *Class* A, the lowest level of minor-league play.

category In the game of Trivial Pursuit, players answer questions in different *categories* such as science or entertainment.

uncover   reveal expose disclose

VERB: to discover and make known.

uncover While digging the hole for the swimming pool, the workmen *uncovered* a huge boulder buried underground. The news reporter has *uncovered* a scandal in the Traffic Bureau in which people pay to have parking tickets fixed.

reveal The Batman character wears a mask so that his identity won't be *revealed.*

expose The capture of secret papers by American troops *exposed* a plot by the traitor Benedict Arnold to surrender his command to the British.

disclose The police supposedly have identified a key suspect in the case, but they have not yet *disclosed* his name.

Antonyms: **cover, hide.**

Roger **uncovered** a trap door while cleaning out his basement.

The door opened to **reveal** a secret underground passage.

under   below beneath underneath

PREPOSITION: lower than or down from.

under I looked for Brad's letter and finally found it *under* a pile of papers on my desk. The sun was strong, and he stood *under* a tree to get some shade.

below After this station the train goes into a tunnel, and then the rest of the trip to the city is *below* ground.

beneath The brown pelican "fishes" by flying above the water and then diving *beneath* the surface to catch its prey.

underneath Rob played a trick on his mom and hid *underneath* the bedcovers so she wouldn't know where he was.

Antonym: **above.**

uninterested   indifferent unconcerned detached

ADJECTIVE: not showing attention or concern; not interested.

uninterested He's totally *uninterested* in politics and has never even bothered to register to vote. She seemed *uninterested* while the speech was going on, so I was surprised that she later remembered everything that was said.

indifferent The actor claims that he is *indifferent* to publicity, but his friends say that he keeps a scrapbook of all the stories about him.

unconcerned The coach was *unconcerned* that his team lost its practice game, because he was just using the game to try out various plans for the regular season.

detached The defendant seemed strangely *detached* in court, as though what was going on in the trial had nothing to do with him.

Antonyms: **interested, concerned.**

union   association alliance federation league

NOUN: a body or group that is formed by combining members.

union For many years the labor leader John L. Lewis was president of the mine workers' *union.* The states that remained loyal to the U.S. government in the Civil War sent troops to fight in the *Union* army.

association More than twenty professional teams from cities all over the U.S. compete in the National Basketball *Association.*

alliance In the War of the Triple *Alliance,* the small country of Paraguay fought against the combined forces of three nations, Argentina, Brazil, and Uruguay.

federation The nation of Canada is a *federation,* with a central government and ten provinces that each have their own local government.

league The *League* of Nations was established after World War I to try to maintain peace among the nations of the world.

unite   combine unify consolidate

VERB: to bring or join together; make one.

unite After the Revolutionary War, the thirteen American colonies *united* to form one nation.

combine To make a cake, you *combine* various raw ingredients and then bake them together.

unify As a result of World War II, Germany was divided into two parts, but in 1990 East and West Germany were *unified* as one country.

consolidate In the Middle Ages, a prince from one kingdom would often marry a princess from another to *consolidate* relations between the two kingdoms.

Antonyms: **separate, divide.**

universal widespread worldwide

ADJECTIVE: of or for everyone or many people.

universal The plays of William Shakespeare have *universal* appeal and have been performed in countries all over the world.

widespread Over 20 million people died in a *widespread* flu epidemic in 1918.

worldwide There was *worldwide* response to the Live Aid concert organized by musician Bob Geldof to benefit famine victims in Africa.

unusual uncommon extraordinary remarkable

ADJECTIVE: not ordinary or common.

unusual A killer whale has *unusual* black and white markings. Charles Dickens's characters often have *unusual* names such as Pumblechook, Wopsle, and Gamp.

uncommon Type AB is an *uncommon* blood type; not even one person in ten has this kind of blood.

extraordinary The performances of ballet dancer Mikhail Baryshnikov became famous for his *extraordinary* leaps, during which he seemed to hang in midair.

remarkable Magician Harry Houdini had a *remarkable* ability to escape from locks, chains, and prison cells.

upset irritate aggravate exasperate

VERB: to make worried, nervous, or unhappy.

upset Carl asked all the boys in his class to his party, so no one would be *upset* about not being invited. The girls were *upset* when they lost the game at the end.

irritate I'm *irritated* when a movie I'm watching on TV is constantly interrupted by commercials.

aggravate Uncle Mike gets really *aggravated* when he's caught in a traffic jam.

exasperate She called and called and kept getting a busy signal, so she finally got *exasperated* and gave up.

use operate employ apply

VERB: to put into action or service for a special purpose.

use Jeff *uses* a dictionary when he writes because he has trouble with spelling. Mom *used* a weed killer to get rid of the plants around the mailbox.

operate The factory has added a night shift and now *operates* 24 hours a day.

employ This experimental car *employs* electrical power rather than gasoline.

apply Mrs. Lee was able to *apply* the things she learned in the summer reading workshop to her own teaching in the classroom.

useful   helpful   practical   worthwhile

ADJECTIVE: having a good use or purpose.

useful These scissors are very *useful;* I use them to cut all kinds of things around the house and even for yard work. Marsha found the typing course to be very *useful,* since she now has to do typed reports for all her classes.

helpful When we first moved here, our neighbor Mrs. Davis was very *helpful* to us in getting to know the area.

practical For Grandpa's birthday we usually get him a *practical* gift, such as a tool for his workshop.

worthwhile She felt that her vacation trip to Europe was a very *worthwhile* experience, because she learned so much about European culture.

The encyclopedia was **useful** to James in writing his report.

The librarian was **helpful** when he needed to find another book.

usually   normally   generally   ordinarily

ADVERB: in a way that is usual; most of the time.

usually I wonder why there are so few cars in the parking lot; it's *usually* full by this time of day. Dad *usually* takes the 5:25 train home, but tonight he worked late and took the 7:10.

normally Children *normally* learn to walk at about the age of one year.

generally Cities in the U.S. *generally* do not allow public gambling casinos, though they are legal in a few places such as Las Vegas and Atlantic City.

ordinarily I was surprised at how talkative and friendly Joey was today, because he's *ordinarily* shy around people he doesn't know.

Antonyms: **rarely, seldom.**

value   importance   worth   merit

NOUN: the quality of something that makes it useful or helpful.

value Diamonds have a high *value* because of their great beauty and extreme hardness. Dr. Bradford gives all her patients a booklet that explains the *value* of a healthful diet and frequent exercise.

importance The city of Venice was of great *importance* in early European history because it served as the link between Europe and Asia.

worth It's definitely true that college graduates earn more money, but the real *worth* of a college education can't be measured just in dollars.

merit The boss always reads letters from customers because he believes that their suggestions and comments have a lot of *merit*.

The museum has a wide **variety** of objects from pioneer times.

They have an unusual **assortment** of old dolls.

variety   assortment   collection   medley

NOUN: a number of things that are different.

variety The actress Meryl Streep has portrayed a great *variety* of characters in her movies. Samantha selected a tie for her father from the wide *variety* the store had available.

assortment For Valentine's Day, John bought his girlfriend a box of candy with an *assortment* of chocolates.

collection The Los Angeles County Museum of Art is noted for a large *collection* of paintings by modern American artists.

medley During his TV concert, the singer sang a *medley* of his hit songs from his long career.

various   assorted varied miscellaneous

ADJECTIVE: not like each other; different.

various At a garage sale, people sell *various* household items that they no longer want. The farmers in this valley grow *various* crops such as corn, tomatoes, peppers, and melons.

assorted The store had wool sweaters in *assorted* styles and colors, and Jeremy couldn't decide which one to buy.

varied This year the football coach wants his team to have a *varied* offense rather than running the same few plays over and over.

miscellaneous Most newspaper columns deal with one subject at a time, but her column is a collection of *miscellaneous* notes about a number of topics.

very   extremely greatly unusually exceptionally

ADVERB: more than is typical or usual.

very San Diego, California is a big city; Los Angeles is a *very* big city. Prime rib is a *very* expensive cut of beef, and we buy it only on special occasions.

extremely Winters in Alaska are *extremely* cold, with the temperature often dropping to thirty degrees below zero.

greatly Last year Darren was struggling to get C's, but this year his work has *greatly* improved and he's on the honor roll.

unusually It was an *unusually* pleasant day for early March, and many people went to the park or the beach to enjoy the sunshine.

exceptionally A hawk has *exceptionally* sharp eyesight and can spot its prey from hundreds of feet above the ground.

▶ We tend to use *very* in speaking whenever we want to emphasize something. But be careful not to use it too often in writing, so that it will be effective when you do use it. Many adjectives are strong enough alone and do not need *very*.

view   sight scene vision

NOUN: something that is seen.

view The hotel is on a cliff above the beach, and it has a great *view* of the ocean. At the football game, a man wearing a big cowboy hat sat in front of me and blocked my *view* of the field.

sight When Grandpa went back to visit his old home town in Connecticut, he was amazed at the *sight* of all the modern stores and houses.

scene The artist Vincent van Gogh often painted colorful *scenes* of the French countryside where he lived.

vision The sun rising over the Grand Canyon was a *vision* of natural beauty.

visitor   guest company caller

NOUN: someone who goes to see a person or a place for a time.

visitor My Aunt Carol lives right across the street from us, and she is a frequent *visitor* at our house. He has two chairs in his office, one that he uses himself and one for *visitors.*

guest Mom says that when we have a *guest* over for dinner we are supposed to serve that person first before we take any food ourselves.

company I saw a car with out-of-state license plates parked in Eddie's driveway; he must be having *company* for the weekend.

caller Grandma says that when she was a little girl her parents used to be "at home" on Sunday afternoon to receive *callers* who came to the house.

▶ **Company** differs from these other words in that it applies only to someone who comes to one's home. A person can be a *visitor* at a school, a *guest* at a hotel, or a *caller* at a business office trying to make a sale. But *company* always refers to a friendly visit at home.

voice   say wish opinion

NOUN: a choice or preference openly expressed.

voice In earlier times, kings and other such rulers held all the power and the common people had no *voice* in the government. Citizens can attend the council meetings to give *voice* to any complaints they may have.

say Our family was trying to decide where to go on vacation this summer, and we all got to have a *say* in the matter.

wish The man wrote a letter to his lawyer saying that it was his *wish* that his art collection be given to the City Museum after his death.

opinion The TV news show has a feature called Editorial Comment, in which one of the newscasters gives his *opinion* on a news issue of the day.

vote   ballot election poll

NOUN: the selection of a candidate or the expression of an opinion.

vote The players on the basketball team took a *vote* and picked Yoshi as captain. The *vote* in the Senate was tied at 50-50, so the Vice President then had to break the tie.

ballot The secret *ballot* is important in a democracy, because it means that no one can force a person to choose a certain candidate.

election Our school is having an *election* this week to choose the student council members for next year.

poll The newspaper took a *poll* to find out whether or not people thought the President was doing a good job in office.

Maria was **waiting** at the corner for her bus to come.

Teddy and his pals were **loitering** on the bench across the street.

wait   remain linger loiter

VERB: to stay in a place or do nothing until something happens.

wait Don't cross the street yet; *wait* until the WALK sign comes on. The train was half an hour late, and a large group of passengers *waited* impatiently on the platform.

remain The pilot asked the passengers to *remain* in their seats until the plane had come to a complete stop.

linger Even after the fire was out, a strong smell of smoke *lingered* in the air.

loiter She doesn't know who robbed her store, but she did see a suspicious-looking man *loitering* across the street earlier that afternoon.

walk   stroll march stride strut

VERB: to move over or through something on foot.

walk Peg lives very close to her office and is able to *walk* to work. The teacher saw us running and told us to slow down and *walk* to where we were going.

stroll She had an hour to wait until her plane came, so she *strolled* around the airport looking at the various shops and displays.

march Jimmy wants to get in the front row to watch the parade; that way he'll have a good view of the soldiers as they *march* past.

stride They thought they had found a nice spot for their picnic, but then a man came *striding* angrily across the field and told them to get off his land.

strut After he scored the touchdown the running back *strutted* past the other team's bench, waving the ball and shouting, "We're number one!"

wall   partition divider barrier

NOUN: a solid, standing structure that separates or closes off an area.

wall Kara put up a picture of her favorite movie star on the *wall* of her bedroom. Tim plays a game where he throws a ball off a *wall* and catches it as it comes back.

partition The company put up a *partition* to make what had been one large office into two smaller ones.

divider The living room and dining room are actually part of the same space, but they use a tall bookcase as a *divider* between the two areas.

barrier The police set up temporary wooden *barriers* to keep the crowd off the street as the parade went by.

wander   roam stray meander

VERB: to go or move around with no particular place in mind.

wander Mom told me not to *wander* on the way back from the store, but to come straight home. While Mrs. Hill was talking to a friend, Billy *wandered* off, and the next thing she knew he was on the other side of the park.

roam On this ranch the cattle are not kept fenced in, but are allowed to *roam* all over the property.

stray While the sheep were being brought in, one *strayed* from the flock, and the sheepdog had to go after it.

meander Ryan's tracks in the snow showed how he had *meandered* all over the field with no route or purpose.

While her mom shopped, Leslie **wandered** around the store.

The manager **roamed** the aisles, checking the product displays.

want   desire crave covet

VERB: to wish to do or have.

want Linda *wants* to learn to play the piano and is going to start taking lessons. Max raised his hand because he *wanted* to get the teacher's attention.

desire The ad for the resort hotel says that it offers every form of vacation fun that a person could possibly *desire.*

crave Sandy *craved* some salted peanuts, but she isn't supposed to have any while she's on her diet.

covet Because Mrs. Tate's property is so close to the new highway, a big building company *covets* the land and has tried to buy it from her.

Antonyms: **have, own.**

war   battle combat warfare

NOUN: a long, serious fight or struggle.

war The Second World *War* lasted from 1939 to 1945 and involved millions of soldiers from many nations. *War* broke out between Spain and the U.S. in 1898, after Spain was accused of sinking an American navy ship.

battle In 1066, the Normans took control of England when their king, William the Conqueror, defeated the English army at the *Battle* of Hastings.

combat American servicemen who are wounded in *combat* receive the Purple Heart medal.

warfare Since the founding of the state of Israel in 1948, that nation has often been involved in *warfare* with neighboring Arab countries.

warm   tepid lukewarm

ADJECTIVE: somewhat hot; not cold but not too hot.

warm When he took the rolls out of the oven, he wrapped them in a napkin to keep them *warm.* Connie wears socks in bed so her feet will stay *warm* at night.

tepid I had expected the lake water to be quite chilly, but it turned out to be a *tepid* 80 degrees and didn't really cool us off at all.

lukewarm Dan likes to eat his soup *lukewarm,* so he always lets it cool off a bit after it's served.

Antonym: **cool.**

▶ These words are also used in ways that do not refer to actual temperature, but that relate to this idea. **Warm** is a positive word, but **tepid** and **lukewarm** tend to be negative, suggesting that something is lacking. A *warm* handshake is friendly, while a *tepid* handshake does not show friendliness. A *warm* round of applause is loud and enthusiastic; *lukewarm* applause is quiet and done just to be polite.

warn   alert caution alarm

VERB: to give notice to avoid something harmful that might happen.

warn Paul Revere rode from Boston to Lexington to *warn* the American patriots that British forces were coming to attack them.

alert As the pilot was waiting in line to take off, he was *alerted* that there would be a ten-minute delay while several other planes landed.

caution A large electric sign over the highway *cautioned* motorists to drive carefully because of slippery road conditions.

alarm Several of the parents became *alarmed* when they heard there was a fire at the school, but it turned out to be only a small brush fire nearby.

The usher **warned** the man to be quiet or he'd have to leave.

The usher **alerted** them that the second act was about to begin.

waste   squander fritter drain

VERB: to use or spend carelessly.

waste Don't leave the hose running like that; you're *wasting* water. Scott was told to stay in his room to study for a test, but he just *wasted* his time building paper airplanes.

squander Gary was supposed to put his birthday money in the bank; instead he ended up *squandering* it all on candy and toys.

fritter When he was 21 he inherited $100,000 from his grandfather, but by the time he was 30 he had *frittered* it all away on bad business investments.

drain In this book, the author complains that we are *draining* the world's supply of energy without any plan to save or replace it.

Antonyms: **save, conserve.**

watch   observe scrutinize eye

VERB: to look at carefully; keep one's attention on.

watch On Sunday afternoons my dad likes to put on the TV and *watch* the pro football games. I *watched* the magician's hands carefully, but I still couldn't figure out how he made the coin disappear.

observe The scientist Jane Goodall spent many years in Africa *observing* the behavior of chimpanzees at close range.

scrutinize The airport security guard *scrutinized* each piece of luggage as it passed through the X-ray check point.

eye Suzie *eyed* me strangely when I walked in, and I suddenly realized that we were wearing exactly the same outfit.

way   method technique means procedure

NOUN: the certain manner in which something happens or is done.

way We should take Valley Parkway; that's the fastest *way* to the city from here. Rex has a *way* of telling a joke that makes you laugh even though he never cracks a smile himself.

method Dad broiled the fish quickly on a charcoal grill with a little lemon juice and butter, which he says is the best *method* of cooking fresh fish.

technique In early times books were lettered by hand, until the German printer Johann Gutenberg invented the *technique* of printing from movable type.

means For many years people dreamed of traveling to outer space, but until powerful rocket engines were developed they had no *means* of getting there.

procedure The instruction booklet explains the *procedure* for programming the VCR to record a show from the TV.

weak   flimsy fragile frail puny

ADJECTIVE: not able to resist wear or strain; not strong.

weak The rope we used to tie up the boat was too *weak,* and with the first strong wind it snapped and the boat floated away.

delicate When I saw the exhibit of Charles Lindbergh's plane, I couldn't believe that something that looked so *flimsy* could ever have flown across the ocean.

fragile These crystal glasses are very *fragile,* so be careful when you wash them.

frail His health has been *frail* ever since he was ill last year, and he has to be careful not to tire himself out too much.

puny Our dog Major was a *puny* little thing when we got him as a puppy, but he's grown up to be big and powerful.

Antonym: **strong.**

weapon arm firearm

NOUN: a tool or device used for fighting or killing.

weapon In early warfare foot soldiers used *weapons* such as arrows, swords, and axes, until modern rifles were invented.

arm The treaty calls on both sides to cut down their supplies of nuclear *arms*.

firearm In our town, it is illegal to shoot off a *firearm* within the city limits.

weather/climate

NOUN: the condition of the outside air in a certain place.

▶ **Weather** and **climate** both refer to conditions outdoors—cold or hot, sunny or rainy, and so on. The difference is in the time span. *Weather* refers to one certain time. *Climate* is the usual weather a place has over a very long period of time.

weight burden pressure strain

NOUN: something that bears down on a person like a heavy load.

weight If you compare a picture of Abraham Lincoln taken in 1861 with one in 1865, you can see how much he aged under the *weight* of his office.

burden When he gave up the throne of England, Edward VIII said that he had found it impossible to carry the heavy *burden* of responsibility of being king.

pressure Because Josh has a strong throwing arm, the coach asked if he wanted to pitch, but he said no—he feels there's too much *pressure* involved.

strain Working during the day and going to law school at night has been quite a *strain* for her.

well competently adequately properly

ADVERB: in a good, correct, or favorable way.

well Carla plays the piano *well,* and her friends often ask her to play at parties. Ellen is a friendly girl who gets along *well* with everyone.

competently The plumber repaired the sink quickly and *competently.*

adequately My father says that reading a newspaper every day is the only way to be *adequately* informed about what's going on in the world.

properly Eric's new riding toy hadn't been put together *properly,* and one rear wheel came loose as soon as he started to ride it.

Antonyms: **badly, poorly.**

▶ The word **good** is not listed here as a synonym, even though it has the same basic meaning as **well.** *Well* is an adverb that tells how a thing was done: Jim did *well* on the math test. *Good* is an adjective that describes the thing itself: Jim got a *good* grade on the math test. It is incorrect to say "Jim did good on the math test."

The dog got **wet** when Mel squirted him with the hose.

Mel didn't watch where he was squirting and his dad got **soaked.**

wet   damp moist humid soaked

ADJECTIVE: covered with water or another liquid.

wet Her hair was *wet* when she got out of the shower, and she wrapped it in a towel. The streets were *wet* and slippery after the sudden rain shower.

damp My shirt was still a little *damp* when I took it out of the dryer, so I put it back in for a few more minutes.

moist She said she was glad summer camp was over, but I noticed that her eyes were *moist* with tears as she drove off with her parents.

humid It was one of those hot, *humid* July days when your clothes stick to your body and you barely feel like moving.

soaked He left his umbrella in the office and got *soaked* waiting at the bus stop.

Antonym: **dry.**

whether   if either

CONJUNCTION: one or the other; yes or no.

whether Kelly can't decide *whether* to wear her blue dress or her green one to the dance. When you go out, check and see *whether* or not the mail has arrived.

if As soon as I have a spare minute, I'll call Donald and see *if* he wants to come to the beach with us.

either *Either* we take the flight at 6:45 in the morning, or we will have to change planes in Dallas, because that's the only nonstop flight.

while/during

▶ **While** and **during** have the same meaning; they both refer to something that happens at the time that something else is also going on. *While* is a conjunction, used to join two sentence parts: It started to rain *while* we were walking home. *During* is a preposition, used to introduce a noun phrase: It must have snowed *during* the night.

whole   complete total entire

ADJECTIVE: having no parts or elements missing; including all of a thing.

whole It rained hard the *whole* day, and all the roads were flooded. Sharon was so thirsty that she drank the *whole* bottle of lemonade.

complete Henry fitted in the last missing piece of the jigsaw puzzle, and it was finally *complete*.

total The *total* number of students in sixth grade in our school is 90; there are three classes of 30 students each.

entire The story was so exciting that Michael didn't want to stop reading, and he finished the *entire* book in one afternoon.

Antonym: **incomplete.**

why

▶ **Why** is used either as an adverb or a conjunction, to ask about the cause or reason for something. As an adverb: *Why* didn't you answer the letter I sent you? As a conjunction: Please tell me *why* you haven't written lately.

wide   broad spacious vast extensive

ADJECTIVE: extending far from side to side.

wide The Hudson River is very *wide* as it flows past New York City, more than a mile from one shore to the other. That old two-lane road will be replaced by a *wide* modern highway with five lanes in each direction.

broad Laura Ingalls Wilder's book *Little House on the Prairie* describes her family's experiences after they settle on the *broad,* empty plains of Kansas.

spacious One thing that the Andersons like about their new house is that it has a *spacious* back yard where the children can play.

vast The *vast* interior of the continent of Australia is almost all desert and dry grassland, with only a few populated areas.

extensive We had thought the fire was limited to a few acres, but there was an *extensive* burned-out area along the whole side of the mountain.

Antonym: **narrow.**

wiggle   squirm fidget twitch wriggle

VERB: to move or twist from side to side in quick, short motions.

wiggle To do this dance, you just keep your feet in one place and *wiggle* your shoulders and hips back and forth.

squirm The cat *squirmed* out of Debra's arms and ran off to hide behind the sofa.

fidget I could tell Ricky was bored with the movie; he kept *fidgeting* in his seat.

twitch The horse stood quietly in the field and stared at us; his only movement was the *twitching* of his tail back and forth.

wriggle Bobby tried to pick up the worm, but it *wriggled* out of his grasp.

The man **wiggled** a hand puppet to try to make the little girl smile.

She didn't want to be photographed and **squirmed** around in the chair.

wild   untamed fierce savage

ADJECTIVE: living in a state of nature; not tame.

wild The dog, a common household pet, is related to *wild* animals such as the wolf, fox, and coyote.

untamed Indian elephants are often used as work animals, but African elephants usually remain *untamed* because they are too hard to control and train.

fierce It's been said that a female grizzly bear defending her cubs is the most *fierce* of all North American animals.

savage The reputation of a tiger as a *savage* beast comes from the fact that it is one of the very few animals known to prey on man.

Antonyms: **tame, domesticated.**

will willpower determination volition

NOUN: the mental power to make a decision and carry it through.

will Jackie Robinson showed a strong *will* as he overcame prejudice to become the first black to play major league baseball. Animals act by instinct alone, but humans have the ability to act according to their own free *will*.

willpower She was totally exhausted, but she finally made it to the top of the mountain by sheer *willpower.*

determination Great Britain was able to resist Germany in World War II, aided by the great *determination* of the British leader Winston Churchill.

volition Many people feel the congressman was pressured to vote for that bill, but he says he did it of his own *volition.*

win triumph prevail

VERB: to gain a victory in a contest or battle.

win In a game of volleyball, the first team to score 15 points *wins* the game.
triumph The combined armies of Britain, Prussia, Austria, and Russia *triumphed* over Napoleon's French army at the Battle of Waterloo.
prevail For many years the Soviet Union controlled all of Eastern Europe, but at the end of the 1980's the cause of democracy finally *prevailed* in the area.
<u>Antonym:</u> **lose.**

wind twist coil curl

VERB: to move in a series of circles or turns.

wind *Wind* the string up into a ball and put it in the drawer. People drive carefully here, because the road *winds* back and forth up the mountain.
twist Allison put her hand to her head and *twisted* her hair around her finger.
coil The snake was *coiled* up on a flat rock, lying still in the heat from the sun.
curl The smoke *curled* up from the chimney in the clear evening air.

wisdom judgment knowledge

NOUN: the ability to decide properly, based on intelligence and experience.

wisdom Several stories in the Bible tell of the *wisdom* of King Solomon. On a gate at the entrance to Harvard College are the words, "Enter to grow in *wisdom.*"
judgment This book on President Eisenhower states that he used good *judgment* in keeping the U.S. out of war during his term in office.
knowledge The writers of the U.S. Constitution had a great *knowledge* of the problems that a free government might face in the future.

wish   desire hope longing yearning

NOUN: the act of saying or thinking that one wants to have something.

wish Matt got a birthday card signed "Love and best *wishes* from Grandma." Shannon tossed a penny into the fountain and made a *wish* that she could come back there again some day.

desire The business leader said that although he was interested in politics, he had no *desire* to run for office himself.

hope Because Mrs. Wright never had the chance to go to college herself, she's always had the *hope* that her daughter would be able to go.

longing After seeing the movie, they had a real *longing* to visit Hawaii and see the places where it was filmed.

yearning The man had a *yearning* to go back and visit the town where he had lived as a small boy.

without   lacking missing

PREPOSITION: not having or doing.

without I've never been to their house, and I don't think we can find it *without* a map. Camels are suited to living in the desert, because they can go *without* water for long periods of time.

lacking The critic gave the mystery movie a poor review, and said that it was completely *lacking* suspense and excitement.

missing This deck of cards is *missing* the jack of diamonds, so we'll have to find another deck somewhere.

Tana is old enough now to ride a bike **without** training wheels.

Her brother's Jet Cycle is **missing** a back wheel.

witness   onlooker bystander observer

NOUN: a person who is present and sees an event take place.

witness When the young ballplayer signed his first professional baseball contract, his father signed alongside as a *witness.*

onlooker A crowd of *onlookers* had gathered on the sidewalk to watch the filming of the movie scene.

bystander The man claimed he had no part in the robbery; he said he was just an innocent *bystander* who happened to be in the bank at the time.

observer While the voting was going on, the United Nations sent *observers* into the country to see that the election was fair and honest.

▶ **Eyewitness** is a more exact word than **witness**. Anyone who has information about a crime can be a *witness;* the information could be anything that relates to the crime. But only someone who actually sees the crime can be an *eyewitness.*

Two **witnesses** told the police how the accident had happened.

Some **bystanders** watched from across the street.

woman   lady female

NOUN: an adult person who is not a male.

woman Sally Ride was the first American *woman* to go into space as an astronaut.

lady Mom told my sister to act like a *lady* and not put her feet up on the table.

female For hundreds of years the famous colleges Harvard and Yale had only male students, but now they have *females* as well.

▶ **Woman** is considered a better word to use than **lady** as a general term for the female sex. Up until recent times *lady* was thought of as a polite word, but now many people object to it as sounding too old-fashioned and "delicate."

wonder   speculate conjecture question

VERB: to think about something without knowing the answer or facts for certain.

wonder When she looks up at the night sky, she often *wonders* if there is life anywhere out there. We didn't get our newspaper this morning; I *wonder* what happened to it.

speculate Many writers have *speculated* on what policies President Kennedy would have followed if he had lived to serve a second term.

conjecture Scientists *conjecture* that people first came to the Americas by crossing a bridge of land that once linked Asia and Alaska.

question Even after reading two books about "Bigfoot," I still have to *question* whether such a creature really exists.

wonderful   marvelous amazing incredible awesome

ADJECTIVE: causing a feeling of great surprise and admiration.

wonderful I think the computer is a *wonderful* invention, because it allows people to do things easily and quickly. The ancient Romans had a *wonderful* system of roads, many of which are still used today.

marvelous Birds have a *marvelous* ability to fly thousands of miles south in the winter and then find their way back to the exact same spot the next spring.

amazing It's *amazing* to think that 400 years before the first airplane flight, Leonardo da Vinci made drawings of aircraft with bird-like wings.

incredible In 1920 Babe Ruth had the *incredible* record of hitting more home runs by himself than any other team in the league hit as a total.

awesome Viewed from the valley below, Yosemite Falls is an *awesome* sight.

▶ These words, and similar ones such as *fantastic, terrific,* and *fabulous,* have to be used carefully. Each has a second, weaker sense that means no more than "very good" or "unusual." Save these words for when a strong word is really needed, and avoid such uses as "a fantastic person" or "an incredible party."

woods   forest grove woodland

NOUN: an area having a thick growth of trees.

woods Mom wants to spend our vacation at the beach, but Dad would rather go camp out in the *woods* somewhere. I often hear owls hooting at night from the *woods* behind our house.

forest The Amazon tropical rain *forest* covers a great part of the South American continent.

grove *Groves* of cottonwood trees were growing along both sides of the river.

woodland Mule deer are often found in the oak *woodlands* of central California.

word   term   expression

NOUN: a small part of language that has a distinct meaning.

word The *word* that is used most often in English is "the." I'm working on a crossword puzzle, and I need a three-letter *word* that means "a female sheep."

term The use of computers has brought many new *terms* into English, such as "software," "byte," and "word processing."

expression In the Hawaiian language, "aloha" is a common *expression* that can be used to mean either "hello" or "good-bye."

▶ A **word** is a single group of letters that has its own meaning, such as "car" or "red." A **phrase** is a separate group of words with some meaning, such as "a red car." A **sentence** is a group of words with a complete meaning, such as "She has a red car."

work   labor   effort   exertion   toil

NOUN: the use of the body or mind to do something or to reach some goal.

work It was hard *work* clearing away all the weeds and bushes along the back fence. Sandra is taking two extra courses in college this semester, so she has to do a lot more *work.*

labor That restaurant seems to run so smoothly, but it actually takes hours of *labor* in the kitchen to make things go that way.

effort Building the pyramids in Egypt required many years and the *efforts* of thousands of workers.

exertion Much less *exertion* is involved in household chores today than in the 1800's, because of modern appliances such as the washing machine.

toil The novels of Charles Dickens made readers aware of the suffering and *toil* of the poor people of London.

Antonym: **play.**

world   universe   creation   cosmos

NOUN: the entire space or area in which people think of themselves as existing.

world The Book of Genesis in the Bible says that God made the *world* in six days and then rested on the seventh day.

universe Scientists do not know the size of the *universe,* but they believe that it is expanding.

creation The blue whale is the largest animal in all *creation,* bigger than any dinosaur that lived in the past.

cosmos The ancient Greek philosophers believed that the *cosmos* was a logical, orderly system that included all things.

worried concerned distressed apprehensive anxious

ADJECTIVE: afraid or upset because something bad may happen.

worried Cathy is *worried* about the big math test and she's been studying hard. Dad said he'd been *worried* about me when I came home late for dinner.

concerned The doctor said it was just a pulled muscle and not to be *concerned.*

distressed During the storm the pilot spoke to the passengers in a calm, quiet way, so no one would be *distressed* about what was happening.

apprehensive The actors were happy that opening night of the play had gone well, but still they were *apprehensive* as they waited to read the critics' reviews.

anxious Matt's a bit *anxious* about tomorrow's tryouts for the basketball team.

<u>Antonyms:</u> **calm, relaxed.**

The boys were **worried** when they saw how fast the other team's pitcher was.

David was **apprehensive** when he went up to bat.

wreck ruin destroy demolish devastate

VERB: to break to pieces or damage greatly; take away the value or usefulness of.

wreck Cornwall, England is known for its dangerous, rocky coastline, and in former times many ships were *wrecked* there.

ruin I *ruined* my blouse when I accidentally left the hot iron on it.

destroy In 1906 the city of San Francisco was almost completely *destroyed* by an earthquake and fire.

demolish The old bus station will be *demolished* and a new building will be put up in its place.

devastate The hurricane *devastated* the town, destroying over half of its homes.

wrinkle   crease fold pleat crinkle

NOUN: a small ridge on a smooth surface, such as cloth or skin.

wrinkle Julie stayed in the pool so long today that the skin on her fingers was all covered with *wrinkles* when she came out. After he washed the shirt, he had to iron it to get the *wrinkles* out.

crease Mr. Dobbs is a neat dresser who makes sure his trousers are always neatly pressed, with a sharp *crease* down the front of each leg.

fold When Marlene finished writing her letter, she made two *folds* in the page so that it would fit in the envelope.

pleat Women's skirts sometimes have sharp *pleats* that run from top to bottom.

crinkle The *crinkles* that show around people's eyes and mouth when they smile are sometimes called "laugh lines."

writer   author

NOUN: a person who writes.

▶ **Writer** and **author** are almost the same. William Shakespeare can be referred to either as an author or a writer. But *writer* has a wider meaning: "Kelly won the sixth grade short-story contest. She's a good *writer.*" We would not refer to Kelly as an author. And the writer of a sports column for a local newspaper would not be called an author. *Author* suggests someone who has published a book, play, or other such work: "In our literature course we read works by *authors* such as E. B. White, Laura Ingalls Wilder, and Virginia Hamilton."

wrong   incorrect false erroneous mistaken inaccurate

ADJECTIVE: not agreeing with the facts; not true or right.

wrong She only spelled one word *wrong;* she wrote "restuarant" instead of "restaurant." He answered that Thomas Jefferson was the second President, but that was *wrong*—it was actually John Adams.

incorrect The teacher puts a red X mark next to each *incorrect* answer, and we have to do the problem over to get it right.

false The statement read "Normal body temperature is 100 degrees," so I wrote *False,* because the normal temperature is actually 98.6 degrees.

erroneous The newspaper ad had some *erroneous* information; it said that the price of the TV set is $99.95, when it's supposed to be $299.95.

mistaken I think you're *mistaken*—the exit we just passed is the one for the road to the city, not that exit up ahead.

inaccurate When medical tests seemed to indicate that the track athlete had been using an illegal drug, he argued that the test results were *inaccurate.*

Antonyms: **right, correct, accurate.**

yell   shout scream call holler

VERB: to say something in a loud voice, or make a loud noise with the voice.

yell Tony saw the bus was about to pull away, so he *yelled* to the driver to wait.

shout The speaker asked the crowd, "My opponent wants to raise taxes. Do you want higher taxes?" And the crowd *shouted* back, "No!"

scream Joey dropped an ice cube down his sister's neck and she started running after him, *screaming* that she was going to get him.

call The coach said that when we go to catch a fly ball we should *call* out, "I got it!" so that the other players will get out of the way.

holler When I took the baby's toy away, he *hollered* like mad until I gave it back.

Randy was too **young** to go on the Cosmic Coaster ride.

It was **childish** of Randy to stop talking to us because of that.

young   youthful childish juvenile immature

ADJECTIVE: not old; showing or suggesting the qualities of childhood or youth.

young It's hard to believe that she's really a doctor; she looks so *young.* The person who answered the phone had a very *young* voice.

youthful There's no date on this picture of Grandpa, but from his *youthful* appearance I'd say it was probably taken while he was in high school.

childish Ryan was really *childish* about the checkers game—when he saw that he was going to lose, he started crying and knocked over the board.

juvenile Skip says that if he doesn't get to be the varsity quarterback he won't play on the team at all, which I think is a *juvenile* attitude.

immature When I teased my sister about watching that silly romantic movie, she said I was just too *immature* to understand what real drama was all about.

Index

The *HBJ Student Thesaurus* contains 800 main entries listed in alphabetical order. This index is a list of all the words that appear as synonyms under those entries. The purpose of the index is to allow you to locate words that are found under other main entries in the book.

If you want to locate a certain word, you should look first in the Thesaurus itself, where the word would occur in alphabetical order. If you do not find the word there as an entry, then check this index. It may be that the word appears as a synonym under some other main entry. You could then use any of the other words given in the entry as synonyms for that word. For example, there is no main entry in this book for the word *actually*. But if you will look at the top of the second column below, you will note that it can be found in the Thesaurus, on page 214. It appears there under the entry for *really*.

Index

Illustration Credits

Lori Anderson: 13, 37, 200, 222; **Kristine Bollinger:** 17, 30, 54, 92, 111, 130, 149, 183, 204, 237, 251, 275, 290; **Stephanie Britt:** 68, 105, 108, 175, 233, 261, 301, 303; **Jim Cummins:** 9, 62, 187, 203, 208, 256, 298; **Toni Goffe:** 28, 51, 61, 107, 122, 134, 172, 188, 206, 225, 244, 287; **Mark Graham:** 6, 48, 152, 242; **Ann Iosa:** 82, 150, 167, 195, 212, 227; **Karen Loccisano:** 10, 27, 45, 71, 85, 95, 112, 144, 176, 193, 240, 280, 293; **Laura Lydecker:** 22, 47, 58, 96, 116, 132, 147, 171, 196, 231, 255, 284; **Stephen Marchesi:** 53, 88, 137, 168, 184, 252, 277; **John Mardon:** 21, 101,143, 15, 161, 219, 266; **Kathleen McCarthy:** 18, 41, 73, 87, 103, 129, 138, 159, 180, 216, 238, 249, 288; **Elizabeth Miles:** 25, 74, 91, 118, 156, 279; **Yoshi Miyake:** 15, 38, 57, 78, 115, 125, 165, 179, 215, 228, 262, 283, 297; **Stephen Moore:** 42, 81, 127, 221, 247, 271; **Cathy Pavia:** 5, 32, 65, 76, 120, 140, 163, 191, 210, 235, 264, 273, 295; **Linda Weller:** 2, 34, 66, 98, 198, 258, 268